Mythic Thinking in Twentieth-Cen

Mythic Thinking in Twentieth-Century Britain

Meaning for Modernity

Matthew Sterenberg

Assistant Professor, Waseda University, Japan

First published 2013 by
PALGRAVE MACMILLAN

Palgrave Macmillan in the UK is an imprint of Macmillan Publishers Limited, registered in England, company number 785998, of Houndmills, Basingstoke, Hampshire RG21 6XS.

Palgrave Macmillan in the US is a division of St Martin's Press LLC, 175 Fifth Avenue, New York, NY 10010.

Palgrave Macmillan is the global academic imprint of the above companies and has companies and representatives throughout the world.

Palgrave® and Macmillan® are registered trademarks in the United States, the United Kingdom, Europe and other countries.

ISBN 978–1–137–35496–9

This book is printed on paper suitable for recycling and made from fully managed and sustained forest sources. Logging, pulping and manufacturing processes are expected to conform to the environmental regulations of the country of origin.

A catalogue record for this book is available from the British Library.

A catalog record for this book is available from the Library of Congress.

Contents

Acknowledgments

One of the thinkers examined in the following pages once suggested that we need intimate knowledge of the past because we need something to set against the present. The resulting contrast reminds us that basic assumptions have been quite different in different periods and shows us that much which seems fixed is only temporary fashion. If this book in any way furthers such intimate knowledge of the past, that is only because the support, encouragement, and assistance of a great many people have enabled me to complete it. I am glad for this opportunity to thank at least some of them.

My first thanks must go to my friend Bill Heyck. From the moment I first proposed to him the idea that became this book, his support, encouragement, and friendship have been unfailing. He remains my role model for what it means to be a scholar and teacher. I trust that by the time he reads this he will again be engaged in his quest to hit "just one crisp iron shot."

Many others have supported this project by suggesting ideas, reading chapter drafts, or helping me develop my ideas in conversation. Ken Alder's enthusiasm for this project has been a constant source of encouragement. He made possible research support for its early stages and offered particularly incisive comments on drafts. Alex Owen was an insightful, challenging, supportive dialogue partner as I tried to develop my thesis. Peter Schakel, Nick Perovich, and Marc Baer planted some of the key intellectual seeds. Marc, who first sparked my interest in British history, offered helpful comments on two chapters. Hunter Heyck, Meredith Veldman, and Ethan Schrum also offered invaluable comments on various chapters. Michael Pelletier, Amy Whipple, Thom Hajkowski, Guy Ortolano, Karl Gunther, and Jana Measells helped me develop some of these ideas when they were still in embryonic form. Larry Siedentop and the late John Burrow graciously took an interest in my work and offered valuable advice. I would also like to thank an anonymous referee for Palgrave Macmillan for thoughtful and constructive comments on the manuscript.

My colleagues at Waseda University's School of International Liberal Studies (SILS) have been a frequent source of intellectual stimulation and support. I am indebted to Graham Law, Adrian Pinnington, Juliann Sivulka, and Koichi Okamoto for their questions, suggestions, and encouragement. Graham in particular offered insightful comments on two chapters and sage advice at a key stage. I am also grateful to Waseda University for research support in the form of a Special Research Projects Grant. One of the best things about SILS is its students. I am particularly obliged to one of them, Tatsuhiko Taketoshi, who has served as a de facto research assistant. I am grateful for his reading of and comments on the manuscript and for his assistance in preparing the index.

It goes without saying that all of those who read the manuscript either in part or in whole offered helpful suggestions (though in some cases my stubbornness has prevented me from following them) and saved me from factual errors. Any errors that remain, however, are my responsibility alone.

I am deeply grateful to my parents, who have always supported me, even when it meant taking their grandchildren an ocean away.

Finally, I thank my wife, Yuko, for her patience, wisdom, grace, good cheer, editorial assistance, and—above all—for being a steadfast ally in all things. You kept the family going during those all-too-frequent times when I was researching, writing, or physically present but mentally in the past. You also secured a prime *masu* at *Hatsubasho* when I needed to put such things aside. Let's make it an annual tradition.

1
Myth and the Modern Problem

Auden's assessment

The chief problem of modernity was an absence of meaning. That was W.H. Auden's conclusion as he reflected on the challenges of modern life in 1948. He explained that inhabitants of the twentieth century were

> faced with the modern problem, i.e., of living in a society in which men are no longer supported by tradition without being aware of it, and in which, therefore, every individual who wishes to bring order and coherence into the stream of sensations, emotions, and ideas entering his consciousness, from without and within, is forced to do deliberately for himself what in previous ages has been done for him by family, custom, church, and state, namely the choice of the principles and presuppositions in terms of which he can make sense of his experience.[1]

Auden's assessment was correct: there was a "modern problem"—or at least many of Auden's contemporaries were convinced that there was. Cultural observers of the time in Britain noted a disorienting absence of given meaning-creating structures, a situation that had ushered in a host of distinctly modern ills. Though catalogs of these ills described the problem in varying terms, assessments of modernity's faults nevertheless tended to emphasize the same family of complaints: science's epistemological pretensions, the spiritual barrenness of modern life, a lack of shared values and traditions, the excesses of consumerism, the banality of mass culture, the alienating effect of contemporary urban existence, and the emotional estrangement produced by the mass media. By the early years of the interwar period, there was a widespread sense in Britain that "modernity" or "the modern age" had eroded a shared set of, to

1

use Auden's terms, "principles and presuppositions." It is no coincidence, for instance, that 1922 saw both the publication of T.S. Eliot's *The Waste Land* and the founding of the BBC. Both endeavors were expressions of a desire to re-establish or replace a cultural unity—based on common principles and presuppositions—believed to have been lost in the transition to modernity.[2]

Much of Britain's intellectual history in the twentieth century can be understood as a series of attempts to come to grips with the modern problem. The responses it provoked were varied. Some, such as G.K. Chesterton or the historians J.L. and Barbara Hammond, longed for a return to a simpler era and hoped to recover a social and moral cohesion that had vanished. Such thinkers imagined a lost golden age that could be recaptured if the right steps were taken. Others, such as the novelist Evelyn Waugh and the historian Christopher Dawson, converted to High Church Anglicanism or Roman Catholicism, seeing such traditionalist forms of Christianity as bulwarks against modernity. And still others, such as the literary critic F.R. Leavis and his epigones, believed that the proper response to modernity entailed replacing Christianity with the humanities as the primary source of cultural values. Even those who launched the BBC were inspired by visions of a cultural unity made possible by modern technology. These responses to the modern problem were all alike in that they developed their interpretations of and responses to modernity by drawing inspiration from the past, whether in the form of an imagined bygone golden age of social cohesion, an ancient faith, or a "great tradition" of literature. They were also alike in sensing that the modern problem was at bottom a problem of meaning and of how to find or construct it in the modern world.

There was, however, a very different, remarkably prevalent, and largely overlooked response to the modern problem that did not look to the past for guidance, but that did place a premium on the question of meaning. This response can be termed "mythic thinking," because it was defined by the belief that myths—explanatory narratives of perennial relevance that deal with ultimate questions—were vital sources of meaning, indispensable frameworks for interpreting experience, and essential tools for coping with modernity. The purpose of this book is to describe the origins, nature, and impact of mythic thinking in the cultural and intellectual life of twentieth-century Britain.

Mythic thinkers tended to view modernity as a rupture in history. They therefore thought that ways of coping with the modern problem that aimed to resurrect the past were obsolete and doomed to failure. This belief marked them as part of a broader twentieth-century reaction against historicity that was also reflected in, for example, literary modernism and analytic philosophy. This sense of a radical break in history that rendered old ways of thinking obsolete connected all mythic thinkers, whether the arch-modernist Eliot in the 1920s, the fantasist J.R.R. Tolkien in the 1930s, the avant-garde novelist J.G. Ballard in the 1960s, or the theologian John Hick in the 1970s. What was needed, mythic thinkers held, was a new way of making meaning that took into account the unique nature of modernity, and they believed that this need could be fulfilled by myth—a concept that was at once conveniently vague and rich with significance. Indeed mythic thinkers defined the modern problem precisely as a debilitating lack of myth. Auden himself expressed this view when he noted how modern culture was characterized by "the disappearance... of a common myth," and Eliot voiced a similar assessment when he described the modern condition as being "barren of myths"—a condition he sought to rectify with his myth-infused poetry.[3]

This study, *Mythic Thinking in Twentieth-Century Britain*, aims to provide a cultural and intellectual history of myth as a mode of thought in order to explain its significance as a recurrent pattern within British culture. Taking a cue from Raymond Williams' insight that cultural analysis begins with the identification of cultural patterns, *Mythic Thinking in Twentieth-Century Britain* sets out to trace the dimensions and salient manifestations of mythic thinking from roughly 1900 to 1980. The central argument of the book is that mythic thinking emerged in the early twentieth century as a way for a variety of thinkers and key cultural groups to frame and articulate their anxieties about a modern era that seemed bereft of transcendent meaning. Mythic thinking is thus best understood as a response to the modern problem identified by Auden. At the same time, mythic thinking was itself a modern project that took place within, depended upon, and existed in fruitful tension with fundamental institutions, features, and tenets of modernity. Its prevalence in twentieth-century British culture is therefore a challenge to the notion that modernity is fundamentally disenchanted and inhospitable to transcendent concerns.

Throughout the period 1900–1980, mythic thinking took the form of works of literature, art, cultural criticism, philosophy, psychology, and theology designed to show that both ancient myths and more recently created mythic narratives had revelatory power for modern life. Most fundamentally and most importantly, *mythic thinking constituted a new mode of making meaning that appealed to the imagination by making the claim that myths communicate timeless truths that cannot be apprehended through reason or science.* Myth therefore signified what its advocates found lacking in both modernity and the alternative responses to it: myth was rooted neither in the past nor in the present but was timeless, it offered wisdom rather than knowledge, unity instead of fragmentation, order in place of chaos, spiritual solace instead of unbelief, and meaning rather than confusion. If, as Auden contended, the modern problem stemmed from an absence of given or inherited presuppositions and metanarratives that imposed coherence on the flow of experience, then mythic thinking was a novel, audacious, and in many ways successful attempt to fill that vacuum.

The domain of myth

The London School of Economics (LSE), the citadel of British social science, is an unlikely place to begin tracing the outlines of the mythic thinking phenomenon. Yet in 1952, the Cambridge don W.K.C. Guthrie, a respected historian of ancient Greek philosophy and religion, took to the dais there to argue that the empirically grounded knowledge produced in the halls of the LSE needed to be balanced by a very different kind of knowledge—the kind that came only from myth. Taking as his subject "Myth and Reason," Guthrie argued that Greek mythology was more relevant now than ever because of the timeless wisdom that it conveyed. Because "Mythical thinking never dies out completely," it was crucial to find ways to make proper use of myth's resources.[4] This entailed eschewing "bad myth"—in the form of contemporary "isms"— which served only to legitimate irrationality by masking it in "woolly and abstract language." However, he continued:

> Good myth is the opposite. It consists in apprehending the profound and universal truths symbolically conveyed by simple stories and images which, just because their mode of expression is concrete, individual and imaginative, are apt to be brushed aside by the devotee of "scientific method" or the latest non- existent *–ism*.[5]

Guthrie's address neatly encapsulates two key features of twentieth-century mythic thinking: (1) the belief that myth offered access to universal metaphysical truths that were deeply relevant to the modern condition and (2) the conviction that these truths complemented, rather than conflicted with, scientific truths.

The year before Guthrie's address at the LSE, Ted Hughes began his studies at Cambridge. It is entirely likely that as an undergraduate

Hughes heard Guthrie lecture on mythical thinking. Moreover, it is quite clear that Hughes' fascination with myth deepened over the years, fed by a fascination with Robert Graves' *The White Goddess*, an interest in the theories of Carl Gustav Jung, and other sources. It is thus not surprising to find Hughes commending the value of myth to the attendees of a conference on children's literature in words that would become widely anthologized:

> The myths and legends, which Plato proposed as the ideal educational material for his young citizens, can be seen as large-scale accounts of negotiations between powers of the inner world and the stubborn conditions of the outer world, under which men and women have to live. They are immense and highly detailed sketches for the possibilities of understanding the two....
>
> Their accuracy and usefulness...depend on the fact that they were originally the genuine projections of genuine understanding....They gave a true account of what happens in that inner region where the two worlds collide. This has been attested over and over again by the way in which the imaginative men of every subsequent age have had recourse to their basic patterns and images.
>
> But the Greek myths were not the only true myths. The unspoken definition of myth is that it carries truth of this sort.[6]

In claiming that "every subsequent age" was marked by recourse to myth's resources Hughes was agreeing with Guthrie's contention that "mythical thinking never dies out completely." For both, emphasizing myth's perennial significance was a way of underscoring myth's ongoing relevance as a means of coping with the challenges of modern life.

Guthrie and Hughes were thus drawn to myth because of their yearning for a kind of truth and meaning that seemed to have been displaced in the modern world. Their studies and personal experiences had convinced them that myth somehow possessed a unique power to provide such truth and meaning by appealing to the imagination. It is worth noting the strong and even categorical language that each uses to underscore this connection. For Guthrie myth apprehends "profound and universal truths" that are expressed in an "imaginative" mode. For Hughes, myths offer "genuine understanding" that has always been appreciated by "imaginative men." They came to this conclusion in part through their contact with late nineteenth- and early twentieth-century anthropological work on myth. Guthrie had both personal and professional connections to the group known as the Cambridge Ritualists, whose work blended classics, archaeology, and anthropology in order to raise new questions about the role of myth in ancient Greek culture and its possible role in modern culture. Hughes switched from studying English to anthropology while at Cambridge, a move that facilitated his increasing fascination with mythology. In being led to a deeper consideration of myth through contact with anthropology, Guthrie and Hughes were by no means atypical; rather they were representative of a common pattern in twentieth-century Britain. Neither were they atypical in thinking that ancient myth had a unique epistemological validity that made it crucially relevant to modern life.

Astute cultural observers began to notice the ubiquity of such mythic thinking by the 1950s. Some, like the American critic Philip Rahv, were implacably opposed to the trend. Rahv, a convinced Marxist, denounced mythic thinkers as "mythomaniacs" who irresponsibly retreated from history.[7] A more equitable observer was the British literary critic Frank Kermode. No one captured the appeal of myth—and the extent of this appeal—better than Kermode, one of the most attentive and incisive observers of British intellectual life during the post-Second World War period. Confronted with a host of thinkers and writers who like Guthrie and Hughes extolled the virtues of myth, Kermode concluded: "our literary culture is saturated with mythological thinking." This state of affairs was a source of both fascination and ambivalence for him, and he devoted much of his attention to the topic during the 1960s. He understood well myth's appeal in a modern age, which he tried to capture in words that could almost be a gloss on Guthrie and Hughes:

> In the domain of myth we can short-circuit the intellect and liberate the imagination which the scientism of the world suppresses.... Myth deals in what is more real than intellect can accede to; it is a seamless garment to replace the tattered fragments worn by the modern mind.[8]

Kermode's assessment goes to the heart of the mythic thinking phenomenon by highlighting its recurrent emphases: myth's appeal to the imagination, its capacity to communicate a higher kind of truth, and the notion that the modern mind is desperately in need of such truth.

"Mythic thinking" is the central concept of this project, yet it is not a familiar term in the historian's lexicon. In order to justify its use, therefore, a more detailed explanation of it is perhaps necessary. The term is admittedly nebulous, in large part because the term "myth" is itself nebulous. I make no attempt to offer a normative definition of myth or to enter debates about myth's status as a genre of unique power or authority. There is a vast and fascinating body of interdisciplinary literature devoted to defining the category of "myth" and to categorizing the myriad theories, examples, and uses of it.[9] As useful as such scholarship may be in some contexts, this study steers clear of the ongoing attempts to validate, quantify, or extol what has been called "myth's abiding power."[10] The focus here, rather, is on explaining why so many in twentieth-century Britain believed that myth had such abiding power. Consequently, instead of offering my own definition of myth, I use the term as it tended to be used by the figures I examine: an explanatory narrative of perennial relevance that deals with ultimate questions. To develop this definition a bit further, most mythic thinkers would have agreed that a myth is a sacred, foundational or archetypal narrative dealing with gods, heroes, cosmology, or the transcendent, which serves to answer perennial questions, reconcile antinomies, guide action, express transcendent truths, diffuse psychological pressures, or legitimate cultural values.

This clearly is an elastic definition and one that allowed for considerable leeway as to what qualified as myth. Indeed, the very vagueness of the concept was part of its appeal. It was commonly thought, for instance, that contemporary writers could create fictions that functioned as myths. Such thinking is one reason the myth scholar Robert Segal has noted that "[Myths] may not even go backward in time but may instead go forward, as in science fiction, or go sideways, such as to other cultures around the world."[11] Mythic thinking thus did not necessarily entail primitivism or an idealization of the archaic cultures that had produced ancient myths.

Instead, mythic thinking was essentially an attempt to exploit myth's supposed unique properties by thinking with or through myth in order to create meaning that was otherwise lacking. Myth became the framework for interpreting experience that Auden claimed moderns needed to construct for themselves. The endeavors of mythic thinkers were premised on the assumption that myth was a narrative genre or a mode of thought that had an indefinable but undeniable gravity, and that it communicated truths that could not be apprehended by any other means. One mythic thinker who tried to put this into words described "myth as profound and suggestive of meanings beyond my grasp."[12] Because this sense of myth's power was widely shared, the term "myth" had significant force as a rhetorical weapon, which contributed to its effectiveness as an instrument in twentieth-century cultural politics. Use of the term, whether in scholarly or non-scholarly discourse, tends to be unavoidably polemical. As historian of religion and myth scholar Bruce

Lincoln has observed, someone who uses the term "myth" is making potent assertions about its validity and authority relative to other types of discourse.[13] These assertions can be approving, by associating myths with, for example, primordial truth or the source of cultural unity. They can also be pejorative, by characterizing myth as, for example, primitive worldview. The mythic thinkers examined in subsequent chapters dealt only in approving assertions about myth: debunking myth or characterizing it pejoratively as merely false story was not part of their project.

Mythic thinking manifested itself mainly in two forms, which often overlapped with each other. First, as Guthrie and Hughes's words above indicate, it often took the form of literary, artistic, and philosophical attempts to show that ancient myths had relevance to modern life. However, it was also manifested in attempts to create new myths and mythic narratives. This second type of mythic thinking was thus largely the province of writers of fiction. The outstanding example of this strain was Tolkien's self-confessed attempt to create a coherent body of mythology for England with his novel *The Lord of the Rings*. Tolkien believed that England's lack of its own ancient mythology was somehow a serious deficiency, a belief that illustrates the very essence of mythic thinking. The notion that British culture needed to maintain contact with myth in order to be stable and healthy was not held by Tolkien alone; it was a fundamental presupposition underlying mythic thinking throughout the period.

For mythic thinkers, then, myth was not one narrative genre among others. It was, rather, a uniquely potent form of discourse that conveyed resources not accessible in other ways. These resources were often revealed by what myth was rhetorically opposed to in cultural criticism. Depending on the particular historical moment and context, the cultural critiques devised by mythic thinkers targeted scientism, excessive rationalism, secularization, mass culture, and the alienation of contemporary urban life. The turn to myth was justified with claims that myth gave access to deeper truths than historical or scientific explanation, and that it offered a unique means of coping with the psychological pressures that modernity brought to bear on the individual. Mythic thinking, then, was in part an idiom through which anxieties about modernity could be articulated and ideas for redressing modernity's deficiencies proposed. Mythic thinkers thus used myth to construct modernity even as they criticized it: for them myth represented all that had been repressed, erased, or fragmented in the transition to modernity. At the same time, mythic thinking was carried out within the rationalist tenets of modernity; it was not part of the "revolt against positivism" described by H. Stuart Hughes.[14] Tolkien, for instance, took great pains to emphasize that the mythic fiction he wrote and advocated "does not destroy or even insult Reason; and it does not either blunt the appetite for, nor obscure the perception of, scientific verity."[15]

Implications

Understanding the nature and scope of mythic thinking can deepen and reshape our understanding of twentieth-century British culture in a number of significant ways. Most fundamentally, identifying and defining the phenomenon of mythic thinking adds a new and necessary category of analysis to our discussions of twentieth-century cultural politics in Britain. Though British studies scholars have long been aware that numerous twentieth-century thinkers were interested in myth, as of yet they have failed to appreciate the breadth and significance of such interest. Two approaches have characterized the investigation of myth in twentieth-century Britain. The first is composed of studies of how the use of myth was a central feature of modernist aesthetics and, in particular, the poetry of Eliot.[16] Though such literature makes invaluable contributions to our understanding of the modernists, by its very nature it cannot help us comprehend the broader dimensions of myth's role in British culture. By contrast, the second approach casts a broader net in attempting to trace the influence of J.G. Frazer's *The Golden Bough*, a method that encompasses the modernists but also goes beyond them.[17] However, this second approach is also limited, as its concerns are largely confined to the influence of a single, albeit iconic and hugely significant, text. In addition to these two main approaches, literary scholars have of course identified a number of other cases where a deliberate use of myth has characterized British literary culture. But there has been no systematic attempt to analyze such instances of preoccupation with myth as part of a broader cultural pattern. Consequently, there has been little effort to see, for example, how seemingly disparate figures like Eliot and Tolkien might have connections that are signaled by their common fascination with myth.[18] The category of mythic thinking allows us to begin to excavate those connections and expose obscured patterns in British culture.

Once the mythic thinking phenomenon is identified and defined, we are then equipped to examine it wherever it surfaces and to describe the role it played in shaping British culture. More specifically, an examination of mythic thinking adds a new dimension to our understanding of how twentieth-century Britons both constructed and experienced modernity. Because the turn to myth was justified with claims that myth was a panacea for a host of modernity's discontents, mythic thinking functioned as a key rhetorical weapon in a cultural struggle that defined twentieth-century Britain: the struggle between modernity's advocates and its critics. Viewing this struggle through the prisms of secularization and the "two cultures controversy," the relevant historiography has represented it as a contest between the sciences on the one hand and Christianity, an imagined past, or the humanities on the other. Traditionally, religious discourse had provided the basis for a critique of modernity, but its plausibility was eroded throughout the century. Consequently many, such as Leavis and his disciples, turned to the humanities as a substitute for religion.[19] Adding mythic thinking to the mix complicates our understanding of this struggle by showing how, in the search for an alternative response to modernity, many thinkers and writers turned to the discourse of mythic thinking instead of to religion, a past golden age, or the humanities.

The ways in which mythic thinkers did this, however, were complex and not understandable in terms of a binary explanatory scheme that opposes modernity and myth. For them myth was not an alternative or antidote to modernity, but something to be held in tension with it. They turned to myth not to escape modernity, but to make space for transcendent concerns within it. The picture is complicated further by the fact that, for some, mythic thinking was a strategy for reinforcing either religion, or the humanities, or both. If in premodern cultures myth is always already there as an unquestioned given, it would seem that one hallmark of modernity is that myth must be sought out critically and self-consciously. The activities of the mythic thinkers examined here show that modernity does not necessitate myth's obsolescence or even skepticism about its truth. It does, however, necessitate that those who would avail themselves of myth must, to recall Auden's words, "do so deliberately for themselves."

The questions at the heart of this work link it to the rapidly evolving body of literature which challenges the view that the processes of rationalization characteristic of modernity were incompatible with spiritual impulses. Modernity is without question a fraught term: historians have been unable to agree on a definition and even offer widely contrasting accounts of when it emerged in history. Nevertheless, some broad lines of agreement can be sketched. Modernity has typically been understood as signifying the interconnected growth of rationalism, scientism, secularism, urbanization, professionalization, urbanization, capitalism, and consumerism—and the list could go on. Not all historians interpret or emphasize these processes in the same way, but as Michael Saler has noted in a recent assessment of the relevant historiography, "There is one characteristic of modernity...that has been emphasized fairly consistently by intellectuals since the eighteenth century: that modernity is 'disenchanted.'"[20] In other words, the advancement of reason, science, and rationalizing processes came at the expense of ways of apprehending the world associated with transcendent meaning, spiritual longing, wonder, and the suprarational; the modern world was a place from which enchantment had been expunged. This was a view most famously expressed by Max Weber in 1917,[21] but it was well-ingrained in western culture before then, going back to the romantics of the late eighteenth century and sustained through the nineteenth century by a range of cultural pessimists from Arthur Schopenhauer to Oswald Spengler.

Saler has gone on to describe an emerging "antinomial" understanding of modernity that aims to avoid the "either/or" logic that has long characterized scholarship on modernity. Instead, a new body of interdisciplinary literature is emphasizing how "modernity is characterized by fruitful tensions between seemingly irreconcilable forces and ideas. Modernity is defined less by binaries...than by unresolved contradictions and oppositions, or antinomies: modernity is Janus-faced."[22] Such new work includes both frontal assaults on the paradigmatic narrative of modern disenchantment, such as Jane Bennett's *The Enchantment of Modern Life*, and more specific historical case studies that expose the inadequacies of that narrative by uncovering fascinating examples of modern enchantment.[23]

An examination of mythic thinking intersects with the new understanding of modernity and enchantment by adding an additional object of investigation to the discussion. Recent works that scrutinize the interaction of modernity and enchantment in modern British history include Allison Winter's *Mesmerized: Powers of Mind in Victorian Britain*, Daniel Pick's *Svengali's Web: The Alien Enchanter in Modern Culture*, Alex Owen's *The Place of Enchantment: British Occultism and the Culture of the Modern*, and Michael Saler's *As If: Modern Enchantment and the Literary Prehistory of Virtual Reality*.[24] Such works offer remarkable insights into the contours of modernity in Britain through examination of mesmerism, occultism, and the ironic imagination in particular. These three objects of investigation were far from the only conduits of enchantment in the modern age. I suggest that mythic thinking can be considered alongside them as an innovative response to modernity—a strategy for maintaining contact with the transcendent in "a secular age."[25] But mythic thinking was more about making space for transcendent concerns within modernity than it was about a revolt against it. Because myth could be conveniently defined as a realm of discourse that was not subject to empirical verification, mythic thinking could articulate spiritual impulses in a way that was thought to be compatible with, not antithetical to, modern rationality.

Finally, this project can also be seen as a contribution to a nascent historiography on the relationship between myth and modernity. As noted above, scholars of twentieth-century literature have long understood that a self-conscious and deliberate use of myth was central to modernist literary culture, and modernist thinking about myth continues to attract scholarly attention.[26] As valuable as such recent works may be, they also have had the effect of reinforcing a sense that the modernists had something like a monopoly on mythic thinking in the twentieth century. In recent years, however, there have been some indications that historians are beginning to examine the interaction of myth and modernity in ways that take us beyond what we know about the modernists in Britain. It is beginning to appear as if a belief in myth as a panacea for modernity's discontents was a common feature of intellectual life in the west from the late eighteenth century on. Perhaps the outstanding example of such recent work is George Williamson's *The Longing for Myth in Germany*, which details how from the Romantic period on intellectuals used myth as a discourse to articulate both regrets over what had been lost in the transition to modernity and visions of a future society in which aesthetic, religious, and public life would be integrated.[27] Williamson seems to believe—on what grounds it is not clear—that mythography manifested itself more intensely in Germany than in other places. This view seems debatable, but it does point up an opportunity for comparative historical inquiry: how did mythic thinking take shape in other contexts and how was it inflected differently in different places? This book represents a step in the direction of such comparative study; the investigation of British mythic thinking offered here can contribute to new insights into myth and modernity when placed alongside studies like Williamson's *Longing for Myth*.

Overview

Each of the following chapters examines a different instance of mythic thinking as practiced by a particular cultural group. Each chapter thus amounts to a case study of how myth was used for specific ends in specific circumstances. Taken together, the chapters reveal both the adaptability and the elasticity of the discourse of mythic thinking, as well as the recurrent emphases and traits that distinguished it as a phenomenon. That is to say, though these groups deployed myth in varying ways, there is nevertheless a family resemblance that marks their uses of myth as being instances of the same cultural phenomenon.

The chapters are arranged in rough chronological order in a way that highlights the emergence of mythic thinking and its subsequent development in different historical moments. Ironically, twentieth-century fascination with myth had its origins in the social sciences—forms of knowledge production that exemplified modernity's rationalist and secularist face. This story is told in Chapter 2, which details how anthropological study of myth prepared the way for later mythic thinking. Central to this story was how two strands of scholarship on myth reinforced each other by exploring ancient subject matter that somehow seemed to speak to early twentieth-century concerns. The first of these was the comparative anthropology that reached its apex in Frazer's magnum opus, *The Golden Bough*. This work's fascinating depiction of a vast array of myths and associated rituals made it a bestseller, and it supplied writers in particular with an inexhaustible stock of mythological themes, images and symbols. Frazer himself, however, saw myth through the lens of his Darwinian presuppositions: to him myths were little more than misguided primitive attempts at scientific explanation. But not all who were dazzled by *The Golden Bough* shared Frazer's late-Victorian rationalism. A case in point was the work of the Cambridge Ritualists, who constituted the second important strand of anthropological scholarship on myth. Motivated in part by dissatisfaction with the spiritual barrenness of the early twentieth century, they studied the religion of archaic Greece in part so they could better understand the nature of humanity's "religious impulse."

As has been amply documented by scholars like John Vickery, the work of Frazer and the Ritualists struck a resonant chord in a post-First World War period characterized by heightened cultural pessimism and a consequent search for spiritual meaning and cultural unity. Chapter 3 takes up this theme by examining the first group to realize that works like Frazer's *Golden Bough* could be mined for ideas, tropes, and images for use in literature intended to make the modern age comprehensible and tolerable—the literary modernists. Eliot's vaunted "mythical method" was the classic case of such a modernist use of myth. According to Eliot the conditions of modernity, in particular cultural fragmentation and the impossibility of religious belief, dictated that myth's role was simply to provide the elements for a pattern or structure in a given literary work. Myth could thus help give aesthetic shape to the chaos of modern life, but it could not convey religious truths or insights in which to believe. But not all modernists presumed with Eliot that religious belief was impossible in the modern age. A number of modernist writers picked up the attitude of spiritual seeking and the critique of instrumental rationality that had been a hallmark of the work of the Ritualists. These writers—John Cowper Powys, Mary Butts, Charles Williams, and David Jones—saw myth as a source of religious truth, a notion they explored by producing literature that drew heavily on the mythology of the Holy Grail. Their willingness to believe in the truth of myth was enabled by their particular response to the late nineteenth- and early twentieth-century scholarship on myth: they refused to accept the secularizing implications of such work, interpreting it instead as an enlightening record of humanity's experience and interpretation of the transcendent. The chapter thus explores the difference between Eliot's mythical method and alternate modernist understandings of myth in order to show that modernists did not solely use myth to supply aesthetic form; they could also believe in it as a source of religious consolation.

Though the modernists who were preoccupied with Grail mythology all attributed a deep spiritual significance to myth, they were not operating as a united front. Chapter 4, however, examines two writers, Tolkien and C.S. Lewis, who worked in concert to develop a form of cultural criticism in which myth played a key role. They stand out as two of the most influential mythic thinkers of the century because of the popularity of the mythic fiction they produced, which not only diffused but also set an example for subsequent writers who conceived of their fiction as a contemporary form of myth. Lewis and Tolkien's use of myth resembled the mythic thinking of Grail-preoccupied modernists in two important ways. First, Lewis and Tolkien turned to myth in an effort to redress what they saw as the spiritual emptiness of a secular age. Second, like the modernists examined in Chapter 4, they refused to see the anthropological scholarship on myth produced by Frazer and others as necessarily corrosive of religious belief. Instead of drawing the common conclusion that *The Golden Bough* had demonstrated that myth-making was little more than a primitive attempt at scientific thinking, they argued that the very ubiquity of myth-making demonstrated myth's perennial relevance as a language for conjuring with the transcendent. Yet their theory of myth was explicitly Christian, and this was a departure from the way most modernists used myth. Lewis and Tolkien conceived of myth as an epistemological category: it was a particular kind of idiom that expressed particular kinds of truths, namely the transcendent truths of religion. Myth was thus a necessary counterweight to science, because it conveyed truths that simply could not be disclosed by empirical investigation. But the mythic thinking that they advocated was something that took place within the rationalist bounds of modernity and freely acknowledged the value of scientific reason. Theirs was a both/and proposition: both scientific rationality and mythic consciousness were necessary components of a healthy culture. Seeking to practice what they preached, Lewis and Tolkien set out to create mythic fictions of their own, an endeavor in part inspired by the fantasy literature they had enjoyed as children.

Tolkien and Lewis developed their conception of myth during the 1930s for the most part, and this is reflected in the particular emphases of their brand of mythic thinking. Chapter 5 shifts to the post-Second World War period to examine how mythic thinking could be inflected in a different context. Nevertheless, the work of Lewis and Tolkien provides a bridge to the mythic thinking of this later period, because the writers examined in Chapter 5 were to some extent inspired by the work of Lewis and Tolkien from the 1930s and 1940s, though they would show how mythic thinking could be modulated and inflected very differently in the 1960s. These writers were known as the "New Wave," and their aim was to create a form of science fiction that functioned as contemporary myth. Their most prominent member was perhaps Ballard, who conceived of his works of fiction as "myths of the near future." Ballard's concern that modernity brought intense pressures to bear on the psyche prompted him to produce contemporary myths that would help individuals cope with these pressures. The work of Ballard and the New Wave was thus distinguished in part by explicitly psychological concerns, and their work can be seen as signaling the reappearance of a recessive gene in the history of mythic thinking: psychological theories of myth.

This recessive gene is examined in Chapter 6. The most influential psychological theorist of myth was of course the Swiss psychologist and psychiatrist Jung. Jung enjoyed remarkable prominence in Britain, and he seemed to gain stature during the postwar period when he came to be seen increasingly as a kind of spiritual sage. And he was seen as such not merely by a countercultural fringe, but by a broad swath of the public. His status as a spiritual sage was directly attributable, at least in part, to his theory of myth. British culture was no stranger to quest myths, from the ancient material of the Grail mythology to modern bestsellers like Tolkien's *Lord of the Rings*. Jung's description of the search for psychological wholeness as a mythic quest resonated in this context.

Jung's influence in Britain was furthered by enthusiastic support from prominent literary figures and intellectuals, as well as Jung's own savvy self-promotion. Finally, the very nature of Jung's thought, which was by nature interdisciplinary, holistic, and open to spiritual and moral concerns, appealed to many at a time of increasing concern about the rift between the "two cultures."

Mythic thinking was not just a matter for poets and writers of fiction, a point taken up in Chapter 7. During the post-Second World War period, mythic thinking became such a prevalent feature of British culture that academic disciplines began to adapt it for their own purposes. Academics began to realize that "myth" was a potent rhetorical weapon that could be used in disciplinary struggles within the university. This was a discovery made by literary critics in Britain as they attempted to stake a claim for their emerging discipline in the context of an expanding university system in which the sciences were ascendant. Literary critics could not plausibly associate their discipline with the authority of science. Nevertheless, they were still in need of a justification for their work and in their search for one they turned to myth. The embrace of myth by literary critics thus grew out of the attempt by the emerging field of English studies to find a discourse of its own that was authoritative without being scientific. Literary critics used myth to construct cultural authority for their discipline by positioning themselves as the interpreters of the mythic significance of literature, and by claiming they were equipped to elucidate that significance and therefore give access to truths that were somehow more real, and more relevant, than the deliverances of science.

Chapter 8 stays within academia, but shifts attention from literary criticism to theology. Like literary critics, academic theologians turned to myth in an effort to demonstrate that their work was relevant to twentieth-century concerns. Christian theologians had long been accustomed to intellectual challenges, but by the mid-twentieth century many theologians concluded continuing to fend off such challenges was no longer tenable. Challenges to Christian belief stemming from modern science and social science, critical history, and analytic philosophy continued to mount. But perhaps, some theologians concluded, the effort to resist modern knowledge on its own terms was the wrong approach: perhaps the territory claimed by modern knowledge should be surrendered and new defensive positions taken. Their strategy amounted to conceding the validity of the modern forms of knowledge production while simultaneously seeking refuge in the seemingly unassailable category of myth. This new strategy burst on the British scene with the controversy provoked by Bishop John Robinson's book-length exercise in popular theology entitled *Honest to God*. However, Robinson was only one of a number of influential theologians who contended that myth was the natural idiom of religion, a form of discourse that transcended the empirical realm, and that as such it was not susceptible to scientific, historical, or philosophical critiques. By defending the religious significance of myth British theologians hoped to sidestep some of the more pointed criticisms of Christian theology, even as they attempted to insulate the faith itself from the intellectual challenges of modernity.

The preceding outline may alert readers to certain omissions in the ensuing pages. The aim here is to provide a cross-sectional overview rather than a comprehensive survey of mythic thinking in twentieth-century Britain, and where omissions were deliberate it was not because I deemed the topic irrelevant to examination of the mythic phenomenon. For instance, I offer no discussion of W.B. Yeats, D.H. Lawrence, or Graves, though all three were undoubtedly significant writers who were by my own definition mythic thinkers. I pass them over not because they are unimportant but because there exist numerous excellent discussions of the role of myth in their thought and because the points I wish to make about the extent of mythic thinking led me in a different direction. The same is true for any number of writers and thinkers who are not examined here. On the other hand, there are a number of mythic thinkers, such as the neo-romantic poets of the "New Apocalypse" group, who remain relatively unexamined, but could not be included within the ambit of this study. The attempt to create meaning for modernity through myth was a broader phenomenon than can be captured exhaustively in a single book.

2

Golden Boughs, Fairy Books, and Holy Grails: The Making of a Myth-Saturated Culture

Introduction

In a 1923 review of James Joyce's *Ulysses*, the young poet and critic T.S. Eliot announced the emergence of a method of criticism and writing that would change both literature and the world:

> In using the myth, in manipulating a continuous parallel between contemporaneity and antiquity, Mr. Joyce is pursuing a method which others must pursue after him .... It is simply a way of controlling, of ordering, of giving a shape and a significance to the immense panorama of futility and anarchy which is contemporary history.... Psychology ... ethnology and *The Golden Bough* have concurred to make possible what was impossible even a few years ago. Instead of narrative method, we may now use the mythical method. It is, I seriously believe, a step toward making the modern world possible for art.[1]

By the time this review appeared, Eliot had already begun his own experiments with the "mythical method" in composing *The Waste Land*, a poem built around sustained reference to various myths. The assumption underlying Eliot's mythical method was that contemporary civilization faced problems that could be redressed by deploying myth.

At about the time that Eliot's review appeared, a young English professor at the University of Leeds was forming his own conclusions about the importance of myth. By 1923, J.R.R. Tolkien had for several years been composing a complex cycle of mythology, a legendarium, which would eventually give rise to two novels, *The Hobbit* and *The Lord of the Rings*. He undertook the project out of a desire to create a body of "mythology" for England. In a letter to his publisher, Tolkien confessed his "passion...for myth" and explained how he had intended

> to make a body of more or less connected legend, ranging from the large and cosmogonic, to the level of romantic fairy-story...which I would dedicate simply to: to England; to my country. It should possess the tone and quality that I desired, somewhat cool and clear, be redolent of our "air"...and, while possessing...the fair elusive beauty that some call Celtic...it should be "high," purged of the gross, and fit for the more adult mind of a land long now steeped in poetry. I would draw some of the great tales in fullness, and leave many only placed in the scheme, and sketched. The cycles should be linked to a majestic whole, and yet leave scope for other minds and hands, wielding paint and music and drama....
>
> These tales are "new," they are not directly derived from other myths and legends, but they must inevitably contain a large measure of ancient wide-spread motives or elements. After all, I believe that legends and myths are largely made of "truth," and indeed present aspects of it that can only be received in this mode.[2]

Tolkien's construction of a "mythology for England" had something in common with Eliot's "mythical method": namely, the assumption that British culture lacked something that could only be supplied by myth.

More specifically, both advocated the importance of myth as a means of understanding and changing the world, and both built aesthetic theories, and developed novel literary approaches, around an emphasis on myth's importance. In doing so, both were building on and engaging with a body of scholarship about myth that had become a significant component of British culture. Eliot's mythical method and Tolkien's mythology for England would have been unthinkable without the work of ethnographers, scholars of comparative religion, and comparative anthropologists going back to the last quarter of the nineteenth century. Both men, for instance, engaged with the work of the various comparative anthropologists who presented the diversity of world mythology in vivid and exhaustive detail. Eliot, as we have seen, underscored the importance of J.G. Frazer's *The Golden Bough* for writers grappling with the modern world. Similarly, Tolkien gave the most detailed explanation of his understanding of myth in a lecture dedicated to Andrew Lang, the late nineteenth-century scholar who was one of Frazer's intellectual forebears in the study of mythology.

The point of juxtaposing the above passages from Eliot and Tolkien is to show that they are both the product of a culture that by the early 1920s had become saturated with popular scholarship on myth. In order to describe the context that produced views like Eliot's and Tolkien's, this chapter seeks to accomplish two objectives in particular. First, it aims to provide a survey of late nineteenth- and early twentieth-century scholarship on myth, in order to build a cumulative case that early twentieth-century Britain by about 1920 was in many ways a myth-saturated culture. Central to this story was the cultural impact of Frazer's *The Golden Bough*. Second, it argues that from early on anthropological work on myth was linked with and motivated by a critique of modern culture, a critique that was premised in part on an approval of "primitivism." There was a distinct strain of anti-modernity in scholarship on myth that came to the fore especially in the work of the "Cambridge Ritualists." For these scholars, the study of myth provided the opportunity to critique British culture and offered intellectual resources for countering excessive rationalism. The work of Frazer, his predecessors, and successors combined with existing elements of British culture to create a precipitate in the form of mythic thinking. This chapter traces that process in order to provide a contextual backdrop for the more detailed examinations in subsequent chapters.

Before *The Golden Bough*: Lang, Tylor, and Smith

Three figures defined anthropology in Britain prior to Frazer: Andrew Lang, E.B. Tylor, and William Robertson Smith. These scholars pioneered a rationalist ethnographic approach to the study of myth in second half of the nineteenth century, developing concepts and methodologies that would become foundational to the work of Frazer and the so-called Cambridge Ritualists that he, in turn, inspired. But beyond their influence on later scholars of myth, they—especially Lang—were instrumental in inundating British culture with popular mythological literature, simultaneously creating and feeding a taste for myth in ways that Frazer and others would perpetuate.

Prior to Lang, Tylor, and Smith the study of myth in Britain was highly eclectic and not beholden to any one systematic approach or method. One reason was the Victorian idealization of the classical past, which made it difficult to conceive of myth as a discrete object of study apart from study of classical culture. When the study of myth did not appear as a branch of classical studies, it was largely subsumed within folklore. If there was a preeminent theory of myth, it was that advocated by Friedrich Max Müller (1823–1900), a German philologist who settled in Oxford. Müller applied the methods of comparative philology to the study of myth. Because the primitive Aryan language could not articulate abstractions, Müller argued, the Aryans were only able to express their religious ideas in metaphors that over time developed and combined to form myths. Building on the so-called Aryan hypothesis, which held that European languages ultimately had their roots in the migration of Aryan peoples from Central Asia, Müller argued that Greek myths derived from Aryan originals could be reconstructed by applying the laws of linguistic change. In Müller's view, as the Aryan language evolved in Europe, the original myths were lost, leaving only the suggestive metaphors upon which they were built. It was this situation—metaphors no longer anchored to what they originally described—that produced Greek mythology. As Hans Kippenberg summarizes:

> when we use a word that was first used metaphorically, without a clear understanding of the steps that led from the original to the metaphorical meaning, we are in danger of mythology; when the steps are forgotten and artificial steps are substituted, we get mythology or what he calls a "disease of language".... Led astray by language men began to imagine natural processes as persons with a gender and started telling stories about these persons.[3]

Because he held that most of the original Aryan myths concerned the sun, his theory of myth was labeled "solarism." One significant implication of solarism was that early humanity's intuitive sense of the infinite had been lost as language evolved.

By about 1860 Müller's theory of myth was the dominant explanation of the phenomenon, but when he died in 1900 his theory, by then subject to increasing criticism, died with him. This was in part because another approach to the study of myth, which was very much in tune with key elements of late Victorian culture, had swept Müller's ideas from the field. Müller's solarism was vanquished by the combined forces of Tylor, Smith, and above all Lang. Their theories of myth, which grew out of an intellectual climate that was deeply shaped by rationalist, progressivist evolutionary social thought, accorded with late Victorian culture in ways that Müller's did not.

The combined effect of the work of Tylor, Smith, and Lang was to replace the philological study of myth with the anthropological approach that would remain dominant well into the twentieth century.

The methods they developed both reflected and reinforced the general trend of evolutionary theorizing across the social sciences that characterized late Victorian culture. Drawing on the work of Jerome Buckley and John Burrow, historian of anthropology Robert Ackerman suggests that the new evolutionary anthropology accorded in some specific ways with the evolutionary trend of late Victorian thought. The passionate Victorian search for origins, inflected through evolutionary thought as a study of the organic growth and modification of all things over time, could readily be adapted to the study of human culture. In addition, evolutionary thought reinvigorated a faltering rationalism by offering a theory of human nature not susceptible to the objections that were undermining the utilitarian theory of human nature. Comparative anthropology reinforced this by purporting to illustrate the universal process of development that governed all human cultures.[4] The new comparative anthropology also reflected the Victorian penchant for incessant fact gathering, inasmuch as it depended on collecting countless examples of primitive thought—readily available from all corners of the empire—in order to illustrate the universality of the laws of cultural development. Finally, the fraught issue of religious belief in late Victorian Britain meant that anthropological work that shed light on the issue of religious belief was deemed highly relevant, since such work could be recruited into debates about the value of religion.

The man who pioneered the evolutionary study of human culture was Edward Burnett Tylor (1832–1917), whose achievements led to a readership in anthropology at Oxford and selection as the first President of the Section for Anthropology of the British Association for the Advancement of Science.[5] A trip to Mexico in the 1850s sparked Tylor's interest in anthropology and led to his first book. He would play a key role in overthrowing the prevailing view that primitive cultures were the degraded remnants of earlier, higher cultures, arguing instead that primitive societies represented an initial stage of human development. His argument rested on three main pillars: the presumption that human nature and human development were universally the same; the comparative method; and the notion of survivals. The first entailed the second: if contemporary primitive peoples were living links in the evolutionary chain, then it was a simple matter to conclude that, as Ackerman puts it:

> to secure the needed dynamic view of prehistoric development, one might string together items of culture taken from the most diverse "primitive" societies if in their totality they showed the steady upward movement of human development.[6]

For Tylor, "primitives" everywhere and at all times could be treated as a homogenous group because they were all at essentially the same stage of human evolution. In assuming that the goal of human cultural development was modern European civilization, Tylor exemplified the tendency of evolutionary anthropologists to interpret human development in terms of liberal British thought.[7] The doctrine of survivals completed the methodology. Survivals were cultural elements that had served a purpose in one developmental stage, but then survived into a later developmental stage in which they had no function. Proper interpretation of these survivals allowed anthropologists to reconstruct the life of earlier developmental stages. Tylor brought this methodology to bear in the 1871 work that made his name, *Primitive Culture: Researches into the Development of Mythology, Philosophy, Art, and Custom*. This was the book that, about 15 years later, would open Frazer's eyes to the explanatory power of comparative anthropology.

Tylor's views on religion and mythology were of greatest interest to most of his readers, and most of *Primitive Culture* was devoted to these subjects. He saw myth as a kind of "savage philosophy" that had its roots in the unique character of primitive mentality. Myth was in fact an attempt by primitive people to explain their experience as rationally as they were able. Incapable of abstract thought, they instead "animated" nature by projecting onto it the primitive doctrine of souls. Tylor coined the term "animism" to describe this attribution of souls or spirits to non-human objects as a way of explaining natural phenomena. This crude philosophy became myth as it was gradually elaborated into "sham history, the fictitious narrative of events that never happened."[8] For Tylor, then, mythology was something like failed science, a primitive attempt to explain the natural world in rational terms. Interestingly, Tylor thought that survivals of animism remained part of modern culture, and he interpreted late Victorian spiritualism, which fascinated him, as a case in point.[9]

For Tylor, then, myth was the product of a certain cognitive state that could not be observed but could be inferred. William Robertson Smith instead built his theory of myth on observable actions, namely rituals. Smith was born in rural Aberdeenshire and before he was 16 he had settled on becoming a minister in the conservative Free Church of Scotland, like his father.[10] He was a brilliant student and scholar who, thanks in part to his studies in Germany with the Old Testament scholar Julius Wellhausen and the eminent theologian Albert Ritschl, became the leading Scottish expert on the Higher Criticism of the Old Testament. He advocated the new German criticism as professor of Hebrew and Old Testament at Free Church College at Aberdeen, a position to which he was appointed in 1870. In 1881 Smith was judged guilty of undermining the authority of scripture by the Free Church as a result of two articles he wrote for the ninth edition of the *Encyclopaedia Britannica*; it was the last successful heresy trial in Great Britain. He was removed from his chair at Aberdeen but became co-editor of the *Encylopaedia Britannica*. Thanks to the interventions of a friend, he was able to join his fellow Scot Frazer at Trinity College, Cambridge in 1883.

Motivated in part by "a Victorian preoccupation with evolutionary origins," Smith wanted to reconstruct the worldview that produced the ancient Semitic religions.[11] Though he appreciated the power of Tylor's comparative method, he saw primitive religion very differently. For Smith primitive religion was a matter of institutions, practices, and rituals rather than belief; performance of sacred acts prescribed by tradition, rather than belief in particular doctrines, was the basis of primitive religion. Smith argued that myths emerge as elaborations on rituals, when the original meaning of the ritual has been lost:

> So far as myths consist of explanations of ritual, their value is altogether secondary, and it may be affirmed with confidence that in almost every case the myth was derived from the ritual, and not the ritual from the myth; for the ritual was fixed and the myth was variable, the ritual was obligatory and faith in the myth was at the discretion of the worshipper.[12]

According to this view, the key to interpreting myths was first understanding the ritual the myth explained, and this meant understanding how the ritual functioned with the social group. The influence of Smith's theory of myth was profound, though its effect was mediated through Frazer:

> It was [Smith's] theory of myth that led to the transformation of classical scholarship wrought by the "Cambridge Ritualists" Jane Ellen Harrison, F.M. Cornford, and A.B. Cook, as well as the Oxonian Gilbert Murray; to the distinctive mythic elements in the works of Yeats, Eliot, Lawrence, and Joyce; and to the "myth and ritual" school of literary criticism represented by Stanley Edgar Hyman. Almost without exception, however, the source acknowledged by these writers was *The Golden Bough* rather than *The Religion of the Semites*.[13]

Smith's role in shaping early twentieth-century thinking about myth was substantial, but largely unacknowledged. Most discussions of Lang, Tylor, and Smith culminate with the last-mentioned. This is because such discussions are concerned with tracing an intellectual lineage in the history of anthropological thought, and Smith was in many ways the intellectual progenitor of Frazer. But when viewed from a broader perspective, Lang emerges as perhaps the key member of the trio. When the question in view is how late nineteenth and early twentieth-century British culture became saturated with mythological writings, Lang's importance comes to the fore. More than any other figure prior to Frazer, Lang *popularized* the reading of world mythology. He did this in two ways: through authoritative scholarship on myth, and through bestselling collections of world mythology that he compiled and edited.

The man who established himself as perhaps the most visible authority on myth in late Victorian Britain was a remarkably prolific scholar and man of letters. Born in 1844 in Selkirk, Scotland, Lang went on to study at Balliol College, Oxford, and subsequently became a fellow of Merton College. He initially made his name in classical scholarship, producing well-received translations of the Homeric epics. Partly inspired by Tylor's work, he turned to the study of myth in the mid-1880s and produced several major works on the subject, as well as the article on myth in the ninth edition of the *Encyclopaedia Britannica*, which offered an extensive critique of Müller's views. His anthropological scholarship was not as original as Tylor or Smith's, but it was opinionated and engaging. During his lifetime, however, Lang's reputation was built on much more than just his scholarship: he was also an active journalist and sometime literary editor for *Longman's Magazine*. His talents as a writer and polemicist made him one of the most sought-after reviewers of the late Victorian period.

In 1889 Lang published his own selection of fairy tales, folk tales and myths called *The Blue Fairy Book*. This was the first of his colored "fairy books" which would appear at semi-regular intervals until 1910, when the twelfth and final volume appeared. The lavishly-illustrated books, which were intended primarily for children, "made him king undisputed of the nursery shelf."[14] Many of the stories collected in the volumes were appearing in English for the first time. In addition, Lang wrote several book-length fairy tales of his own, which remained popular into the 1940s.[15] Along with works by William Morris, Kipling, George MacDonald, E. Nesbit, J.M. Barrie, and Kenneth Grahame, Lang's work in this vein was one of the main tributaries feeding the widespread late Victorian and Edwardian taste for the fantastic. In a unique way, Lang bridged the gap between the scholarly and the popular in his advocacy of myth. Children absorbed his fairy books, the middlebrow public learned from his plentiful essays and reviews, and other scholars drew inspiration from his work—not least among them Harrison, the pioneer of Cambridge Ritualism.[16]

Although Lang, Tylor, and Smith shared the evolutionary assumption that myth-making was characteristic of a primitive stage of cultural development, their work could leave readers with the opposite impression. Their comparative method proceeded by the sheer amassing of examples from as many different cultures and time periods as possible. Lang demolished Müller's theory by producing numerous examples showing that cultures from all over the world—with no possible connection to the ancient Aryans—had versions of the same myth. One seemingly inescapable consequence of this was that myth-making was a *universal human trait*; humans were by nature myth-makers. What had helped primitive man make sense of the world might help modern man do the same. Indeed, once this conclusion was drawn, it could overshadow the intended point that myth-making was a primitive, passing evolutionary stage. There was thus an instability and tension at the heart of the comparative anthropological approach to myth: in trying to establish a universal, primitive mythical stage of human cultural evolution, such scholarship could leave the impression that myth-making was more universal than primitive. This unintended consequence would become apparent in responses to Frazer's work and would be exploited by some of the Cambridge Ritualist scholars of myth who were the intellectual descendents of Lang, Tylor, and Smith.

J.G. Frazer and *The Golden Bough*

The importance of Tylor, Lang, and Smith in popularizing the study of myth was surpassed by the work of a classics don who turned to comparative anthropology after encountering their work. This was James George Frazer, whose monumental study of primitive mythology was to exercise a profound influence on the imagination and vocabulary of the twentieth century. Almost immediately after its many volumes first began to appear in 1890, *The Golden Bough*'s influence began to suffuse both literature and popular culture.[17]

One of the first to take the measure of Frazer's cultural influence was the American critic Stanley Edgar Hyman, who in 1962 published a book that he considered his magnum opus, *The Tangled Bank: Darwin,*

Marx, Frazer and Freud as Imaginative Writers.[18] Hyman chose four figures that he thought had deeply shaped contemporary thought by providing basic metaphors for understanding the world. Hyman's choice of figures is indicative of how Frazer's cultural significance was estimated by many in the 1960s. Hyman identified Frazer as a scholar of myths who was himself a modern myth-maker, because his great work was in the form of a "mythic quest" by humanity for the Grail of rationality. Hyman noted something that other students of Frazer had been noting for decades: his influence was negligible within the field of anthropology, but was profound beyond the borders of that discipline. In trying to explain this odd fact, Hyman drew attention to the epic sweep, universality, and enduring imagery of *The Golden Bough*:

> *The Golden Bough* is not primarily anthropology, if it ever was, but a great imaginative vision of the human condition. Frazer had a genuine sense of the bloodshed and horror behind the gaiety of a maypole or a London-bridge-is-falling-down game . . . . The key image of *The Golden Bough*, the king who slays the slayer and must himself be slain, corresponds to some universal principle we recognize in life. It caught the imagination not only of Freud and Bergson, Spengler and Toynbee, but of T.S. Eliot, and produced *The Waste Land.*[19]

Hyman was correct to emphasize the compelling imagery of *The Golden Bough*, because one of the primary reasons for the work's cultural impact was the range of potent metaphors it contained. Scapegoating, cycles of death and rebirth, cycles of drought and fertility, ritually effica-cious violence, dying and reviving gods, the tension between reason and irrationality—all these key themes of Frazer's book came to be seen as apt metaphors in a period bracketed by world wars. What is more, the final volume of the third edition was an index, which effec-tively turned the work as a whole into a ready reference for authors in search of strange customs, rituals, or myths that might serve as useful tropes. In short order, leading modernist writers began to pro-duce works that relied heavily on material drawn from *The Golden Bough*.

The irony is that one of the most influential books of the century was originally intended to answer a straightforward and even incon-sequential question: explaining why the high priest of Nemi in Aricia took office by killing his predecessor. But to understand how Frazer transformed such a simple task into an epic quest it is necessary to understand something of his background.[20] Frazer was born in Glasgow in 1854 to pious Free Church parents and enjoyed a happy childhood that was saturated by religion. In the Frazer household, daily worship was the norm, which in part explains why an attempt to explain the mental processes behind religion would be central to Frazer's work. When he was 16 Frazer entered Glasgow University, where he developed an abiding allegiance to the power of disciplined rationality and decided to pursue classics as a career. He won a scholarship to Trinity College, Cambridge, where he matriculated in 1874. Trinity College would be Frazer's home for the rest of his life. When his thesis on Plato earned him a fellowship in 1879, Frazer seemed poised for an ordinary career as a classics don, but a fortuitous encounter with anthropology would open up an intellectual world to him beyond the editing of classical texts.

At the urging of a friend, Frazer read Tylor's *Primitive Culture* and soon after became friends with Smith, who came to Cambridge in 1883 to take up a post as Reader in Arabic at Frazer's own Trinity College. Through Smith's influence, Frazer realized that anthropological study might shed light on classical culture, and Smith's patronage enabled him to pursue his burgeoning interest in anthropology. As editor of the ninth edition of the *Encyclopaedia Britannica*, Smith commissioned Frazer to write articles on both classical and anthropological subjects. It was at this point that Frazer began collecting a mass of anthropological material that he solicited through industrious correspondence with foreign travelers who had been in contact with primitive peoples. These included explorers, missionaries, and colonial officials; hence he became the great exemplar of armchair cultural anthropologists. This mass of material would provide the basis for *The Golden Bough*, which proved to be a tremendous success. Each edition was more successful than the last and Frazer's reputation outside the academic world continued to grow throughout his career.

The Golden Bough's remarkable sales figures testify to its popularity. It was a huge financial success for both author and publisher, and enjoyed a sustained popularity rarely achieved by multivolume works. Between March 1911 and November 1922, at least 36,000 copies of all volumes of the twelve-volume third edition were printed. In the 11 years after the abridged edition appeared, it sold at least 33,000 copies annually. The third edition remained in print throughout the 1920s, with each volume being reprinted two or three times.[21] Beginning with the second edition, the book's influence was amplified by the extensive critical attention it received—almost all of it positive. As one of Frazer's biographers has written:

the new and not-so-well-educated middle class were told by the news-papers that *The Golden Bough*, at least in its abridged form, was one of those books that any thoughtful person had to know about; the self-educated among the working class and aspiring intellectuals and radicals read *The Golden Bough* for its explanation of how society and religion had begun in primitive confusion and misunderstanding.[22]

In her examination of the book's reception, Mary Beard has shown that by the turn of the century, the press treated Frazer not just as an author-ity, but as a veritable oracle whose every utterance on the exotic or the primitive must be heeded. The press's consistent invocations of Frazer's unique authority played a crucial role in creating a middlebrow "craze for Frazer" and elevating the status of *The Golden Bough* as a text.[23] Indeed, Frazer's cultural authority became so entrenched that, well into the 1960s, his critics and opponents within the field of anthropology were driven to extremes of vituperation in an attempt to kill off his influence.[24]

The Golden Bough's popularity certainly had much to do with its exotic subject matter, but it was also successful because of how Frazer treated and explained the strange myths, customs, and rituals he sur-veyed. Frazer combined in a unique way several intellectual trends of the late nineteenth century. To begin with, the most obvious charac-teristic of *The Golden Bough*, especially the twelve-volume third edition, is that it is an encyclopedic, exhaustive collection of "facts." Frazer's book epitomized the Victorian predilection for rational fact gathering. These facts bolstered a Darwinian attempt to illustrate the universal laws governing the development of human culture. At a time when the evolutionary outlook was ubiquitous and evolutionary thinkers like Huxley and Spencer immensely popular, this approach helped give *The Golden Bough* cultural purchase. Though he was not a dogmatic believer in progress, Frazer's view of human cultural evolution was optimistic. Human cultures, in his view, would inevitably progress from savagery to civilization by passing through the ages of magic and religion before ultimately arriving at the age of science. This process was driven by evolutionary adaptation: cultures abandoned magic, for instance, when they realized that it did not work. In a related way, *The Golden Bough* also catered to the Victorian enthusiasm for historical explanations. Frazer's epic tale of humanity's journey from savagery to civilization appealed to late Victorians who were trying to come to terms with their place in history. Throughout the book Frazer describes and illustrates recur-ring patterns of historical development while illuminating the origins of central components of Victorian culture such as Christianity, which Frazer argued had its origin in primitive fertility cults.

Finally, Frazer raised the comparative method to new heights, though critics charged the edifice was rickety, tenuous, and inconsistent.[25] Mountains of diverse facts were compiled and subsumed under Frazer's theory. Never had a work of anthropology seemed to explain so much, to bring into focus such a wide range of human experience. In its final edition *The Golden Bough* moved from an initial examination of the magical role of priest-kings, to a consideration of taboos, dying and reviving god myths, fertility myths and rituals, and scapegoating rituals, before returning again to priest-kings.[26] Frazer's comparative method depended on a principle he termed "the law of similarity," an idea he borrowed from the nineteenth-century German scholar Wilhelm Mannhardt. According to this principle, similar customs in different societies were assumed to be motivated by the same mental state. It is this principle that gave Frazer license to adduce such disparate evidence to support his assertions. Because of its scope, for many, Frazer's book represented a unique achievement in the human sciences. As one commentator remarked: "If here and there he was mistaken, if on this doubtful detail or other his guess has been discarded, the substance of his argument stands erect among the noblest scientific monuments of a century that knew how to build in the grand manner."[27]

Frazer's comparative method further reinforced the cultural relevance of *The Golden Bough* by allowing him implicitly to link together and comment on a number of concerns that were central to late Victorian culture. Frazer was equally willing to juxtapose and compare examples of customs and rituals from Australia, India, Mexico, rural Britain, Italy, Germany, central Europe and ancient Greece; neither time nor geography were barriers to his comparative approach. As Mary Beard observes:

> By bringing together these different areas of study, he set the subject of imperialism within the context of other central issues in the culture of Late Victorian Britain: the changing face of British traditions in the face of growing industrialization; the role and importance of the classical past. Through *The Golden Bough*, questions about British imperial domination became implicated in other questions about the relations between the peoples of the empire and those of rural England, about the nature of the rural and urban, the nature of the foreign, the domestic, and the past. The extraordinary appeal of *The Golden Bough* derived from the power of this combination: from its

weaving together so many central problems of late Victorian, early twentieth-century Britain.[28]

This multivalent relevance, Beard suggests, helps explain not just why *The Golden Bough* became a bestseller, but also why Frazer the man was so honored and, in fact, adored in his lifetime.

Frazer always maintained that the book was "not a general treatise on primitive superstition,"[29] but rather a work of science that attempted to solve only one problem: explaining the custom whereby the high priest of Nemi in Aricia took office by killing his predecessor. The larger and more unwieldy *The Golden Bough* grew, however, the more its faults and inconsistencies became apparent. In the preface to the third edition, Frazer contends that even if his explanation were to collapse, "its fall would hardly shake my general conclusions as to the evolution of primitive religion and society."[30] Any reader of *The Golden Bough* soon realizes that Frazer's scholarly objectives are far more numerous than simply explaining the priesthood of Nemi. It is clear, for instance, that he is interested in developing a theory of myth. Strangely, though, Frazer was never able to decide for himself what myth was and how it worked. As various scholars have pointed out, Frazer veered back and forth between endorsing at least three different incompatible theories of myth. Ackerman argues that "On no matter did he change his mind more often than on the nature and origin of myth and its relation to ritual."[31] At one moment he would describe myth as something like Tylor's savage philosophy (intellectualism), at another he would take the view that myths grew out of stories about past heroes and kings (euhemerism), and at still another he would argue that myths arise to explain rituals that have fallen into disuse (ritualism).

Frazer's work, and especially his use of the comparative method, drew increasing criticism from professional anthropologists in the years immediately following the appearance of *The Golden Bough's* third edition. Both his evolutionary assumptions and the conclusions they produced were called into question. For instance, Frazer's contention that the magical worldview was always and everywhere the first stage of human mental evolution was refuted, as was the underlying assumption that magical, religious, and scientific stages of mental evolution could be distinguished. Whereas Frazer's faculty psychology emphasized the study of mental states and of cultural practices as indicators of mental states, the emerging social anthropology rejected psychologism and tried to understand primitive cultures by studying the social function of cultural elements. Frazer's comparative method had little regard for cultural context, but the new social anthropology argued that cultural practices could *only* be understood in terms of their cultural context.[32] Though an emerging generation of professional anthropologists saw Frazer's approach as uncritical and naïve, this criticism did little to diminish the influence of *The Golden Bough*.

Ultimately, then, *academic* disputes about Frazer's assumptions and methods could do little to undermine the *literary* influence of *The Golden Bough*. In particular, it was the mythic material in *The Golden Bough* that gave the work its purchase in British literary culture. In fact only by emphasizing the appeal of this subject matter can certain ironies about *The Golden Bough's* reception be understood. The appeal of *The Golden Bough's* mythic subject matter escaped Frazer's presuppositions and explanatory apparatus. What endured in readers' minds was not so much Frazer's explanations of how various myths embodied various primitive beliefs, but rather the myths themselves in their many vivid permutations. Thus what impressed the first generation of writers who took inspiration from Frazer was not his argument that myths of dying and reviving gods had their roots in fertility rituals, but instead the power and perceived relevance of the dying and reviving god myths. In John Vickery's view two factors above all explain the book's literary influence: "one was the subject-matter or content of *The Golden Bough* itself, and the other, its singular appropriateness to prevailing literary tastes."[33] In the preface to the second edition of *The Golden Bough*, Frazer expressed the hope that even if his hypotheses should sooner or later break down or be superseded, "I hope that my book may still have its utility and its interest as a repertory of facts."[34] This was not quite correct: it was not as a repertory of facts but as a repertory of myths that *The Golden Bough* was able to remain relevant.

Frazer described *The Golden Bough's* comparative method as an artillery battery that would obliterate primitive beliefs and superstitions including, presumably, Christianity.[35] The irony is that by cataloguing those beliefs so compellingly, he revivified them by awakening literary intellectuals to the imaginative power of myth. The myths that Frazer sought to destroy took on new life first in the works of modernists and subsequently in the works of many others. But the fact that *The Golden Bough* was important to the work of modernist writers only reinforced its authority by leading many to conclude that a work that inspired—and was recommended by—so many important writers must be highly significant.

The First World War, its aftermath, and tensions of the interwar period served as an ideal context for reception of the mythic material in *The Golden Bough*. This was a period in which many of Britain's intellectuals tried to come to grips with forces of irrationalism and disorder that seemed to threaten the very continuation of civilization in Europe. To many, the myths presented in Frazer's work offered both a key to understanding this irrationalism and an antidote to it. Frazer, following on the heels of Tylor, Smith, and Lang, drove home the point to a culture steeped in the classics that myths were more than adornments of the glory that was Greece. *The Golden Bough* played a key role in creating and feeding the desire for primitive as opposed to classical myth. As Vickery has put it, thanks to Frazer, "Myths broadened their significance from that of a predominantly ornamental beauty to a dynamic illumination of the wellsprings of the human imagination."[36] And those wellsprings that Frazer illuminated were often savage, violent, and dark.

Frazer himself was apprehensive about reason's fate in Europe; his belief in progress was conventionally Victorian, yet tenuous. As more than one commentator has noted, *The Golden Bough* is a kind of ode to the progress of human reason "in the face of the forces of gigantic unreason."[37] But, though Frazer never abandoned his evolutionary faith in the progress of reason, there were moments when he worried whether this progress was reversible: "Will the great movement which for centuries has been slowly altering the complexion of thought be continued in the near future? Or will a reaction set in which may arrest progress and even undo much of what has been done?"[38] And he worried elsewhere about how "A mass, if not the majority, of people in every civilized country is still living in a state of intellectual savagery, that, in fact, the smooth surface of cultured society is sapped and mined by superstition."[39] Frazer was haunted by the fear that a resurgence of unreason might damage modern civilization. Yet many students of *The Golden Bough* saw in its myths a means of channeling and coping with unreason, and they were given encouragement in thinking this by the work of a group of scholars, the Cambridge Ritualists, who drew inspiration from Frazer while taking the comparative study of myth in new directions.

"Reason is not everything": Primitivism and the Cambridge Ritualists

A few brooding interludes aside, *The Golden Bough* was marked from beginning to end by Frazer's optimistic, confident Victorian outlook. It is ironic, then, that some of the most prominent anthropologists who owed an intellectual debt to Frazer did not share his Victorian faith in rationality and the progress of science. In fact, several of Frazer's epigones produced work that was marked by a distinct strain of antimodern primitivism that emphasized the limits of reason and the dangers of an over-reliance on rationality. Because of the university at which most of them worked and the theory of myth they held, these scholars have been labeled the "Cambridge Ritualists," and the approach they took to the study of myth afforded an opportunity to critique Victorian bourgeois complacency.

For the Cambridge Ritualists, the study of the ritual origins of myth was an opportunity to expose the incomplete, self-serving picture of classical civilization that was central to the Victorian cultural establishment. The Ritualists recognized that one of the props to Victorian bourgeois culture was an idealization of Greek classicism and associated values.[40] Investigating the ritual origins of myth—and thereby exposing the irrational, Dionysian background of classical civilization—allowed the Cambridge Ritualists to suggest that what they perceived as a narrow bourgeois mentality was in fact built on a false foundation. Far from representing the epitome of enlightened rationality, the Cambridge Ritualists suggested, Hellenic civilization had contained within itself deep currents of ecstatic emotion and religious feeling—currents that were perhaps worth reappropriating. At the end of her vast study of ancient Greek religion, Harrison quoted her friend and erstwhile collaborator Gilbert Murray: "Reason is great, but it is not everything. There are in the world things, not of reason, but both below and above it, causes of emotion which we cannot express, which we tend to worship, which we feel perhaps to be the precious things in life."[41]

The reversion to irrationality that Frazer feared was a source of fascination to Harrison, a brilliant scholar who drew inspiration directly from his works. But there was a difference. For Frazer, religion belonged to an earlier stage of evolution, to the childhood of humanity; for Harrison it spoke to human cultural maturity. Whereas Frazer saw irrational superstition as a threat to civilization, Harrison saw it as a link to vital experience that could reinvigorate an emotionally arid civilization.

Students of Harrison's life—from admiring contemporaries like Virginia Woolf to more recent biographers—are alike in approaching her with a mixture of fascination and admiration, whatever opinions they might have of her work and ideas.[42] Born in 1850 into a Nonconformist Yorkshire family, Harrison belonged to the first generation of women to attend university in England. In 1875 she entered Newnham College, Cambridge, where, unlike most Newnham students, she read for the classical Tripos. She expected to be invited to join the Newnham staff as a lecturer in classics after passing her Tripos in 1879, but she was passed over as too independent-minded. Harrison was crushed, and after a year of teaching at a girls' school she settled in London. She soon mastered German so that she could keep abreast of classical scholarship, and spent time studying in both Continental museums and the British Museum. She supported herself by writing and lecturing on classical culture. Harrison had a particular gift for making Greek art come alive and her lectures were very popular. Around 1887 she underwent a personal and intellectual crisis, which she herself described in explicitly religious terms. The details of this crisis remain uncertain, but she eventually emerged from a period of depression, loneliness and guilt with a renewed passion for her vocation and an entirely new perspective on it. In her scholarship, this personal transformation was evident as a new interest in the origins of religion.

One of the main factors in bringing Harrison out of her crisis was an 1888 trip to Greece during which she observed ongoing archaeological excavations in Athens. It was a moment in the history of classical studies when younger scholars were controversially attempting to establish that archaeology was a source of valuable information about antiquity—not simply a supplement to classical literature but a rich body of evidence in its own right. This was an affront to the nineteenth-century status quo position that the way to approach classical culture was through its literature. Harrison had gravitated toward the archaeological position in the 1880s, and her visit to Greece convinced her that archaeology offered a means of getting beyond the idealized Victorian picture of classical civilization. On this trip she hit upon what would become one of her central ideas: "Some of the loveliest stories the Greeks have left us will be seen to have taken their rise, not in poetic imagination, but in primitive, often savage, and, I think, always *practical* ritual."[43] She put forth this view in *Mythology and Monuments of Ancient Athens*, which was the fruit of her trip to Greece. She acknowledged that in adopting such a view she was taking a cue from Lang, among others. Later she would discover Smith, whose work would serve as further inspiration. *Mythology and Monuments* earned Harrison some measure of scholarly renown, which was no small feat for a woman in what was then one of the most conservative fields of scholarship.[44]

The idea that rituals provided the basis of myths would remain central to all of her subsequent work in classical studies, work that was stimulated and supported by a group of like-minded scholars. In 1898 she returned to Newnham College as a lecturer in Classical Archaeology. There she met Gilbert Murray and Francis Cornford, and later

A.B. Cook. This group of classicists, who shared an interest in Frazer and were methodologically indebted to Smith, formed a group that would later be called the Cambridge Ritualists. From about 1900 to 1915 they together pursued a new course in the study of Greek religion and drama, each shaping and contributing to the work of the others. The year 1912, when three of them published major works, represented a high point in their association. Together these scholars took iconoclastic aim at an idealized nineteenth-century portrait of the Greeks, and tried to put flesh and bones on a merely skeletal understanding of the culture and religion of Archaic Greece.

If myth had its origins in ritual, then in order to understand myth it was necessary to understand what the primitives did, rather than simply what they thought. A hallmark of Harrison's approach was thus an emphasis on religion as performed and felt rather than as believed—religion as, in her words, "social custom, embodying social emotion."[45] She was at pains to emphasize this distinction in her work, and her desire to understand and communicate to her readers the felt nature of religion led her to embrace "the newest irrationalist Continental sociology, psychology, and philosophy" as found in the works of Durkheim, Freud, and Bergson.[46] To this was added a career-long interest in Nietzsche. Harrison's sense that beneath the placid surface of classical Greece moved darker currents had first been mooted by Nietzsche in *The Birth of Tragedy*, which Harrison had read with interest. This openness to other thinkers marked her as one of the most intellectually voracious writers of the late Victorian and Edwardian periods; the latest work from various fields and in several languages became grist for her mill.

Harrison's two main works were *Prolegomena to the Study of Greek Religion* (1903) and *Themis* (1912). The former exposed the dimly understood religious stratum underneath the Olympian pantheon, while the latter extended this line of inquiry with the help of the theories of Durkheim and Bergson. The event that sent Harrison down the road that would lead to her *Prolegomena* was another encounter with archaeology. Around 1900 her friend Arthur Evans, an archaeologist, introduced her to Cretan artifacts—clay impressions of seal rings—that illuminated the pre-Olympian goddess cults of ancient Greece. The impressions depicted Greek religious rituals prior to the worship of the Olympian gods, and the rituals were very different than those of Olympian religion—much darker, more pessimistic, and colored by a deep sense of evil. Whereas in the Olympian religion believers performed sacrifices in order to maintain a coolly rational cycle of gift exchange between believers and gods, the rituals she saw depicted in the impressions were ecstatic, intended to avert divine wrath and ensure fertility, matriarchal (centered on a Great Mother goddess rather than a Zeus-figure), and chthonic (earthly as opposed to heavenly). This was the turbulent reality that lay behind the placid façade of Olympian religion. Thus, Harrison's *Prolegomena* highlighted the irrationality at the heart of archaic Greek civilization. And she did not make a great effort to conceal the fact that she felt something had been lost in the transition from the archaic cults to the Olympian pantheon. As Hans Kippenberg has put it, she felt that "With the victory of the Olympians, intellect triumphed over feeling, cold rationality over female power."[47]

From about the turn of the century, the limits and misuses of reason became a running theme of Harrison's work. For Harrison reason was a tool, helpful only to the extent that it furthered understanding by producing unified, synthetic explanations of the phenomena to which it was applied. She thus reacted strongly against scholarship that only fragmented and atomized its subject matter. For her this intellectual tendency indicated a deeper cultural malady: analysis that only deconstructed, which merely broke down a subject into its constituent facts, was indicative of a society that was socially atomized and lacking in fellow feeling and a sense of common life. For her, the collective thinking and feeling that characterized archaic Greek religion seemed far preferable to the social atomism of her day. This was a point she emphasized in *Themis*, which highlighted the group-unity that undergirded totemism in terms that imply a clear critique of the individualism of early twentieth-century Britain:

> [Totemism's] basis is group-unity, aggregation, similarity, sympathy, a sense of common group life, and this common life, this *participation*, this unity, extended to the non-human world in a way that our modern, individualistic reason, based on observed distinctions, finds almost unthinkable. (emphasis in original)[48]

In order to explain religious practices—such as totemism or mysterygod cults—that seemed inexplicable to moderns, Harrison turned to Durkheim's theories about the social function of primitive religion. Durkheim convinced her that "the form taken by the divinity reflects the social structure of the group to which the divinity belongs."[49] Likewise, Bergson's notion of durée, "that life which is one, indivisible and yet ceaselessly changing" helped her see primitive Greek religion as an instinctive, intuitive attempt to express such oneness, in contrast to Olympian religion, which was "not an intuitive expression, but a late and conscious representation, a work of analysis, of reflection and intelligence."[50]

In *Themis* Harrison applied this insight to the mystery cults of Dionysus and Orpheus, which to her mind represented genuine religious expressions, in contrast to the Olympian gods of Homer. Understanding the myth-ritual nexus revealed in the mystery religions was for Harrison the key to transcending the false picture of Greek civilization that came from emphasizing the intellectual achievements of the Greeks. *Themis* attempted to show that by an examination of rites and rituals (*dromena* in Harrison's terminology), it is possible to see Greek myths for what they originally were: something like scripts that governed the performance of religious rituals; ritual was enacted myth, even though this fact was obscured by historical change. As she put it:

> In the study of Greek religion it is all important that the clear distinction should be realized between the comparatively perma-nent element of the ritual and the shifting manifold character of the myth.... This does not, however, imply, as is sometimes supposed, that ritual is prior to myth; they probably arose together. Ritual is the utterance of an emotion, a thing felt, in *action*, myth in words or thoughts. They arise *pari passu*. The myth...does not arise to give a reason; it is representative, another form of utterance, of expres-sion. When the emotion that started the ritual has died down and the ritual though hallowed by tradition seems unmeaning, a reason is sought in the myth and it is regarded as aetiological.[51]

The implications of this view of myth were explored in two sections of *Themis* contributed by Harrison's fellow Cambridge Ritualists, F.M. Cornford and Gilbert Murray. Cornford showed how the Olympics Games emerged from a ritual that welcomed the new year. Murray's contribution was briefer but more significant, because it was the first attempt to apply the key idea of the myth and ritual school to liter-ary criticism. Murray aimed to expose an underlying mythic pattern in Greek tragedy by making an historical argument about how it had developed out of Dionysian religious ritual. This attempt to find mythic patterns in other literary forms would become the central principle of later myth criticism.

Harrison's depiction of Greek religion, which emphasized its com-munal, emotional, and irrational aspects, was linked to an explicit critique of British culture. Virtually every point that Harrison empha-sized about the connection between myth and ritual in ancient Greece corresponded to her anxieties about Britain's pressing cultural needs. Three examples in particular stand out. In her scholarship she depicted religion as enacted emotion rather than as Victorian belief in dogma; she described a culture united by a communal experience of shared emotion rather than a British culture marked by individualism and fragmentation; and she saw the vital emotion exemplified by the ancient Greek cults as a salutary contrast to the rationalism and intellectualism of her day. If the work of scholars like Tylor, Smith, and Frazer had demonstrated the universality of myth-making as a feature of human culture, Harrison was the first to argue that the study of ancient myth could reveal resources for dealing with contemporary needs. In fact, this conviction was the source of the urgency and zeal that suffused her work. As one of her biographers has written, "She wrote with a passion that came from seeing her research as intensely practical. She believed that to study the origins of Greek religion was to discover the essence of the nature of religion."[52] To Harrison, rediscovering the true nature of religion was a precondition for the religious reawakening she believed her age needed, a belief she came to in part through her research for *Themis*. In her introduction to the work she confessed:

> I have come to see in the religious impulse a new value. It is, I believe, an attempt, instinctive and unconscious, ... to apprehend life as one, as indivisible, yet as perennial movement and change. But, profoundly as I also feel the value of religious impulse, so keenly do I feel the danger and almost necessary disaster of each and every creed and dogma....

> The only intelligible meaning that ritual has for me, is the keeping open of the individual soul ... to other souls, other separate lives, and to the apprehension of other forms of life.... Whether any systematized attempt to remind man, by ritual, of that whole of life of which he is a specialized fragment can be made fruitful or not, I am uncertain.[53]

By the time she published *Epilegomena to the Study of Greek Religion* in 1921, this uncertainty had become something more like hope. The influence of Bergson was palpable as she declared that there was one present form of religion that was "vital, creative" as primitive Greek religion had been. This was immanentism, the principle of which was "you, that is the best in you, is one with God, is God, your work is the divine activity."[54] In immanentism she saw something close to the spirit of primitive Greek religion: "It is very near to that primal mystery, the impulse of life, which it was the function of primitive religion to conserve."[55] Rather than group ritual, the core of this immanentism was "the practice of asceticism," though she failed to specify what this asceticism entailed.[56] Despite this vagueness, Harrison's zeal was evident: the final chapter of the book was a passionate plea for immanentism achieved through ascetic discipline.

Harrison was not alone in parlaying her study of myth and ritual into a call for spiritual renewal. Similar themes were sounded by Harrison's exact contemporary, Jessie Weston.[57] And, as Ackerman has pointed out, there are further parallels between their careers. He notes that both women were deeply influenced by Frazer's *Golden Bough*, both moved from an initial interest in aesthetics to comparative religion and anthropology, and both used evidence in similar ways.[58]

Though Harrison and Weston knew and admired each other's work, they were not acquainted. For her part, Weston was deeply indebted to the work of the Cambridge Ritualists and openly acknowledged this, singling out the work of Frazer, Murray, and Harrison in particular.[59] Weston was the first to see that the Ritualist approach could be applied to literature that did not have its roots in ancient Greece. In 1920 she published *From Ritual to Romance*, which, as the title suggests, argues that the Grail legend derives from pre-Christian pagan fertility rituals. Weston also offered a mystical interpretation of the Grail quest, arguing that for moderns it can represent the quest for self-realization.

Weston's religious reading of the Grail bears more than a passing resemblance to Harrison's praise of immanentism in *Epilegomena*. Both Weston and Harrison were motivated by deep religious impulses and both saw their scholarship as part of an effort to reconceptualize religion for the needs of their contemporaries. Weston followed Harrison in concluding that one reason for the spiritual poverty of the modern age was reliance on a rationality that only dissected its subject matter, rather than allowing a holistic understanding of it. Such "criticism by isolation" had prevented a proper understanding of the Grail material in Weston's view.[60] And, like Harrison's, Weston's scholarship is marked by a deeply personal tone and a sense that ancient myths and rituals have contemporary relevance. At the outset of *From Ritual to Romance* she offered a defense of primitive religion: "The more closely one studies pre-Christian Theology, the more strongly one is impressed with the deeply, and daringly, spiritual character of its speculations."[61] Weston herself was active in occult circles, and she took her experience of the occult as confirmation for the ideas she advanced in her work. After making her name with *From Ritual to Romance*, she was in demand as a commentator on religious issues and could be found giving public lectures on such topics as "The Vital and Vitalizing Spirit of Religion."[62] As with Harrison, for Weston the study of ancient myth was bound up with a desire for a spiritual reawakening in Britain.

Weston's book seemed to mark a tipping point in the saturation of British literary culture with mythic ideas. Her application of the myth and ritual approach to a myth with British connections was a decisive intervention. The ritualist method applied to Arthurian legend catalyzed literary interest in myth. Moreover, the aspects of the Grail legend that Weston chose to emphasize, such as the Waste Land; her emphasis on the power and importance of symbols like the Grail, lance, sword, and stone; and her idealization of the primitive religious imagination, were all particularly appealing to modernists and writers with modernist inclinations. Richard Barber, in his encyclopedic and authoritative study of changing beliefs about the Grail, describes Weston as someone who "unleashed" powerful images in twentieth-century literature, images which have "haunted twentieth-century literature to a degree quite disproportionate to [their] basis in fact."[63] Though Barber is certainly correct to see *From Ritual to Romance* as a catalyst for Grail mania in Britain, it is worth remembering that Weston was also capitalizing on an interest in Arthuriana—fascinatingly documented by Marc Girouard in *Return to Camelot*—that was already present in Edwardian culture.[64] The two decades after *From Ritual to Romance's* appearance saw an unprecedented proliferation of Grail-themed literature, whose authors frequently acknowledged their debt to Weston. Eliot's *The Waste Land* is the best-known case, but there were a host of novels as well, including Arthur Machen's *The Secret Glory* (1922), John Cowper Powys' *A Glastonbury Romance* (1932), Mary Butts' *Armed With Madness* (1928), and Charles Williams' *War in Heaven* (1930). Weston's work was thus one of the formative elements of an intellectual climate in which, as Barber has observed, "insistence on the limitations of rational thought and on the value of personal mystical experience untrammeled by the bonds of ritual and doctrine was to be one of the main influences on Grail literature in England in the early twentieth century."[65]

Conclusion

By 1920, when *From Ritual to Romance* appeared, scholars of comparative religion, folklorists, classicists, and, above all, anthropologists had produced a wealth of scholarship that both compiled myths from various cultures and times and sought to explain the purpose and meaning of those myths. John Vickery has suggested the term "classical anthropology" to encompass the diversity of work produced by the scholars whose era of productivity is marked by Lang's career on the one hand and Bronislaw Malinowski's on the other.[66] The mass of material produced by these classical anthropologists, much of it aimed at a popular audience, could not but have wide cultural repercussions. By 1920 British culture was saturated with this cultural production on myth, and literary deposits began to form from this saturation. This process was complex. Works on myth by scholars like Lang, Frazer, Harrison, and Weston were popular in their own right, but the cultural influence of these and related studies of myth was dramatically amplified by authors and poets who drew inspiration from them and produced a body of literature driven by the belief that myth had a pressing contemporary relevance. The group of writers who initially did the most to build on the work of classical anthropologists were the modernists.[67] They were able to powerfully and influentially articulate the contemporary relevance of myth in both works of imaginative literature and aesthetic theory.

Why the modernists were drawn to myth has much to do with how Frazer and the myth and ritual school wrote about it. In particular, the theme of primitivism in their work exerted a powerful influence on British literary culture, first with the modernists in the interwar period and later with literary critics in the postwar period. The supposed virtues of "the primitive mind" and of the myths produced by it proved attractive to both groups. After examining the central assumptions of the myth and ritual writers, one commentator offered his assessment of why their primitivism was so influential:

> On the basis of these assumptions, critics are prepared to argue that the literature of Western civilization can be understood and evaluated by establishing its connection with, or similarity to, the religious rituals of an assumed world-wide primitive society and primitive mind, the last being an important idea, since it is assumed that the primitive or unspecialized mind has a greater contact with, a more complete view of, total reality than the modern mind.[68]

For those disenchanted with a modernity that seemed disenchanted, the primitive mind depicted by Frazer and the Ritualists seemed not just appealing, but worth rediscovering and reawakening. Harrison and Weston in particular had complained that the modern intellect fragmented all that it analyzed, while the primitive mind saw life more accurately as a whole. And, the Ritualists argued, seeing life as a whole entailed communal spiritual experience that gave identity to the self, in contrast to a modern age when the self had no certain place, no stable identity. Writers and critics with similar complaints found depicted in ritualist scholarship a mode of experiencing life that had been sacrificed to modernity, and they acquired from ritualist scholarship a set of images, tropes, and analytic categories that could be used to articulate their discontent with modernity and seek new meaning within it.

3

"The Grail Is Stirring": Modernist Mysticism, the Matter of Britain, and the Quest for Spiritual Renewal

Introduction

In 1937 Faber & Faber published the first literary effort by David Jones, a Welshman who until that time had been known primarily as a painter, illustrator, and engraver. The book, entitled *In Parenthesis*, defied easy characterization with its unusual mix of poetry and prose, but this did not stop T.S. Eliot from penning an admiring introduction. *In Parenthesis* was Jones's attempt to make sense of the events he had witnessed as a soldier in the First World War. Using literary techniques that Eliot himself had pioneered in *The Waste Land*, Jones tried to give his war experience meaning by linking it to a pattern of mythical references. He even used the image of the waste land to describe the war landscape that he had inhabited, thus adapting for his own purposes the symbol that Eliot had made an iconic representation of the modern condition. Yet Jones's use of myth was not merely an attempt to impose order on "the futility and anarchy which is contemporary history," as Eliot had famously described "the mythical method."[1] For Jones myth was much more that a source of literary form: it was a narrative matrix in which religious truths were accumulated and preserved throughout the ages. Myth could not only bring order to a work of literature, it could also disclose a perennial spiritual order that existed independently of the artist.

Jones's *In Parenthesis* exemplifies a particular modernist approach to myth that has been largely ignored or obscured in the existing scholarship on modernism. This scholarship has based its explanation of the modernist engagement with myth almost exclusively on analysis of the works of four key modernist writers—Eliot, Yeats, Lawrence, and Joyce—who are treated as representative of modernism as a whole.[2]

The presumption implicit in this scholarship is that there was a typical modernist understanding of myth based on a shared modernist reaction to anthropological scholarship. According to the standard view, modernists held that the conditions of modernity dictated that myth's role was simply to provide elements for a pattern or structure in works of literature, not to convey religious truths or insights in which to believe. In short, recourse to myth was essentially an attempt to seek the consolations of a coherent aesthetic form given that the consolations of religious belief were unavailable. Though there are significant elements of truth in this line of argument (many modernists *did* seek the consolation of literary form as a substitute for religion), it places far too much weight on the dictates and examples of a few canonical modernists.

Two prominent examples of this approach are Michael Bell's penetrating monograph *Literature, Modernism, and Myth* and Andrew Von Hendy's meticulous study *The Modern Construction of Myth*. Bell, through examinations of early Eliot, Joyce, Yeats, and Lawrence, concludes that the belief that one may commit to a worldview while still acknowledging its relativism was central to modernist aesthetics.[3] In Bell's view, Frazer's *The Golden Bough* contributed to this awareness by both fostering a skepticism toward myth and encouraging a degree of nostalgia for it—a set of circumstances that essentially gutted the meaning of "belief" and reinforced the modernist commitment to coping with modern fragmentation by imposing order on it through art. Von Hendy's discussion of modernist engagement of myth is also limited to the quartet of Eliot, Yeats, Lawrence, and Joyce—though he contrasts the last-mentioned with the first three. He emphasizes how the first three were alike in interpreting *The Golden Bough* as demonstrating "the permanent presence of the archaic within each human consciousness."[4] For them, Frazer had demonstrated the existence of a mythic stratum in the human mind that could facilitate coping with modernity. One result was Eliot's mythical method, which Von Hendy describes as "something like the artist's apprehension of his chaotic world through the frame of a traditional sacred narrative so as to fix upon it by means of his artistic 'form' a public 'order' that isn't otherwise there."[5]

My intention here is not to disparage the work of Bell and Von Hendy. On the contrary, their books are rich with insights that significantly advance our understanding of the modernist use of myth. The point, rather, is that studies of the modernist use of myth that rely almost entirely on examination of the Eliot-Yeats-Lawrence-Joyce quartet are limited in ways that inhibit a robust historical understanding of the culture of modernism. An exclusive focus on how canonical modernists employed myth has produced several deficits in our understanding of interwar modernist literature. To begin with, it has led us to marginalize a number of key authors who were, in actuality, quite conspicuous in their day. Furthermore, it has prevented us from fully appreciating the significance of cultural patterns, such as the Grail obsession that characterized much of interwar literary culture. Most importantly, perhaps, it has perpetuated an incomplete understanding of how modernist writers conceived of the relationship between faith, knowledge, and art in the modern world. To put it bluntly, focusing our attention on modernists who believed that art (supported by myth) *creates* order and meaning in the world has caused us to ignore those modernists who believed that art (supported by myth) *reveals* an order and meaning that exists independently.[6]

In an effort to enhance and deepen our understanding of the modernists' engagement with myth, in this chapter I make three inter-related arguments. First, I seek to show that some modernists saw myth as a source of spiritual meaning, not simply as a means of imposing form on a work of art or imposing coherence on history. Second, I argue that these modernists believed that this spiritual meaning was not a human creation, but an independent reality that myth revealed. Third, I argue that this understanding of myth as a source of spiritual meaning was enabled by a particular interpretation of anthropological scholarship on myth. The writers examined in this chapter did not see modern anthropology as necessarily corrosive of faith. Modern anthropology may have led some modernists away from faith, but it helped others sustain or even find it.

I advance these arguments by examining how four modernist writers, John Cowper Powys, Mary Butts, Charles Williams, and David Jones, engaged during the 1920s and 1930s with the mythology concerning the Holy Grail—a mythology that was attractive to them because it was familiar, indigenous, and spiritually suggestive. These writers turned to Grail mythology not simply as a source of fragmentary raw material to be reshaped for literary purposes, but also as a source of spiritual consolation. For them, unlike many other modernist writers, myth in general and the Grail mythology in particular revealed an order and meaning— a spiritual dimension of reality—that existed independently of them. They were able to use the Grail mythology this way because of the way they responded to and adapted the relevant anthropological scholarship of the late nineteenth and early twentieth century. Though many modernists drew skeptical conclusions from such work, the Grail writers examined here found it an illuminating and spiritually encouraging record of how various cultures had experienced the divine.

The Grail in early twentieth-century Britain

One of the remarkable features of modernist writing is the spate of work based on the Grail myth produced during the interwar period. Almost immediately after the First World War, the Grail myth became an all-purpose metaphor for modernist writers in search of aesthetic resources for coping with modernity. The are a variety of reasons for this boom, including a postwar context in which the Grail's healing properties resonated as a powerful symbol; the influence of anthropological literature on myth and ritual, particularly Jessie Weston's *From Ritual to Romance*; and the British associations inherent to the Grail mythology, which suited an introspective cultural moment during which many writers were grappling with questions of Britishness and Englishness. Above all, by reworking the mythology surrounding the Grail, modernist writers were able to articulate their desire for spiritual renewal, and the Arthurian corpus proved to be an ideal idiom for expressing this desire. It is no coincidence that many of the writers who were fascinated by the Grail myth also explored spiritual matters through involvement with various forms of spiritualism, religious seeking, or the occult, as will be detailed further below. Arthur Machen, whose novel *The Secret Glory* (1922) was one of the first of the modernist Grail novels, was a member of the Order of the Golden Dawn. Mary Butts, whose novel *Armed with Madness* (1928) explores the revitalizing power of the Grail, had explored the occult with Aleister Crowley. Charles Williams, who wrote both poetry and novels that draw heavily on Grail mythology, was also a student of the occult and a member of the Fellowship of the Rosy Cross, a Rosicrucian order. Powys and Jones had their own interests in religious matters. Powys moonlighted as a religious philosopher and Jones was a convert to Catholicism.

The popularity of the Grail myth among modernist writers is noteworthy in part for the way it illuminates the influence of myth scholarship on twentieth-century British literary culture. Indeed, the subgenre of modernist Grail literature is unimaginable apart from the late nineteenth- and early twentieth-century anthropological and archaeological work that had illuminated so much about ancient myth and ritual. Not only did works like Weston's *From Ritual to Romance* and A.E. Waite's *The Hidden Church of The Holy Graal* (1909) suggest the Grail myth had greater historical significance than previously thought, recent archaeological discoveries held out the prospect that the Grail itself might actually be discovered. As Richard Barber has written:

> The idea that the actual Grail, the dish of the Last Supper, might be found again was strengthened by the rise of archaeology and the spectacular discoveries of the late nineteenth century. If legendary cities such as Troy could be resurrected, why should the Grail be beyond reach? The Catholic relics which claimed to be the dish or chalice of the Last Supper were ignored, and new candidates emerged.[7]

Several of these candidates emerged in Britain. The early twentieth century saw a number of celebrated cases of supposed Grail discovery in Britain, and the current association of Glastonbury with the Grail myth is attributable in part to two of these cases. These causes célèbres were reinforced by respectable scholarly works that lent credibility to certain key elements of the Grail mythology, such as R.G. Collingwood and J.N.L. Myres' *Roman Britain and the English Settlements* (1936). This volume in the *Oxford History of England* by respected Oxford dons suggested that a historical personage corresponding to the King Arthur of myth might well have existed. It all served to reinforce the notion that the Grail myth was a distinctly British inheritance, and one that might well have some basis in fact. Modernist meditations on the Grail myth thus took place in a context in which the possibility of finding the actual Grail was widely entertained.

The Grail myth derived added appeal from its association with ancient Celtic traditions and with actual British places. For instance, there were clear parallels between the Grail mythology and some parts of Celtic mythology. The Grail mythology's supposed roots in ancient Celtic mythology only made it a more attractive source of material for modernist writers. The more ancient the roots that the Grail myth could be shown to have, the more it could be disentangled from the supposedly superficial elements that had been added to it by the writers of medieval romances. Not only did ancient Celtic origins give the Grail mythology an added profundity, it also linked the mythology firmly to the British Isles while providing a convenient pretext for dismissing Continental versions of it.[8] The Grail mythology was deemed special in part because it was a British myth.

Disentangling the various strands of the Grail mythology, however, was no easy task for those who chose to undertake it. Though the mythology itself existed in numerous different versions of varying provenance, age and complexity, all the versions shared a number of common, richly symbolic elements that appealed to the imaginations of modernist writers. The most fundamental of these was the Grail itself, thought to be the cup used by Christ at the Last Supper. The Grail is invested with a number of magical properties, including the ability to restore life or vitality to those who drink from it. The Grail is kept in a castle (often identified as Carbonek or some variation thereof) ruled by the Fisher King, who is sometimes identified as Pelles, Pellam, or Pellehan.[9] Perhaps as punishment for some sin, the King has suffered a "dolorous blow" to his leg or groin and, inexplicably, his woundedness reacts on his kingdom, rendering it barren and infertile and his subjects miserable. The portion of Athurian and Grail mythology set in Britain is known as "the Matter of Britain" to distinguish it from corresponding mythology set in Continental locales. It was this Matter of Britain that modernist writers would turn to again and again in attempts to invest their work with mythic significance.

Belief, form, and T.S. Eliot's "mythical method"

Before considering modernist writers who were able to sustain some form of religious belief and explore it through the Grail mythology, it will be helpful to consider Eliot's mythical method as a striking contrast. As we have seen, Eliot first broached the possibility of a "mythical method" in his 1923 review of James Joyce's *Ulysses*, which would become the most famous and oft-quoted statement on the relationship between myth and literature.[10] The narrative method, based on the premise that reality was coherent and unified, might have been suitable for a past era, but the modern era, in which reality was chaotic and fragmented, required a new method. Underscoring the significance of anthropology, in his review Eliot pointed out that the mythical method "was impossible" until the work of Frazer appeared. Also significant is how Eliot's proposal was haunted by questions of belief and meaning, which he saw as central to the crisis of modernity. As one Eliot scholar has put it, "Eliot usually discusses the modernist crisis in terms of an absence in contemporary life. Sometimes he calls the missing factor belief, sometimes myth, sometimes tradition."[11] As he himself wrote elsewhere, "now there is nothing in which to believe.... Belief itself is dead,"[12] yet he was equally convinced that some substitute for religion was urgently needed. Understanding Eliot's sense that religious belief was impossible helps explain his concern with "giving a shape and a significance to the immense panorama of futility and anarchy which is contemporary history." If moderns could not look to religion for an explanation of the world, they would, out of pragmatic necessity, have to generate meaning themselves.

Eliot's review of *Ulysses* appeared in the November issue of the *Dial*, which also included a newly completed poem by Eliot; he did not simply define the mythical method and recommend it to others, he himself put it into practice in his epochal poem, *The Waste Land*.[13] The poem shows us the mythical method at work, as Eliot attempts to address what he conceived of as the central modern problem: the lack of a given framework—whether from religion, tradition, or myth—that made sense of reality. This problem is at the heart of *The Waste Land*, expressed pointedly in the lines "I can connect/Nothing with nothing" (ll. 301–02). The poet's only recourse, however, is to find some way to make connections, to impose an order on the chaos of experience. Thus the necessity of the mythical method, and in the case of *The Waste Land* Eliot claimed to draw his mythic raw material from two sources in particular, as the very first of his notes on the poem makes clear:

> Not only the title, but the plan and a good deal of the incidental symbolism of the poem were suggested by Miss Jessie L. Weston's book on the Grail legend: *From Ritual to Romance*.... Indeed, so deeply am I indebted, Miss Weston's book will elucidate the difficulties of the poem much better than my notes can do; and I recommend it...to any who think such elucidation of the poem worth the trouble. To another work of anthropology I am indebted in general, one which has influenced our generation profoundly; I mean *The Golden Bough*.... Anyone who is acquainted with these works will immediately recognize in the poem certain references to vegetation ceremonies.[14]

Though Eliot explained that his work was indebted to Weston's "book on the Grail legend," the Grail never actually appears in what is the most famous Grail poem of the century. In *From Ritual to Romance* Weston had emphasized the theme in Grail mythology involving the "dolorous blow" which wounded the Fisher King and laid waste to his lands. This story, she argued, was central to the lost ritual from which the symbol of the Grail had eventually emerged. In Eliot's poem, however, the Grail is evident only by its absence and no restoration occurs. Late in his life Eliot expressed some regret that his endorsement of Weston's work had contributed to the Grail enthusiasm of the

1920s and 1930s. By invoking Weston, he had meant to recommend her method rather than inspire any belief in the mythical objects like the Grail.[15]

Eliot was thus emphatic that the point of the mythical method, in theory and in practice, was not the reinforcement of belief but rather the production of meaningful, significant literary form that made sense of contemporary chaos. The mythical method did not disclose meaning but rather was a means of creating it. Eliot's description of his modernist procedure as a "method" is highly significant, indicating in essence a scientific approach to producing relevant art. As Jewel Spears Brooker explains:

> For years, he had been working on some method that would enable him to construct a great poem without using a framework borrowed from religion or philosophy.... In *The Waste Land*, instead of borrowing a framework, Eliot borrows a method. Using the comparative method of modern science, particularly of anthropology, he tries to force the reader to construct the abstraction that will serve as the framework of the poem.[16]

When properly applied, then, the mythical method resembles a kind of inductive scientific reasoning, whereby seemingly disconnected fragments of data are compared and analyzed in order to generate meaningful conclusions. It was similar to the method Frazer had applied to his disparate ethnographic evidence, which he in turn had adapted from Darwin. Eliot regarded anthropology as yet another force that eroded the credibility of religious belief. It did this by placing all myths on the same plane, granting privileged status to none. Hence all were relativized, existing in the modern world solely as the fragmentary remnants of past cultures, meaningful only if given their meaning by an artist.[17]

As we leave Eliot to consider other modernist writers, a key point to keep in mind about his mythical method is that it was developed out of an absence of religious belief: it was a method for generating meaning and order out of chaos that could serve as a substitute for the consolations of religion, a surrogate for faith. For Eliot, at that stage in his intellectual development, there was no myth that merited or commanded belief, but myth could supply art with raw material—images, symbols, themes, tropes—that could be shaped into useful works of art, works that could help moderns cope with their experience. But not all modernists were willing to relinquish belief, not all were willing to reconstruct literature as science, and not all were willing to treat mythic symbols like the Grail as mere material for a method.

"Symbol of the beyond-life": John Cowper Powys's quest for the meaning of the Grail

Though Eliot's views on myth were unquestionably influential, they did not necessarily determine how his fellow writers approached the question of myth. A telling case in point was the remarkable writer John Cowper Powys, who respected Eliot but nevertheless developed his own powerful interpretation of myth's role in the modern world. Attempts to categorize Powys and his work are inevitably complicated by the very strangeness of the man. Yet for all his uniqueness, his Grail-focused meditations on myth linked his work to that of contemporaries working along similar lines. Powys is perhaps best described as a spiritually ambitious modernist mystic who in the mid-1920s decided to disseminate his religious philosophy by writing novels, which he considered to be "simply so much propaganda ... for my philosophy of life."[18] Central to that philosophy of life was an emphasis on the necessity of myth.

Powys was born in 1872 to parents who embodied what would become two of his most prominent personality traits: deep religious sensibility and an urge to write. His father was a firmly Evangelical clergyman, and though Powys would reject his father's faith, he retained a strong religious sensibility that ultimately developed into his own idiosyncratic belief system. His mother was a descendent of both John Donne and William Cowper, and with such a lineage it is perhaps unsurprising that Powys and three of his ten siblings became writers.

At the age of ten, Powys was sent to Sherborne public school and after that went on to Cambridge, where he took a second in history. After completing his studies he traveled the country as a University Extension lecturer, giving one-night public lectures on a variety of subjects, from literary and philosophical topics to moral and social issues. During these years he did quite a bit of writing, publishing works of poetry, criticism and philosophy. In 1910 he headed to the United States, where he continued his career as a highly popular itinerant lecturer, returning each summer to England. This pattern would continue until 1936 when he moved to Wales, where he remained until his death in 1963. Powys did not turn to fiction writing until he was in his forties, but he proved remarkably prolific and ultimately published 15 novels. He has been classed with Lawrence, Joyce, and Woolf as belonging to "that essentially 'modern' tradition of the novel that thinks in terms of symbol, and of the fluidity of personal awareness and relationships."[19]

All of Powys's novels were written as expressions of an elaborate, mystical personal philosophy that he referred to as his "mythology."[20] Powys's work as a lecturer obliged him to keep abreast of intellectual trends and developments, and he read avidly in a broad range of fields. Driven by a desire to resolve his spiritual questioning, much of his reading encompassed the fields of philosophy, religion, mythology, and anthropology; he was well acquainted with the religious texts of South and East Asia, was a devoted student of world mythology, and was strongly influenced by the Cambridge Ritualist school of anthropology. Though Powys could be critical of modern science and was often wont to rail against the excesses of the "machine age," these attitudes were something more than a reflexive antimodernism. They were, rather, part of Powys's elaborate personal philosophy, one fundamental postulate of which was that matter itself had consciousness.

Powys was an unusual mix of pantheist and polytheist, seeing a flame of immortality in all things and believing in the existence of divine beings to whose status humans could aspire. His belief in the vitality and consciousness of all matter was linked to a dualistic conception of the universe as a product of the struggle between malice and love in every individual's soul; in his words, "Its duality comes from the duality in us."[21] To comprehend the nature of reality, Powys argued, was to be confronted "with the spectacle of innumerable 'souls,' human, sub-human and super-human" who are part of a universe "which in their interaction with one another they have half-created and half-discovered."[22] This metaphysical truth about the universe could only truly be grasped by what Powys termed "the complex vision," which was achieved by individuals in those rare moments when reason and sense experience were balanced with imagination, instinct, and intuition.

The foremost example of malice was "the illusion of dead matter," which in the modern world tended to be encouraged by scientific reasoning. Succumbing to the illusion of dead matter resulted from visualizing "the world through the attributes of reason and sensation alone," neglecting imagination, instinct and intuition.[23] The result was a deep sense of spiritual isolation and alienation from the natural world. It was not modern science itself that Powys objected to, but rather "the heresy that underlies modern attitudes to science, the heresy that denies a man's derivation from, and participation in, a physical universe as alive as himself."[24] The rational and sensory faculties from which science derived were of great benefit to humanity, but only when balanced by the faculties of imagination, intuition, and instinct.

The only way to break free of the illusion of dead matter, according to Powys, was to restore the complex vision by a rebalancing of the faculties. This could be done by partaking of myth, which exemplified how rationality, sense experience, imagination, intuition, and instinct could be held in equipoise. The complex vision could not be attained by the use of "pure reason divorced from poetic imagery," because the fundamental nature of reality simply could not be apprehended by normal categories of thought. The best, albeit imperfect, way to describe the nature of reality was with symbols, images, and metaphors borrowed from mythology: "The mythological symbolism of antique thought was full of this pictorial tendency and even now the shrewdest of modern thinkers are compelled to use images drawn from antique mythology."[25] Powys accorded special importance to the mythological symbol of Christ, whom he interpreted as the supreme symbol of how love could transcend malice, and therefore an ideal for all who strove to realize the complex vision. As the "embodiment of Love itself," Christ testified to the benevolence of the gods, testimony which could be trusted even though his connection to the actual figure of Jesus was uncertain.[26] For Powys, Christ was a symbol that had all the reality of the thing itself, whether or not the thing itself had existed in history. In a passage that conveys well the unique flavor of his philosophical style, Powys explained:

> We arrive … at the very symbol we desire, at the symbol which in tangible and creative power satisfies the needs of the soul. We owe this symbol to nothing less than the free gift of the gods themselves; and to the anonymous strivings of generations…. [O]nce having been reached this has become…a definite objective fact, whose reality turns out to have been implied from the beginning.[27]

The fact that Christ-figures were common throughout world mythology was of little concern to Powys. Having read Frazer he acknowledged that this was the case, but he argued that this did not diminish the power of the symbol of Christ. Making an intellectual move common to so many of his contemporaries, he argued that other dying-and-reviving god myths culminated in, rather than undermined the force of, the Christ myth: "In him all mythologies and all religions must meet and be transcended. He is Prometheus and Dionysus. He is Osiris and Balder. He is the great god Pan."[28]

The passage is indicative of Powys's general attitude toward mythology, which he saw as a record of human experiences of the transcendent or the divine, not, as the anthropologists would have it, a record of pre-scientific superstition. As such, mythology represented a vast body of data about humanity's spiritual history that modern thinkers ignored to their detriment. A philosophy that failed to "include and subsume" such data "has eliminated from its consideration one great slice of actual living fact."[29] The complex vision that Powys advocated was thus premised on a recovery of myth:

> And it is in this aspect of the problem...that the philosophy of the Complex Vision represents a return to certain revelations of human truth—call them mythological if you please—which modern philosophy seems to have deliberately suppressed. In the final result it may well be that we have to choose, as our clue to the mystery of life, either 'mathematica' or 'mythology.'[30]

Powys put these views into practice with his novel *A Glastonbury Romance*, perhaps the most remarkable piece of Grail-themed literature to appear in the interwar period. This immense tome is almost impossible to summarize, dealing as it does with a vast cast of characters (more than fifty), a host of plotlines, and a wide range of key themes and ideas; in most editions the novel runs to well over 1000 pages. What holds *A Glastonbury Romance* together is "a constant undercurrent of secret reference to the Grail legends, various incidents and characters playing roles parallel to those in the old romances of the Grail, not without furtive dips into that world of weird ritual and mythology made so much of in T.S. Eliot's 'Wasteland.'"[31] Powys was obsessed with Grail-related mythology and was preoccupied with the symbol of the Grail, which he took to represent life itself. In fact, Powys thought of his own life as a sort of Grail quest, and in his diaries he often remarked on what he saw as mystical correspondences between his life and the history of the Grail. Much of his knowledge of mythology came from Frazer and from the Cambridge Ritualists,[32] whose work crops up repeatedly in his novels in the form of allusion and borrowed ideas. His studies of mythology led him to conclude that the Grail was far more ancient than Christianity, with counterparts in various mythologies from Asia to Greece to Wales and Ireland.[33] The Grail was the ultimate symbol of "conscious identity after death" of "the beyond-life" that could not be believed in with certainty, but that could be glimpsed through the intimations that came via myth.[34]

For Powys the Grail was inseparable from a particular, mystically powerful place: Glastonbury and its environs. The point of *A Glastonbury*

Romance was to examine, according to Powys, "the effect of a particular legend, a special myth, a unique tradition, from the remotest past in human history, upon a particular spot on the surface of this planet."[35] Like his contemporary Butts, Powys was a believer in the power of certain parts of the English landscape to bring about spiritual renewal, and no place exemplified this more than Glastonbury. The Grail myth had "not only stained, dyed, impregnated the atmosphere of this particular spot but has associated itself with every detail of its local history."[36] In the novel, then, Powys is keen to explore how a particular myth–locale nexus might bring spiritual renewal to England.

To work out this theme the novel dramatizes a conflict, played out against the backdrop of the myth-suffused Glastonbury landscape, between myth on the one hand and scientific modernity on the other. The latter is represented in the novel by Philip Crow, a wealthy industrialist with dreams of transforming Glastonbury "from an idle show-place into a prosperous industrial centre."[37] He wants to do so in part to eradicate the mythology associated with Glastonbury, which he despises as nonsense that stands in the way of scientific progress. To break the power of the myth he knows he must somehow remake the very landscape; destroying the power of the myth and destroying the landscape itself are to him inseparable objectives: "Arthur and the Holy Grail, Abbey Ruins and Saint Joseph—he was the man to blow them all sky-high!"[38] Enthralled by modern technologies such as the airplane, he dreams of a world "dominated absolutely by Science" and remade by industry.[39] Opposed to Crow are two main protagonists, both questers for the Grail in their own ways. One, Sam Dekker, renounces his love for the married Nell Zoyland, commits himself to a life of ascetic devotion to others, and is eventually rewarded with a vision of the Grail. The other, John Geard, is an itinerant preacher and spiritualist who wants to make Glastonbury the center of a religious revival. Caught up in the events of the novel is John Crow, a relative of Philip's who is a modernist intellectual and Grail-skeptic.

As mentioned above, Powys was deeply influenced by the Cambridge Ritualists, and once wrote that his "imagination inevitably converts every mental process which is at all important to me into a ritualistic symbol."[40] His daily life was structured around dozens of personal rituals including, during the time he was writing *A Glastonbury Romance*, ritual reenactments of the waste land myth.[41] It is unsurprising, then, that Powys chose to structure the climax of his novel's first half around a fertility ritual premised on enacting the Grail myth. It is with good reason that one of Powys's most perceptive interpreters has remarked that "His work partakes more of anthropology than prophecy."[42] Powys's use of insights derived from anthropology to structure his narrative is perhaps what led him to describe the novel as "mythological and yet modern."[43]

The ritual, which constitutes the climax of the book's first part, takes the form of a pageant-play orchestrated by Geard, who has become mayor of Glastonbury. The pageant enacts a variety of episodes connected to the Grail myth and, though its actual performance turns out to be a chaotic, virtually incoherent mess, it nevertheless brings about real renewal for Glastonbury. Prior to the pageant the town was dying: it was a waste land, an image that preoccupied Powys no less than it did Eliot. However, after the Grail-based fertility ritual it begins to revive, not just spiritually, but socially and economically as well. Suddenly in Glastonbury "there began to spring up—out of the void as it almost seemed—a very exciting and most original school of Glastonbury design . . . an art for which the whole western world seemed especially to thirst for, an art which embodied in it . . . the new religion of Glastonbury's Mayor!"[44] The revived town becomes of a symbol of the possibilities for how a belief system that draws on Britain's mythic past can temper the barren, rationalist secularity of modernity. The dying town is not saved by the industrial schemes of Philip Crow, who wants to demolish everything related to the area's mythic past. Instead, it is saved by Geard, who embraces that mythic past and taps its power to unleash forces of renewal—a renewal that is not merely spiritual. What is revived at Glastonbury is a coherent culture unified around a spiritual center; the town becomes economically and socially healthy because it is spiritually vibrant. This revival of Glastonbury thus serves Powys's purpose of creating a modern retelling of the Grail myth that would help his readers navigate the challenges of modernity.

Ultimately the revival of Glastonbury does not last, and when the novel closes the town's future is uncertain. The novel concludes with an immense flood that sweeps away both the religious edifices built by Geard and the industrial projects of Philip Crow. Neither the forces of imagination, instinct, and intuition, nor the forces of rationality and scientific modernity triumph. Instead, a balance between the two is restored for the time being. All that remains of the Glastonbury revival is the way it has changed certain individuals like the skeptical intellectual John Crow, who finally has to admit that Glastonbury does indeed possess an undeniable spiritual power. He begins to cope effectively with the fragmenting pressures of the modern world, and for the first time begins to build healthy relationships with those close to him. According to Powys, the purpose of the book was to examine the effect of a particular myth on the inhabitants of twentieth-century civilization. He seems to conclude that the effect can be profound, but that it can in the end only be measured by its lasting impression on human hearts and minds.

"Come Out, Grail": The modernist mysticism of Mary Butts

Powys's work testifies to the modernist penchant for constructing novels around the significance of the Grail. Another such novelist was Mary Butts, a writer whose career and concerns also intersected with Eliot's in significant ways. Though Butts was a respected writer and reviewer in her day, a long period of scholarly neglect has only recently given way to a renewed interest in her life and work, such that a recent observer has spoken of a "Butts renaissance."[45] Butts was co-owner of the press that published Eliot's second book of poems, *Ara Vos Prec* (1920), and believed that she and Eliot were working along similar lines to examine the spiritual state of the culture through use of the Grail. After reading Weston, she noted in her journals, "A fruitful book, cf. Eliot, & as Jane Harrison & Frazer are to me. (Eliot & I are working on a parallel.)"[46] This brief comment serves as a succinct summary of the key influences on Butts's thought. She was deeply indebted to the anthropological and classical scholarship of Frazer, Gilbert Murray and Jane Harrison, whose work fed both her fascination with classical antiquity and her interest in things spiritual and mythical. Butts idolized Harrison, borrowing much of her conceptual vocabulary from Harrison's work and turning to it in times of spiritual and personal distress.[47]

Butts's career was likewise characterized by an ongoing fascination with Frazer's *Golden Bough*, a text which haunted her imagination like the Grail. After reading Waite's book on the Grail in 1925 she observed somewhat cryptically, "he cannot conceive the answer—no one yet has—that has to be made to *The Golden Bough*."[48] In a subsequent journal entry she clarified what she meant by an "answer" to *The Golden Bough*: "as for our anthropologists—they will write up the facts of every belief in every quarter of the globe; but even the best of them, Frazer hardly, gives one the least idea, the least suggestion of the passion, the emotion that made men behave like that." But, she concluded, where the anthropologists fell short, writers like herself could step in: "It is for art to take over the anthropologist's material."[49] Butts, then, saw her vocation in part as working out the implications of anthropological research through literature, with the aim of constructing a response to the cultural fragmentation and spiritual emptiness of modernity. Jane Garrity puts it well when she observes,

"Like other modernists, Butts laments the cultural and economic dispossession of life in postwar Europe—'everywhere there was a sense of broken continuity'—looking to mythic structures and contemporary anthropology to help her re-order an England that appeared not only chaotic and faithless, but seduced by plasticity."[50]

Butts was convinced that Britain both desperately needed, and stood on the brink of, a new age of spiritual renewal, and she avidly sought such renewal on a personal level through her extended involvement with the occult and various forms of spiritualism. She was tutored in magic by Philip Heseltine and Aleister Crowley and was a frequent participant in séances, automatic writing, and astral journeys. Though she remained interested in the occult for most of her career, she eventually drew more spiritual solace from the classical past, the world of myth, and the work of fellow writers.

Butts was bothered by the sense that, however fascinating scholarship on the Grail might be, it always failed to explain the spiritual power of such symbols. Taking her cue from Harrison, Butts concluded that the rationality exhibited by modern forms of scholarship had distinct limitations. It was the realm of the spiritual that highlighted these limitations: anthropologists and psychologists simply could not explain the depth and persistence of the human religious impulse.[51] For all the erudition displayed by Harrison, her works failed to convey "What gave greek myth & the beliefs of all mankind their power to save or kill."[52] This criticism of the limits of certain disciplines did not mean that Butts demeaned the sciences and modern forms of rationality. On the contrary, in addition to her avid interest in anthropology, she was deeply interested in the physics of Einstein and Eddington, the philosophy of Russell and Whitehead, and the psychology of Freud and Jung. To Butts, the work produced by such figures was spiritually provocative and full of suggestions and intimations about a spiritual world that she was certain lay just beyond the reach of modern forms of inquiry. Though immensely valuable, modern rationality could ultimately only produce flawed, reductionist accounts of spiritual realities:

Our state today is due to the fact that we are trying to make purely intellectual formulae do the work they were not intended to do. We take the non-intellectual factors & try & describe them intellectually, i.e. we take man's "infra-rational nature," emotional, imaginative or mystical, & derive it, by assumption, from nothing but animal instinct.

[W]e want to try & reduce all things to order. Only it's essentially un-intellectual—this applying of reasonable intelligence to subjects it has nothing whatever to do with.[53]

Butts longed for a discovery of spiritual realities that would force science to revise its materialist account of reality. Speaking of the supernatural beings of Celtic myth she wrote, "What I should like to see most in the world. Proof that the Sidhe exist, & all the others & the scientist having to square up with it."[54] Butts, however, was able to transform her frustration with the scientific reductionism into inspiration for her own literary work, which she conceived of as something like a science of the spiritual, capable of producing a "formula for the whole truth; not intellectual truth only."[55]

Throughout her life Butts struggled to make sense of the spiritual yearning that she repeatedly termed "this mysticism of mine."[56] This ongoing endeavor led eventually to disillusionment with occultism, which she came to see as self-indulgent, rooted in an excessive subjectivism, and motivated by a desire for control.[57] She was similarly critical of self-serving spiritual philosophizing, and dismissed "People who chat airily about esoteric Buddhism & its advantages."[58] Toward the end of her life, Butts took the path previously taken by Eliot and converted to Anglo-Catholicism. A key factor in her conversion was her ability to resolve a conundrum that had long troubled her: the relation between recent anthropological scholarship and Christianity. The myth scholars—Harrison, Murray, Weston, et al.—whose work she revered seemed to cast doubt on the validity of the Christian myth, yet the longevity of that same myth seemed to indicate that at the very least it encapsulated some significant spiritual truths. She was able to resolve the problem when she was suddenly struck by

> another reason why Christianity clicked; that it helped give a final shape to the other beliefs in gods & heroes who were born of virgins & who lived & died for men. The idea was about, had always been about.... Christianity gave it a personality, books, gossip even; exalted it & brought it nearer home.[59]

This interpretation of Christianity as a culmination of other dying god myths was a reversal of the anthropologists' view that the Christian myth was a late and unremarkable example of ancient near-Eastern vegetation god myths. Butts was thus an avid appropriator of late nineteenth- and early twentieth-century anthropology who, like Powys, refused its relativizing implications.

At the center of Butts's literary attempts to examine the spiritual condition of British culture and make sense of her own mysticism stood the Grail and the myths surrounding it. Along with associated images like the waste land, the Grail was one of her favorite symbols, and considerations of its meaning surface with regularity throughout her journals. While still in her youth she concluded that the Grail was "the most wonderful thing to think about in the world."[60] Her thinking about the Grail was catalyzed by a visit to Glastonbury in the summer of 1918 and she remained deeply interested in it until her death in 1937. She seems to have envisioned herself as engaged in a Grail quest, seeing her purpose as a writer as plumbing the true meaning of the Grail, perhaps in a way that would even lead to discovery of the physical Grail itself. After Butts moved to Cornwall in 1932, the intensity of her meditations on the Grail seems to have increased, fed by the influence of a landscape that had connections to the Grail myth. In December of that year she enigmatically remarked, "I think that the Grail might be seen here this winter. It is time anyhow." Convinced that the land she had moved to was truly "the Grail Country," she reiterated a month later, "I believe the Grail is stirring at [the village of] Sancreed." A few months later she implored "It is a wild night. Come out, Grail."[61] Butts's fascination with the Grail made her an avid reader of Grail scholarship, including Waite's *The Hidden Church of The Holy Graal* and Weston's *From Ritual to Romance*, a work she reread annually. Her work as a reviewer exposed her to a steady flow of new works, so she was quick to take note of any new literature that touched on the Grail. It was in this way that she discovered the work of Charles Williams, whose novels and literary criticism would become a source of fascination and inspiration for her.

Butts gave expression to her meditations on the significance of the Grail in her novel *Armed with Madness*, which centers on the Grail's power to bring about spiritual renewal. *Armed with Madness* is probably her best known novel and, as she herself acknowledged, it explored the power of the Grail in ways that intersected with Eliot's explorations in *The Waste Land*. Both Eliot's poem and Butts's novel depict barren landscapes that are reflections of spiritual barrenness in the characters. The significant difference is that the Grail is conspicuous in Eliot's poem by its absence, whereas the characters in *Armed with Madness* are, in their own ways, desperately seeking the Grail and its revivifying powers; the novel has been summarized as a search for life by characters trapped in a waste land.[62] Butts's willingness to entertain the possibility that the Grail offered real solutions to modernity's spiritual emptiness, along with her linking of the Grail's power to the power of the English land-scape, place her work closer to that of Powys than that of Eliot. Like Powys, she was far less equivocal about the Grail than Eliot, and this in part derived from her ability, also like Powys's, to see anthropology as an ally rather than an enemy of belief. As Butts scholar Roslyn Reso Foy has summarized Butts's intentions: "Clarification of the significance of the Grail and its offer of spiritual truth…becomes the core of her novel and a means of resisting the spiritual depravity of civilization."[63]

Armed with Madness centers on a group of five men and one woman, most of them alienated artists and intellectuals, who have gathered in a remote country house; they constitute a community of Grail knights. One of them has stolen, and subsequently hidden, an ancient cup from his father's collection. This prompts a search for the cup that temporarily transfigures the characters and enchants the locale. Butts invests the two main characters with mythic significance; their names, Scylla and Picus, indicate how she interweaves classical with Grail mythology.[64] The echo of myth and ritual scholarship is evident in how Butts frames questions of the of the cup's significance. The characters' search for it, motivated by their inchoate desires for rebirth and renewal, is described as "some-thing like a ritual," a point Butts reinforces throughout the novel with a constant stream of ideas about the power of ritual drawn from the work of the Cambridge Ritualists.[65] Butts also links the power of the cup to the power of the land itself. As Jed Esty has perceptively noted, when at one point in the novel it appears as if the cup is of Indian, rather than English, origin, it immediately loses its value and appeal.[66] The charac-ters ultimately abandon their "quest"; the rebirth offered by the Grail is deferred, awaiting a day when its questers are better prepared to receive it. The novel thus concludes on a note that is open-ended, an ambiguity underscored by the fact that it is never clear whether or not the cup the party is searching for is indeed the Grail or merely a stand-in for it. What is clear is that in England spiritual realities are ready to be awakened and that something like the Grail is needed to shatter the arid intellectual-ism that Butts saw as the main obstacle to the spiritual revival she hoped for and expected.

"The central matter of the matter of Britain": The Grail in Charles Williams' Christian mysticism

In the last few years of her life, Butts became enamored by the work of a poet and novelist whose work seemed to have many affinities with her own. This was Charles Williams, a gifted writer who worked in a variety of genres, writing poetry, plays, novels, criticism, and even history. The two began corresponding, eventually met, and struck up a friendship that was cut short by Butts's premature death in 1937. There were good reasons for Butts to think that she and Williams were working along similar lines. Like Butts, Williams had a background in occultism and was deeply concerned with matters spiritual. Williams was also preoccupied with the mythology of the Grail, a symbol he approached with a spiritual reverence that Butts herself knew well. He was proudest of his two books of Grail-themed poetry, *Taliessin through Logres* (1938) and *The Region of the Summer Stars* (1944) in addition to writing best-selling novels and essays that also dealt with the Grail. Butts and Williams were connected by another significant link, their common acquaintance with Eliot. Eliot and Williams became close friends while the latter was an editor at Oxford University Press in the 1930s, and they admired and published each other's work. Williams's novels, which began appearing in the early 1930s and for which he was well-known during his lifetime, blended the conventions of pulp fiction thrillers with weighty mythological and spiritual subject matter. Williams was thus in his day a significant figure in modernist literary networks and a writer who was able to effectively disseminate his ideas about myth through highly popular novels.

Despite Williams's prominence in the literary world of the 1930s, and a recent revival of interest in his life notwithstanding, his work has certainly become, in the words of one commentator, "marginal to today's modernist canon."[67] Another scholar has described Williams as "an odd and charismatic man about whom it is difficult to write with justice or even clarity."[68] This difficulty is in part due to Williams's unusual ability simultaneously to inhabit very different literary circles, which has caused problems for scholars seeking to place Williams within a literary taxonomy of the interwar period. In addition to his modernist connections, Williams was part of the "Inklings" or "Oxford Christians" circle that included C.S. Lewis and J.R.R. Tolkien, and his work is often viewed in relation to theirs. However, the greatest difficulties in approaching Williams stem largely from his oddness and charisma, characteristics which were closely related to his spiritual explorations. Friends and acquaintances noted that there was something strangely compelling about being in his presence, and when Eliot attempted to describe this effect he linked it to Williams's spiritual gravitas, remarking that he "seemed to me to approximate, more nearly than any man I have ever known familiarly, to the saint."[69] In short, Williams's life and work can simply not be understood without appreciating his background in Christian mysticism, a mysticism that was heavily influenced by the Grail-oriented, Christianized hermeticism associated with the writer, scholar, and Grail enthusiast Waite. Richard Barber has remarked that "the attempt to involve the Grail in occult matters is an important element in its image in the twentieth century, with wide artistic repercussions,"[70] a trend that is amply illustrated by Williams's life and work.

As already noted, Waite, author of the widely read *The Hidden Church of the Holy Graal*, was a key figure in creating the wave of Grail enthusiasm that was building in the early twentieth century. Waite was in part a product of the resurgence of Rosicrucian orders that ensued in the 1880s after Madame Blavatsky was discredited, bringing her Theosophical Society into disrepute. One result was the emergence of new hermetic groups that tended to emphasize the mystical rather than the occult and paranormal. Such groups, like the Hermetic Society or the better known Order of the Golden Dawn, attracted a number of disenchanted Theosophists and prominent literary figures, the most famous of which was W.B. Yeats. Such orders promised initiation into moral and religious truths as preserved in ancient rituals. Waite founded his own Rosicrucian order in 1915, the Fellowship of the Rosy Cross, which Williams joined two years later. Waite's innovation was to make the Grail central to his mysticism; previously it had not been a prominent feature of Rosicrucian philosophy and practice. This reflected his attempt to effect a synthesis of Rosicrucianism and Christianity. The Fellowship of the Rosy Cross has been described as "mystical rather than magical; its membership was open to those desiring 'knowledge of Divine Things and union with God in Christ.' "[71]

It was this synthesis of the hermetic and the Christian that impressed Williams when he first read Waite's *Hidden Church of the Holy Graal* between 1912 and 1914.[72] In that book Waite argued, with scholarly seriousness, that there was a secret, mystical tradition in Christianity that was connected with the Grail. This tradition, involving a supposed original, primitive form of the Eucharistic rite, was outside the bounds of official church teaching and, according to Waite, was kept alive by an unidentified "Secret School of Christian Mystics." This group understood the Grail's power as a master key to ecstatic mystical union with God. "All sacred symbols," wrote Waite, "serve at need to open figurative gates and everlasting portals" to the world of mystical experience, and of these the Grail was paramount.[73] At the time he encountered *The Hidden Church*, Williams was a young poet, and this interpretation of the Grail within a hermetic framework seemed to open up an entirely new realm of significance for the symbol. His subsequent literary use of the Grail would owe much to the ideas advanced in *The Hidden Church*.

The influence of hermetic ideas on Williams's interpretation of the Grail is clearly evident in his 1930 novel *War in Heaven*, which deals with the events that ensue when the Grail is discovered in an English village. One of the novel's interesting leitmotifs is its implicit critique of skeptical anthropological understandings of myth. Williams seems to have been suspicious of anthropological research on myth, and he was critical of those scholars who, making a fetish of their objectivity, failed to appreciate the spiritual realities to which the Grail pointed. This attitude shapes his portrayal of the cynical adventurer-archaeologist-folklorist Sir Giles Tumulty. Tumulty's scholarly training (he has just authored the book *Historical Vestiges of Sacred Vessels in Folklore*) enables him to locate and identify the Grail, but it has also made him indifferent to moral questions of good and evil. He views the Grail in the same way he does the occult: with the detached curiosity of a scholar. Nevertheless, he falls in with a group intent on obtaining the Grail and using it magically for evil purposes. They are thwarted by an impromptu alliance of three who are aided by Prester John, the legendary priest-king. It is largely through the eyes of these protectors that the Grail's true nature is revealed: "In one sense, of course, the Graal is unimportant—it is a symbol less near Reality now than any chalice of consecrated wine. But it is conceivable that the Graal absorbed, as material things will, something of the high intensity of the moment when it was used, and of its adventures through the centuries."[74] The novel concludes with Prester John performing a mass using the Grail as the chalice, enacting the very theory at the heart of Waite's book.

Williams continued to develop his ideas about the Grail in his two collections of Arthurian poetry, *Taliessin through Logres* and *The Region of the Summer Stars*, which deal with the efforts of Arthur, the Welsh bard Taliessin, Merlin, and others to bring order to Logres (Britain) by means of the Grail. Williams wrote the poems in order to bring coherence to the sprawling mass of Arthurian mythology by centering it on the symbol of the Grail, "the central matter of the Matter of Britain."[75] Failure to deal with the Grail "in all its meanings and relationships" left "a much smaller myth."[76] The cycle of poetry that Williams produced is simply too intricate and even opaque to examine here. The significance of his Arthuriad for this investigation is that it testifies to the strength of Williams' conviction that the Grail be recovered for twentieth-century Christians as a deeply meaningful symbol. Throughout the cycle of poems, the Grail is efficacious only for those who rightly understand its meaning. But in the poems, the power of the Grail is linked to distinctly modernist concerns about a fragmented culture, though these concerns are inflected through Williams's Christian presuppositions. Any attempt to redress the fragmentation of modern culture, he seems to suggest, may require a recovery of Christianity's vision of the power of self-sacrifice, a concept symbolized in the cup of Christ.[77]

Given his convictions about the importance of the Grail for Christian belief, Williams was at pains to underscore the cup's origins in Christian theology, arguing that it subsumed all analogous symbols in European mythology. This was in part because it could be associated with identifiable historical events, whereas the magic cauldrons and enchanted vessels of European myth belonged to an indefinable mythic prehistory. But a deeper reason was the power attributed to the Grail, which exceeded the powers attributed to the other magical vessels of European myth. In his uncompleted study of the history of the Grail myth he describes it as "that Cup which in its progress through the imagination of Europe was to absorb into itself so many cauldrons of plenty and vessels of magic."[78] Williams was thus hostile to those scholars who argued that the Grail's origins were not in Christian theology but rather in pre-Christian fertility cults. Though he does not name Weston, he likely had her in mind when he wrote:

> Something perhaps should be said...about those fabulous vessels, which from Celtic or whatever sources, emerged into general knowledge. There has been much controversy about them...and they have been supposed by learned experts to be the origin of the Grail myth. That...they certainly cannot be. Cup or dish or container of whatever kind, the Grail in its origin entered Europe with the Christian and Catholic Faith.[79]

In the end, though, for Williams any powers possessed by the actual Grail were less important than the Christian ideas it symbolized.

Beyond the mythic method: David Jones and the uses of Arthurian myth

Williams's work and Arthurian imagination were deeply respected by the Welsh poet and artist David Jones. Jones's work can be linked to Butts's and Powys's as well, insofar as they took similar attitudes to anthropology and the spiritual power of the Grail mythology. The work in which Jones first began to make use of Grail mythology at length was *In Parenthesis* (1937), an unusual mix of verse and prose that he referred to simply as a "writing."[80] In 1952 Jones published another major work called *The Anathemata*. Though it received mixed reviews largely due to its difficulty, it was also acclaimed by a number of influential critics including W.H. Auden, who regarded it as the most important long poem in English of the twentieth century.

Jones initially made his name as a visual artist and he continued to produce visual art throughout his life. Born in 1895 to a Welsh father and an English mother, he showed an affinity for art at a young age and attended Camberwell Art School, where he first became acquainted with recent trends in art. After the First World War began he enlisted in the Royal Welch Fusiliers and served with that regiment from January 1915 until the end of the war. Jones's battalion was involved in the assault on Mametz Wood during the First Battle of the Somme, and he depicts this fighting strikingly in *In Parenthesis*. After demobilization, Jones continued his artistic training at the Westminster School of Art. A period of postwar spiritual seeking ended in 1921 with his conversion to Catholicism, after which he quickly became involved for a time with the Guild of St. Joseph and St. Dominic, a group of artists founded and run by the Catholic artist Eric Gill. During the late 1920s and early 1930s Jones enjoyed increasing success as an illustrator and engraver. Despite his success as an artist, it is for his writing that Jones is best known today. After the war he made several abortive attempts to produce a literary work based on his war experiences, but it was not until *In Parenthesis* that he first began to put his ideas about myth into a literary form. The work is Jones's attempt to make sense of his experiences as a soldier in the First World War between December 1915, when he arrived in France, and July 1916, when the Somme offensive began.

The mythology that informs *In Parenthesis* above all others is that surrounding King Arthur and the Grail. Though there were a number of reasons why Grail mythology recommended itself to Jones, one in particular made it an especially natural choice. The regiment Jones served in was composed largely of men from London on the one hand and Wales on the other. It was an inauspicious combination for, in Jones's words, "no two groups could ever be more dissimilar." Yet the war revealed a fundamental unity between these two groups who "bore in their bodies the genuine tradition of the Island of Britain."[81] This bonding of the Welsh and the English both touched and impressed Jones, and it is little surprise that he concluded there was no better way to illustrate this almost mystical British unity than by drawing on that body of myth known as "the Matter of Britain."

In building *In Parenthesis* around a frame of mythological references, Jones both followed the example set by Eliot in *The Waste Land* and went beyond it. A key emphasis of Eliot's mythical method was the use of myth to generate meaning from chaos by means of a pattern of references to myth. Jones was drawn to this notion, which seemed to fit neatly with key elements in the Grail mythology. He felt, for instance, that Arthur, as "the Lord of order carrying a raid into the place of Chaos," symbolized myth's ability to bring meaning out of disorder.[82] *In Parenthesis* is shot through with a constant stream of mythological references, which might be too esoteric or subtle to catch, were it not for the fact that their meaning is disclosed in the copious annotations that Jones provided at the end of the work. Moreover, in true Eliotic fashion, Jones's explanations are often backed by references to scholars like Frazer and Weston.[83]

Up to this point Jones appears to be a prototypical practitioner of the mythical method, yet some probing reveals that he had a much more robust understanding of myth than Eliot. For Jones, though, myth was more than a consoling source of literary form, it was also a mode of discourse that communicated wisdom deriving from "true, immemorial religion."[84] After establishing his literary reputation with *In Parenthesis*, Jones was increasingly in demand as an essayist and reviewer, work that gave him the opportunity to elaborate on his understanding of myth. In two essays from the 1940s on the history and relevance of "the Myth of Arthur," Jones made clear that he considered the entire body of Arthurian myth to be a cultural artifact of great importance. But the myth was more than a cultural artifact for Jones; it was also a repository of wisdom that had perennial relevance. Seeking to capture the function of myth in a single, rambling sentence he explained:

> To conserve, to develop, to bring together, to make significant for the present what the past holds, without dilution or any deleting, but rather by understanding and transubstantiating the material, this is the function of genuine myth, neither pedantic nor popularizing, not indifferent to scholarship, nor antiquarian, but saying always: "of these thou hast given me have I lost none."[85]

Jones emphasized the distinctly British nature of Arthurian and Grail mythology and expected that each generation would appropriate it in ways that served its present needs. By countering the philosophical materialism of the machine age, the mythology offered resources for coping spiritually with the "confusion and complexity" of the contemporary world.[86]

As one who had read extensively in modern anthropological scholarship on myth, Jones was well aware of the attempts to debunk myth by painting it as a primitive thought form. Though he valued such scholarship, he did not accept many of its presumed implications. He did not, for instance, believe that Jessie Weston's work vitiated the Christian associations of the Grail. He conceded that

> It was salutary and necessary that fairly recent scholars—the name of the late Miss Jessie Weston suggests itself—should have concentrated on the supposed or actual derivation of elements in the theme from origins in primitive ritual and symbolism; to have directed our attention…to horns of plenty, inexhaustible cauldrons and life-giving dishes.

Nevertheless, Jones maintained, "nothing of all this invalidates the identification of the grail with *the* Horn of Plenty, *Calix sanguinis mei.*"[87] This had been the position of Charles Williams, who for Jones was the exemplary modern exponent of Arthurian/Grail mythology. According to Jones, Williams had distinguished himself among appropriators of the mythology by successfully integrating in his work recent scholarly insights into the "whole complex of myth and ritual" with a relevant response to "the very convulsions and stress which have characterized fairly continuously the lives of all of us living today."[88] In doing so, he had demonstrated how anthropology need not necessarily rob symbols like the Grail of their spiritual force and meaning. Jones thus saw in Williams's work a validation of his own view that anthropological research had "in fact assisted a re-appreciation of some of the deep validities of the Faith."[89] In short, Jones drew inspiration from myth and ritual anthropology that reinforced rather than undermined his own religious beliefs. For Jones, as for Williams, the works of Weston and others only made the Grail a more mysterious and powerful symbol by revealing its continuing appeal through the ages and by illustrating the Grail's "historic ability to absorb, integrate, develop, [and] fulfil [sic]" its pre-Christian or non-Christian analogues.[90]

Conclusion

The modernist recourse to myth was one of the most salient symptoms of a deeper loss of faith in the idea of a shared reference point that provided the common ground for cultural unity or spiritual renewal. Brooker has helpfully described the modernist project in terms of an attempt to cope with this predicament: "The herculean effort to cope with the loss of a shared reference point, involving ingenious attempts to retrieve or to discover or to create substitutes, characterizes modernism in all the arts."[91] To many, the work of the late Victorian anthropologists had contributed to this sense of loss by relativizing European beliefs. If myths were simply relics of a primitive stage of human development, and if all cultures produced remarkably similar myths, then what validity could be claimed by the Christian myth at the heart of European culture? Some modernists, such as Eliot, attempted to make a virtue of this necessity by using the primitive relics of mythology as so much suggestive raw material, to be shaped into something meaningful by the artist.

The work of Powys, Butts, Williams, and Jones, however, testifies to an alternative modernist approach, one that both complicates and enriches our understanding of the culture of modernism. Their work shows how modernists could use myth to conjure with questions of belief in ways that belie the common characterization of modernist poetics as concerned with form rather than belief. They did this in part by creatively drawing on forces usually understood as being aligned with the secularizing tendencies of modernity, in particular anthropology. Importantly, the context in which Powys, Butts, Williams, and Jones tried to work out the relationship between myth and belief followed close on the heels of a period during which, as Alex Owen has recently shown, notions of what counted as "belief" had undergone significant revision.[92] Consequently, these writers benefited from a new openness that freed them to think in new ways about myth's relevance to their predicament. Their work invites us to reconsider received interpretations of modernity as strictly inimical to religious belief. On the contrary, characteristically modern forms of knowledge production like anthropology could and did enable new forms of spiritual seeking and religious speculation, of which the meditations on the Grail examined above are but one strain.

4
"The Mythical Mode of Imagination": J.R.R. Tolkien, C.S. Lewis, and the Epistemology of Myth

Introduction

In June 1942 *Time and Tide* reported that the Nazi party had chosen Hagen over Siegfried as their national hero. Passing over the noble but credulous hero of the Niebelungenlied, the Nazis instead identified a scheming, malicious villain as the epitome of the Germanic spirit. When he heard the news, C.S. Lewis could barely suppress his elated laughter. Lewis had long been an admirer of the Niebelung mythology, and in the years leading up to the Second World War he had watched with increasing dismay as the Nazis appropriated it for their own ideological purposes. "It was," he wrote, "a bitter moment when the Nazis took over my treasure and made it part of their ideology."[1] But with the news that the Nazis had chosen Hagen, Lewis's dismay was replaced by a relieved amusement: "[N]ow all is well. They have proved unable to digest it. They can retain it only by standing the story on its head and making one of the minor villains the hero.... [T]hey have given me back what they stole."[2] Lewis observed that the Nazis' attempted appropriation of Norse mythology was part of a no less ridiculous attempt to appropriate "the Nordic" as a whole: "What business have people who call might right to say they are worshippers of Odin? The whole point about Norse religion was that it alone of all mythologies told men to serve gods who were admittedly fighting with their backs to the wall and would certainly be defeated in the end." The Nazis' use of mythology left him baffled: "How is it that the only people in Europe who have tried to revive their pre-Christian mythology as a living faith should also be the people that shows itself incapable of understanding that mythology in its very rudiments?"[3] In Lewis's view there was truth in Nordic mythology, but the Nazis had utterly failed to grasp it.

Lewis's friend and colleague J.R.R. Tolkien was of a similar mind about the Nazi appropriation of Nordic mythology, but could not bring himself to view it with amusement. For years Tolkien had been at work on his own legendarium that drew heavily on the body of myth the Nazis were now claiming as their own. Moreover, he was a scholar of this very material, and he took scholarly offense at the way Hitler and his followers were distorting it. Writing to his son in June 1941, he gave vent to his frustration:

> I have spent most of my life...studying Germanic matters (in the general sense that includes England and Scandinavia). There is a great deal more force (and truth) than ignorant people imagine in the "Germanic" ideal.... You have to understand the good in things, to detect the real evil.... I have in this War a burning private grudge...against that ruddy little ignoramus Adolf Hitler.... Ruining, perverting, misapplying, and making forever accursed, that noble northern spirit, a supreme contribution to Europe, which I have ever loved, and tried to present in its true light.[4]

In reality, Tolkien's anger indicated more than a "burning private grudge." His irritation stemmed from his conception of myth's proper function, a conception that Lewis largely shared. Both believed that myth had a unique ability to communicate moral and religious truth that distinguished it from any other form of discourse.[5] This explains their reaction to the Nazi use of myth: Hitler's abuse of myth to disseminate blatant falsehood was, in the eyes of Lewis and Tolkien, a perversion of myth's true function.

Lewis and Tolkien's reaction to the Nazi appropriation of Nordic mythology thus brings into focus some of the key assumptions underlying their understanding of myth's significance. The most important of these was the conviction that myth was a vehicle for communicating significant truths. By the early 1940s, Lewis and Tolkien were already in the midst of an extended literary project premised on, and intended to demonstrate, myth's unique epistemic functions. A related premise was that the health of a culture is indicated by its relationship to myth. A healthy culture, they held, was one which availed itself of myth's benefits by attending to the perennial truths that myth conveyed. Lewis and Tolkien were convinced that Britain was in danger of losing a proper relationship with myth. This is why Tolkien sought to create a mythology that he "could dedicate... to England; to my country" and why Lewis insisted that "myth is relevant as long as the predicament of humanity lasts."[6]

The problem both saw was that the increasing cultural authority of science was displacing myth's proper cultural function. They found this trend troubling because a culture in which science alone defined what counted as knowledge was a culture in which people were inclined to dismiss myth as a source of truth. More specifically, this meant that the culture was not receptive to the Christian ideas Tolkien and Lewis sought to communicate, because Christianity was inescapably tied to myth and thus viewed skeptically by many. In short, Tolkien and Lewis were concerned about a culture in which the advance of science had conditioned people to see it as the only valid source of knowledge and to ignore myth—and by extension Christianity—as a source of truth. This state of affairs led Lewis to observe in the mid-1950s that "the apologetic position has never in my life been worse than it is now."[7] Already by the 1930s Lewis and Tolkien had concluded that their culture was dangerously out of touch with myth in general and with the Christian myth in particular. Consequently, they engaged in an extended attempt to rehabilitate myth's authority as a source of moral and religious truth. For them, then, the question of myth's function was an epistemological question, for they believed that myth conveyed truths that could not be apprehended through other forms of discourse.

The aim of this chapter is to show how myth played the central role in Lewis and Tolkien's campaign to reshape a British culture in which, they believed, science had exceeded its proper bounds and threatened to usurp the proper role of ethics and metaphysics. This campaign was conducted at the level of epistemology, as they tried to establish through both polemic and example myth's credentials as a vehicle of moral and religious truth, an endeavor which obliged them to confront the late Victorian and Edwardian anthropological work that had sought to dissolve myth's status as a privileged form of discourse. Though he does not examine Lewis and Tolkien's theory of myth, literary historian Jed Esty has come close to capturing the motivations behind it when he observes that their "vision of the writer's role was determined neither by market relations nor by freestanding aesthetic ideologies but by the production of a complete allegorical system of truth that would resonate with an English audience's latent Christianity."[8] Esty's assessment captures the epistemological thrust of their project: not only did they contend that myth communicated truth in a unique way, they also sought to exemplify this with their fiction. They hoped thereby to counteract the influence of science, reorient the culture's moral bearing, and even reawaken an interest in Christianity.

The making of a myth-maker: Tolkien's background and early views on myth

The foundations for Tolkien's interest in myth were laid early in his life, and many of the features of the mythology he would develop grew out of his childhood experiences. Ironically, the man who would construct a mythology that glorified the beauty of England was born in 1892 in Bloemfontein in the Orange Free State, a dusty town surrounded by the open veldt that could not have been more different from the West Midlands countryside that he would later come to think of as his true home.[9] Though John Ronald Reuel's parents, Arthur and Mabel, had roots in Birmingham, they had moved to South Africa for the sake of Arthur's career. In 1895 young Ronald, his mother, and his younger brother left Bloemfontein to visit England, leaving Arthur behind. While they were in England they received news that he had suffered a severe hemorrhage and died.

Tolkien's first teacher was his mother, and during their lessons it became clear that he had a strong emotional and aesthetic response to the sound and appearance of words and language. He was "excited by the Welsh names on coal-trucks, by the 'surface glitter' of Greek, by the strange forms of the Gothic words... and by the Finnish of the *Kalevala*."[10] He also was fascinated by fairy tales, especially those collected in Andrew Lang's fairy books and William Morris's retellings of Norse mythology, which Tolkien would later devour during his undergraduate years.[11] His fascination with, and strong aesthetic response to, language and fairy stories would prove to be key factors in motivating him both to develop a theory of myth and to craft one of his own.

In 1896 the family moved to the Warwickshire hamlet of Sarehole, where the English countryside became inscribed on Tolkien's imagination. A few years later Mabel Tolkien converted to Catholicism and was essentially disowned by her family. In 1904 she died suddenly after collapsing into a diabetic coma. Tolkien felt afterwards that she had been driven to her death by the cold treatment she received after her conversion, and this drove him to cling to the Catholicism she had passed on to him. Tolkien's biographer has suggested that "after she died his religion took the place in his affections that she previously occupied."[12]

After his mother's death, Tolkien was also helped by the good companionship he found at King Edward's School in Birmingham, especially with a group of three or four other boys known as the T.C.B.S. This was an informal club devoted to reading, discussion, and intellectual exploration in general.[13] The friendship among the core members of the group survived their departure from school, and they took with them a conviction that they had been brought together so that in the future they might spark some kind of cultural renewal.[14] It was this shared belief that encouraged Tolkien to first think of himself as a creative writer and poet.

Tolkien was fascinated with myth from an early age, and this fascination was closely linked with his interest in language. His interest in the relationship between myth and language took on more concrete form after he began his studies at Oxford in 1911. Tolkien read Classics and chose Comparative Philology as his special subject, a decision that brought him under the influence of the charismatic Professor Joseph Wright. Wright focused and directed Tolkien's nascent interest in philology, while encouraging him to pursue his interest in languages, such as Welsh, that had long fascinated him. Indeed, Tolkien eventually switched from reading Classics to English because this allowed him to study Old and Middle English and other Germanic languages that interested him. The language that captured Tolkien's imagination above all others, however, was Finnish. His encounter with the tongue convinced him that England lacked the sort of rich mythology found in the Finnish epics, and he began to yearn for "something of the same sort that belonged to the English."[15]

The Great War proved to be the crucible in which these various inclinations and enthusiasms were brought together. Tolkien would later say that his "taste for fairy-stories was wakened by philology on the threshold of manhood, and quickened to full life by war."[16] In June 1915 he completed his final examination, earning a First that positioned him for an academic career once the war was over. Several months earlier he had enlisted under a scheme that allowed him to complete his degree before taking up a commission, so almost immediately after finishing at Oxford he was posted to the 13th Battalion of the Lancashire Fusiliers. His work as a signaling officer played to his longstanding interests in codes, alphabets, and language.[17] In March of 1916 he married and less than three months later his battalion was sent to France as part of the buildup for the Somme offensive. Though Tolkien's company was involved in a series of bloody engagements, including the infamous assault on the Schwaben Redoubt, he survived the offensive uninjured, and in November he was invalided home with trench fever. Two of his closest T.C.B.S. friends, however, died in the fighting on the Somme.

Rather than giving in to despair, Tolkien decided to impose a shape and meaning on the tragedy of the war. His experience of war thus impelled him to create the mythology that he had been contemplating for some time, and while recuperating from trench fever he began to write the first of the stories that would provide the basis of his mythology. All that he had seen in the war—the bleak landscapes, the corpses, the destructive capabilities of modern technology, the violence, and the heroism and self-sacrifice—would be given meaning by becoming part of a vast mythology. Begun in the shadow of one world war, Tolkien's mythology would be brought to completion in the shadow of a second; it is no coincidence that his fiction is pervaded by war and the threat of war.[18]

At the same time, by creating his mythology Tolkien felt that he would be supplying what England sorely lacked: a mythology of its own. After his undergraduate days he became more deeply convinced of "the poverty of my own beloved country: it had no stories of its own (bound up with its tongue and soil), not of the quality that I sought, and found (as an ingredient) in the legends of other lands."[19] He resolved to remedy this deficiency, using his philological expertise and his own invented language to give his mythology the tone and air of the stories that had long fascinated him. His myth-making project was thus initially driven by a range of motivations, from the intimately personal to the almost ridiculously grandiose. Tolkien's surname derived from a German word meaning "foolhardy," a word that many would think an apt description of his intention to single-handedly provide a mythology for England.

At the same time that he was developing his mythology, he began to develop a theory of how myth functioned as a form of discourse in order to explain the strange power it seemed to have. His development of that theory would be aided by friendship with a man who spent much of his career as Tolkien's colleague at Oxford.

Gods and heroes, atoms and evolution: Lewis's background and early views on myth

Like Tolkien's, the roots of Lewis's fascination with myth went back to a childhood marked by tragic loss. Clive Staples Lewis was born in Belfast in 1898 to parents who both had Irish roots, though they were vaguely Anglican in religion. His father was a successful solicitor and his mother something of an intellectual who had taken a B.A. in mathematics at Queen's College, Belfast. It was a book-loving family and the young Lewis quickly developed a love of reading. He was particularly fond of fairy tales, E. Nesbit, Beatrix Potter, and anything with the flavor of myth and legend. The family was happy until Lewis's mother died in 1908. From that point much of the stability in Lewis's life was gone, and he took increasing refuge in the imaginative side of his personality—the side that was drawn to myth and fairy tale.

Lewis was thus intrigued by myth from an early age, and until the 1930s two somewhat contradictory instincts shaped his thinking on the subject. One was a love of any literature that had the flavor of myth or the fantastic. The other was a rationalistic skepticism about the epistemic value of myths, which he saw as essentially beautiful lies. The former instinct he became aware of as an adolescent while reading Henry Wadsworth Longfellow's translation of a poem on the death of the god Balder. The poem's opening lines, "I heard a voice, that cried/Balder the Beautiful/Is dead, is dead!" would remain with him for the rest of his life.[20] The imaginative intensity of this experience drove him to seek out literature—such as work by William Morris and George MacDonald—that would produce a similar effect, though none of it satisfied his appetite for mythology that smacked of what he could only describe as "Northernness." He did not encounter the same mythic quality again until, as a teenager, he discovered the mythology behind Wagner's Ring Cycle of operas. Mere synopses of the operas in the magazine *The Soundbox* set him off on a quest to acquire and read everything possible on the subject of Norse mythology, including, like Tolkien, Morris's versions of Norse myths.

However, Lewis's appetite for the mythical was countered by an anthropological skepticism about myth. This skepticism was instilled in him by William T. Kirkpatrick, the family friend who privately tutored Lewis before he went up to university. A ruthless dialectician, Kirkpatrick was the man Lewis credited with teaching him how to think. Kirkpatrick had grown up in Ulster and trained to become a Presbyterian minister before losing his faith, in part through the influence of J.G. Frazer's *Golden Bough*. In Lewis's words, "[H]e was a 'Rationalist' of the old, high and dry nineteenth-century type.... At the time when I knew him, the fuel of Kirk's Atheism was chiefly of the anthropological and pessimistic kind. He was great on *The Golden Bough* and Schopenhauer."[21]

Kirkpatrick had been convinced by Frazer's argument that Christianity was but one among many dying god myths, and this became Lewis's own belief, providing a rationalization for his own loss of faith a few years earlier. In encountering Frazer, Lewis was also glad to discover that there existed a body of scholarship that aimed to explain the mythopoeic impulse in human culture. Though the young Lewis was convinced by Frazer's materialist explanation that myths emerged as a way of giving meaning to the cycle of the seasons, his reading of scholarship on myth did not end with Frazer. Throughout his career he kept up with scholarship on myth produced by a variety of disciplines, and he would later credit the Cambridge Ritualists, Freud, and Jung, among others, with offering important insights into myth.

As a young man, then, Lewis was of two minds on the subject of myth: on the one hand he had an imaginative taste for myth that he fed at every opportunity, and on the other he was convinced that all myth was ultimately false and meaningless. A significant theme of Lewis's autobiography is the evolution of his thinking about myth. He wrote there of how

> the two hemispheres of my mind were in the sharpest contrast. On the one side a many-islanded sea of poetry and myth; on the other a glib and shallow 'rationalism.' Nearly all that I loved I believed to be imaginary; nearly all that I believed to be real I thought to be grim and meaningless.[22]

He summed up, "Such, then, was my position: to care for almost nothing but the gods and heroes, the garden of the Hespirides, Launcelot and the Grail, and to believe in nothing but atoms and evolution and military service."[23]

Lewis tried to resolve this conflict by exploring the occult. His "passion for the Occult" was sparked by a school matron who was deeply involved in spiritualism of various forms: "Theosophy, Rosicrucianism, Spiritualism; the whole Anglo-American Occultist tradition."[24] Another way to resolve the dilemma seemed to be offered by the religious ideas of Yeats, whose occultism began to intrigue Lewis as a young man. Occultism was appealing because it offered a potential answer to a question that continued to nag him: why did myth affect him so powerfully if indeed it was false? Because occultism acknowledged the existence of unseen, deeper, preternatural forces, it seemed to Lewis like a philosophy that could accommodate and even explain the power of myth. Though he never fully embraced the spiritualism of his school matron or the occultism of Yeats, his willingness to consider such possibilities reflected a compulsion to make sense of myth's power.

Lewis's thinking about myth remained very much unresolved in 1917 when he began his studies at Oxford, which were quickly cut short by the war. Lewis had enlisted in the Officers' Training Corps and in

November 1917 he was sent to the front near Arras. He came home in the spring of 1918 after being wounded by a British shell that had fallen short of its target. The same shell killed a close friend and fellow Oxford undergraduate, a loss that would help push Lewis into a postwar pessimism. Though he was generally reticent about his experience during the war, it clearly affected him—not least by catalyzing his desire to write creatively. During his spare time at the front and while recovering from his wounds, he began to write a cycle of poems in an attempt to make sense of his experiences, and he would continue to write creatively for the rest of his career.

After recuperating he returned to Oxford to resume his studies at University College. He took the path of a future academic, taking a Double First in Honour Mods and Greats, after which he applied for a fellowship in philosophy. When the fellowship went to someone else, he decided to take another degree in English. It was, he rightly recognized, a rising subject, and it would not hurt to add another string to his bow.[25] After taking his English degree he filled in for a year as a don at University College before being elected as a fellow in English at Magdalen College in 1925. One year later, Tolkien would also come to Oxford as an English don.

Tolkien, Lewis, and the epistemology of myth

Thus by the mid-1920s both Lewis and Tolkien were young dons at Oxford, and the friendship that developed between them would help both men clarify and refine their views on myth. This was particularly true of Lewis, whose conversion to Christianity in the early 1930s would turn on the issue of whether or not myth conveyed truths about reality. In the end, thanks to Tolkien's influence, Lewis concluded that myth was a unique form of discourse that conveyed profound truths in ways that other forms of discourse could not. At the same time, friendship with Lewis pushed Tolkien to refine his own ideas of the nature of myth. The well documented story of Lewis's conversion thus highlights the importance of myth to the epistemology that would become central to their work, and reveals how the work of the late Victorian anthropologists continued to shape debates about myth in Britain, for Lewis and Tolkien developed their theory of myth in reaction to scholars like Frazer and Lang. The shared understanding of myth that they developed during repeated conversation and argument in the late 1920s and early 1930s would become foundational to their work as writers for the rest of their careers.

When the two met in the spring of 1926 at a meeting of the Oxford English faculty they did not warm to each other. At the time there was upheaval among the faculty about what the structure of the English curriculum should be, and Tolkien and Lewis were on opposite sides of this debate. Tolkien suspected that Lewis was in the "Lit." camp, which defended the study of literature as a field of serious scholarship, while Lewis knew that the philologist Tolkien was in the "Lang." camp, which saw the study of Anglo-Saxon and Middle English as the only rigorously academic part of the English curriculum.[26] And on Lewis's side there were other reasons for mistrust: "At my first coming into the world, I had been (implicitly) warned never to trust a Papist, and at my first coming into the English Faculty (explicitly) never to trust a philologist. Tolkien was both."[27]

Nevertheless, the two men ended up becoming fast friends, and what brought them together was a shared interest in myth. When Tolkien learned that Lewis had an interest in Norse mythology the mutual suspicion that divided them began to dissolve. In the late 1920s Tolkien started an informal group devoted to studying, reading and discussing Icelandic sagas. Lewis immediately joined, eager for the chance to read in their original language the myths that had long fascinated him. After the sessions ended, Lewis would typically remain behind with Tolkien to continue the discussion well into the night.[28]

One of the central issues in these late-night discussions was the unique power that myth seemed to possess. Lewis, having imbibed the skepticism of Frazer and others, insisted that whatever power they might have, myths were still "lies," even though "breathed through silver."[29] By about the summer of 1929 Lewis had moved from his earlier agnosticism, through a brief dabbling in occultism, to a vague theism. This added a theological dimension to their discussions of myth. Though Lewis conceded that myths could be deeply moving and powerful on an emotional level, he could not accept Tolkien's Christian understanding of myth's significance. Following Frazer and Kirkpatrick, Lewis saw the Christian story as but one dying and reviving god myth among many. In short, for him myths were beautiful, but ultimately false; his appreciation for myth was aesthetic rather than philosophical.

Lewis reversed this approach when assessing the Christian myth, however, taking little interest in it because he found it philosophically unconvincing. In his attempt to defend Christianity, Tolkien sought to expose this seeming inconsistency in Lewis's views. This took place in an extended conversation on September 19, 1931, when Tolkien, Lewis, and Hugo Dyson, a lecturer at Reading University, again took up the question of myth's significance. A few weeks afterward Lewis gave an account of the conversation in a letter to a friend:

> Now what Dyson and Tolkien showed me was this: that if I met the idea of sacrifice in a Pagan story I didn't mind it at all: again, that if I met the idea of a god sacrificing himself to himself... I liked it very much and was mysteriously moved by it: again, that the idea of the dying and reviving god (Balder, Adonis, Bacchus) similarly moved me provided I met it anywhere *except* in the Gospels. The reason was that in the Pagan stories I was prepared to feel the myth as profound and suggestive of meanings beyond my grasp even tho' I could not say in cold prose "what it meant."[30]

Lewis thus concluded that "the story of Christ is simply a true myth: a myth working on us in the same way as the others, but with this tremendous difference that *it really happened.*"[31] Moreover, Tolkien had convinced him that the myths had power because they reflected, albeit imperfectly, profound truths. Myth was the language of describing truth, a language that humans could speak by virtue of the fact that they had been divinely created. In the words of one of Tolkien's biographers, "just as speech is invention about objects and ideas, so myth is invention about truth."[32]

This was a view that Tolkien worked out in verse a few days after the momentous discussion of September 19. In a poem he called "Mythopoeia" that was framed as an appeal to Lewis, he elaborated his views on the innate truth of mythology.[33] But Lewis was already largely convinced; he had come to embrace a view of myth that resolved the aesthetic and philosophical issues with which he had wrestled: aesthetically, myth did have unique power, but this ultimately derived from the truth it conveyed. And, standing Frazer on his head, he now believed that the Christian myth was not one myth among many, but the myth to which all others pointed. In accepting the Christian myth, he thus made an intellectual move similar to that made by Mary Butts prior to her conversion.[34] Thus Lewis's conversion to Christianity, and a precipitous moment in his friendship with Tolkien, centered on the *epistemic* status of myth, that is, on questions relating to its truth value.

Their friendship and shared understanding of myth would prove to be highly conducive to literary creativity; without the friendship between Tolkien and Lewis it is unlikely that they would have produced the body of fiction they did.[35] Lewis's prompting and encouragement of his friend played a key role. Sometime in the late 1930s Lewis suggested to Tolkien that they both begin writing mythic fiction. "[T]here is too little of what we really like in stories," Lewis observed, "I am afraid we shall have to try and write some ourselves." They agreed that Lewis should try to produce a space travel story and that Tolkien should produce a time travel story. They also agreed that their stories should communicate truth through myth.[36] The result of this agreement was Lewis's *Out of the Silent Planet* (1938), the first volume of his Space Trilogy. Tolkien never finished his time travel story, but his attempt convinced him to take up the mythology that he had been developing intermittently since the 1920s.[37] Lewis was one of the first to read early chapters of what would become *The Lord of the Rings*, and his enthusiastic encouragement combined with pestering helped Tolkien eventually to complete the novel.[38]

Coming to a shared understanding of myth's significance was one thing, but developing a theory of how their own fiction could function as myth was a task that required further thought. Tolkien was the first to take on this problem, one he had pondered since his undergraduate years. Unable to shake the sense that in his fiction he was somehow recording "a sudden glimpse of the underlying reality or truth," he decided to work out a theory of how and why myths came to be written.[39] We have seen that already by 1931 Tolkien had worked out a theory of myth's epistemic function that was sufficiently robust to convince a skeptical Lewis, in part because he contested explanations of mythology offered by philologists and anthropologists. A few years later, Tolkien alluded to these themes in his lecture *Beowulf: The Monsters and the Critics*. Tolkien was keen to show that the fantastic elements in *Beowulf* were in fact essential to the mythic power of the poem, rather than regrettable and disconcerting stylistic flaws as many critics alleged. This prompted a brief aside on "the mythical mode of imagination":

> The significance of a myth is not easily to be pinned on paper by analytical reasoning. It is at its best when it is presented by a poet who feels rather than makes explicit what his theme portends; who presents it incarnate in the world of history and geography, as our poet has done. Its defender is thus at a disadvantage: unless he is careful...he will kill what he is studying by vivisection.... For myth is alive at once and in all its parts, and dies before it can be dissected. It is possible, I think, to be moved by the power of myth and yet to misunderstand the sensation, to ascribe it wholly to something else that is also present: to metrical art, style, or verbal skill. Correct and

sober taste may refuse to admit that there can be an interest for *us*—
the proud *we* that includes all intelligent living people—in ogres and
dragons.[40]

Tolkien's comments on the inability of contemporaries to appreciate the
fantastic elements of *Beowulf* are strikingly similar to arguments that
were being developed at the same time by R.G. Collingwood. This is significant because Tolkien and Collingwood were colleagues at Pembroke
College in the 1930s, and they seem to have been on friendly terms with
each other. It seems likely that Tolkien and Collingwood shaped each
other's views about how a naïve scientism led to reductive explanations
of myth and folktale.[41]

Tolkien further developed his explanation of myth's epistemic function in a 1939 address entitled "On Fairy Stories." This address, the most
thorough statement of his views on the nature of myth and the sort
of fantasy stories that he composed (*The Hobbit* had been published in
1937), was given as the twelfth Andrew Lang Lecture at St. Andrews
University.[42] In it Tolkien explained his objections to the theories of
myth offered by scholars such as Max Müller and Lang. As a boy, Tolkien
had read with enjoyment Lang's compilations of fairy tales, but had also
come to object to Lang's attitude toward such mythic material. Here was
a chance to defend the value of "fairy-stories," by which he meant essentially myths in literary form; throughout the lecture he often used the
terms "myth" and "fairy-story" interchangeably. As the most extensive
and detailed expression of Tolkien's views on the topic, views which
were shared substantially by Lewis, it merits a thorough analysis.

In order to discern the proper use of myth it was first necessary
for Tolkien to clear away mistaken views on the subject. The two
approaches at which he directed his criticism were the philological
approach represented by Müller and his follower George Dasent and the
anthropological approach of Lang. Though these two schools of myth
interpretation were at odds with each other, from Tolkien's perspective
they committed the same error: approaching mythic stories with strictly
scientific motivations. Philological, folkloric, and anthropological theories of myth were produced by "people using the stories not as they were
meant to be used, but as a quarry from which to dig evidence, or
information."[43] Tolkien acknowledged that there was a place for scholarly inquiry into the origins and development of mythic tales, but
maintained that such investigations did little to reveal the meaning,
power, and value of "the story as it is served up by its author or teller."[44]
By emphasizing the internal coherence and integrity of mythic stories

as works of literature, Tolkien was setting the stage for one of his central points: that myth-making was a fundamental human activity; it was not a primitive pursuit which humans outgrew as Lang argued, nor was it a "disease of language" as Müller had claimed. On the contrary, Tolkien argued, "Mythology is not a disease at all.... You might as well say that thinking is a disease of the mind."[45] Myth was an inevitable and perennial product of interactions between the human mind and language. Language gave the human mind the means to form imaginative visions into stories, thereby injecting the world with "fantasy." The wood with silver leaves, the ram with a golden fleece, and the dragon with fire in its belly were all products of the human tendency to remake the world through imagination. Human life and myth-making went hand-in-hand; thinking mythically was constitutive of being human.

Establishing that humans were myth-makers by nature still left the question of "what, if any, are the values and functions of fairy-stories now?"[46] First, Tolkien confronted the common charge that fairy stories were suitable only for children, a view that reflected how unwarranted condescension trivialized myth. Lang perpetuated this notion by patronizing both the presumed "primitives" who had originally produced many myths and fairy tales, and the children who read fairy tales in modern times. Tolkien singled out one sentence that encapsulated Lang's attitude: "Their taste remains like the taste of their naked ancestors thousands of years ago; and they seem to like fairy-tales better than history, poetry, geography, or arithmetic."[47] Lang's false sentimentality toward children prevented him from recognizing that "the association of children and fairy-stories is an accident of our domestic history."[48] Children did not as a rule gravitate toward such stories and had not made the decision to stock Victorian nurseries with volumes of them.

Against Lang, Tolkien contended that fairy stories were "a natural branch of literature."[49] As such, well-written fairy stories could have at least the same value as any other form of literature, although they were also unique in some very significant ways. Specifically, they offered "Fantasy, Recovery, Escape, Consolation, all things of which children have, as a rule, less need than older people."[50] Tolkien's argument here depended on a distinction between what he termed the "Primary" and "Secondary" worlds, the former being the everyday world and the second being a world created in imaginative literature by writers acting in their capacity as "sub-creators." This notion of the fantasy writer as a sub-creator had been broached by Tolkien earlier in his debates with Lewis about the nature of myth. The concept was at bottom a theological one. In "Mythopoeia," his polemical poem to Lewis on the subject, he had argued that by making stories humans were acting on a divinely implanted impulse; having been created in God's image humans themselves were driven to create.[51] This impulse in fact lay behind all forms of artistic creation, but was most evident in the secondary worlds of "fantasy" stories, a term that Tolkien used as a synonym for "fairy story."

Fantasy was thus, according to Tolkien's Christian anthropology, a natural human activity. Moreover, it was an activity by no means at odds with human reasoning capacities or scientific pursuits. Tolkien maintained that fantasy "does not destroy or even insult Reason; and it does not either blunt the appetite for, nor obscure the perception of, scientific verity.... For creative Fantasy is founded upon the hard recognition that things are so in the world as it appears under the sun; on a recognition of fact, but not a slavery to it."[52] For Tolkien, then, mythic fantasy offered a way of coping with the modern world by providing a venue for the imagination to create a secondary world that offered both a respite from, and different perspective on, the primary world. As Michael Saler has observed, "For him, re-enchantment through fantastic Secondary Worlds was not a rejection of modernity, but rather a corrective to its one-sided emphases."[53] Fantasy was able to convey truths that life in the primary world could all too often obscure.

It is here that the fairy story's capacity to offer what Tolkien called Recovery, Escape, and Consolation came into play. He defined Recovery as "regaining a clear view."[54] Creative fantasy could wipe clean the windows of perception by freeing the everyday world "from the drab blur of triteness or familiarity."[55] By drawing on the material of the primary world to create their secondary world, writers of fantasy presented those materials in a new light, counteracting the disenchantment of daily life. Similarly, fantasy's ability to offer Escape offered another avenue of enchantment. Escape denoted the fairy story's capacity to provide a temporary imaginative satisfaction of the perennial human desire to transcend the limitations and constraints of life. Tolkien was at pains to distinguish Escape from escapism, the former premised on a healthy relationship to the primary world, and the latter characterized by a desire to ignore the primary world and its problems. Finally, Tolkien argued that fairy stories were distinguished by their capacity to offer Consolation; just as tragedy was the truest form of drama, the happy ending was the truest form of the fairy story. He coined the word eucatastrophe—"the good catastrophe, the sudden joyous 'turn' "—to describe this aspect of successful fairy stories.[56] Eucatastrophes offered "a piercing glimpse of joy" that seemed to transcend the story itself, and this was the essential "mythical fairy-story quality."[57] Tolkien concluded with an epilogue in which he ascribed theological significance to the glimpses of joy offered by fairy stories. The joy stimulated by the best fairy stories—those that presented internally consistent and convincing secondary worlds—in fact testified to truths of deep significance: "The peculiar quality of the 'joy' in successful Fantasy can ... be explained as a sudden glimpse of the underlying reality or truth."[58] The consoling joy in successful fairy stories was at bottom an intimation of a world in which all sorrows would be abolished; in other words, the eschatological future that Tolkien's faith led him to anticipate.

Tolkien's understanding of myth offers an interesting contrast to that of Yeats. Andrew Von Hendy helpfully suggests that during the first half of his career Yeats had a romantic view of myth that emphasized "constructing a national culture around a newly refurbished indigenous mythology."[59] Clearly there is some point of contact here with Tolkien's desire to create a mythology for England by weaving together pre-Norman Conquest linguistic and cultural fragments. Though both writers were anti-imperialists and both explored questions of national identity, as actually written Tolkien's legendarium seems much more interested in moral questions than political ones. Moreover, Tolkien's view of the epistemic function of myth contrasts sharply with that of the later Yeats, who in *A Vision* identified "the tragedy of his own life with the tragic pattern of dying gods in vegetation myth" and invented a "spatializing metahistorical system" to rationalize that identification.[60] For Tolkien myth was a vehicle for truth that exists independently of the knower, but in *A Vision* Yeats seems to force his own idiosyncratic philosophy onto history. As one critic has put it, "*A Vision* perhaps shows Yeats at his worst, where the author rigidly tries to prove the validity of his system."[61] Tolkien saw his exercises in myth creation as anchored in and constrained by the greater myth of Christianity, but would likely have seen the later Yeats as attempting to forge an artificial myth (though in *A Vision* he labors to forestall this misapprehension, presenting the book's contents as impersonal revelations).

It is not difficult to understand why Lewis found the views Tolkien expressed in "On Fairy-Stories" so amenable. He had already made them his own through conversation with Tolkien well prior to 1939, and once the revised piece appeared in print in 1947 he recommended it enthusiastically to others as the final word on the power and function of mythic fantasy. Lewis was convinced on both an emotional and intellectual level by his friend's explanation of how the genre facilitated coping with modern life and communicated truths in ways that other genres did not. As he explained in an essay on science fiction:

The Fantastic or Mythical is a Mode available at all ages for some readers; for others, at none. At all ages, if it is well used by the author and meets the right reader, it has the same power: to generalise while remaining concrete, to present in palpable form not concepts or even experiences but whole classes of experience, and to throw off irrelevancies. But at its best it can do more; it can give us experiences we have never had and thus, instead of "commenting on life", can add to it.[62]

Though Lewis also agreed with the epistemological thrust of Tolkien's Lang lecture, he felt compelled to work out some of the philosophical implications that Tolkien did not make explicit. Lewis was always more philosophically inclined than Tolkien, and he was especially eager for any opportunity to challenge the linguistic philosophy and logical positivism ascendant in the Oxford of the 1930s, 1940s, and 1950s. He took particular exception to logical positivism and its claims that myth was essentially meaningless. Articulating the epistemological import of myth was therefore precisely the kind of task he welcomed.

One of the clearest examples was a 1944 essay in which Lewis tried to elucidate just what myth communicated and how it did so. The reason for the air of profundity that myth evoked was that myths actually provided contact with reality in a deeper, more direct way than did other forms of knowledge. To establish this, Lewis pointed out that all thought was "incurably abstract" whereas "the only realities we experience are concrete."[63] That is, while bearing pain or enjoying pleasure humans could not simultaneously intellectually apprehend those sensations. Here he was drawing on the ideas of the former Oxford metaphysician Samuel Alexander, whose work had made a strong impression on Lewis early in his career.[64] In Lewis's view, then, humans found themselves in a dilemma: they were unable both to experience and contemplate simultaneously, causing reality to dissipate by the very act of grasping at it. Thankfully, though, "Of this tragic dilemma myth is the partial solution. In the enjoyment of a great myth we come nearest to experiencing as a concrete what can otherwise be understood only as an abstraction."[65] By bridging the immediacy of experience and the abstraction of thought, what myth provided access to was not merely truth, which was after all an abstraction, but reality itself:

What flows into you from myth is not truth but reality (truth is always about something, but reality is that about which truth is).... Myth is the mountain whence all the different streams arise which become truths down here in the valley . . . . Or, if you prefer, myth is the isthmus which connects the peninsular world of thought with that vast continent we really belong to. It is not, like truth, abstract; nor is it, like direct experience, bound to the particular.[66]

Myth, as a unique medium of meaning, offered access to reality in a primeval, unified form.

Lewis's views here reveal the influence of his close friend Owen Barfield, a poet, critic, and amateur philosopher who had helped convince Lewis to embrace theism.[67] In his 1928 book *Poetic Diction: A Study in Meaning*, Barfield had explored the connection between myth and meaning in language by way of arguing that all meaningful language contains a poetic element. He posited an earlier stage of human consciousness in which mythic language enabled direct, undifferentiated perception of reality. At this stage, concrete and abstract meanings were not separated, but rather fused in myth. Lewis did not agree with Barfield that human consciousness had passed through evolutionary stages, but he was influenced by at least three key aspects of Barfield's view: his resistance to the idea that only science could offer true knowledge, his emphasis on the importance of the imagination in producing knowledge, and his insistence that myth communicated truth in a unique way.[68] Barfield's influence, mediated through Lewis's Christian presuppositions, is evident in the following lines from his book *Miracles*, "Myth in general is not merely misunderstood history (as Euhemerus thought) nor diabolical illusion (as some of the fathers thought) nor priestly lying (as the philosophers of the Enlightenment thought) but, at its best, a real though unfocused gleam of divine truth falling on human imagination."[69]

History, science, and myth

Though Lewis and Tolkien were convinced that myth was a form of discourse with a unique capacity to communicate truth, this does not explain why the need for myth struck them as a matter of pressing cultural significance. The answer involves how they viewed their culture's relationship with history and science. Their views on both history and science revealed their sense of how myth could redress certain cultural imbalances that characterized modernity.

Lewis and Tolkien's conception of myth's significance was intricately bound up with their understanding of history. Both lamented the narrow horizons of their own age and drew most of their inspiration from what might be called "old books," for lack of a better term. For the most part, they were not given to what Lewis once called "rash idealization of past ages," but both were in many ways more at home intellectually in the past.[70] Tolkien dreamed of a life in the era before the advent of the "infernal combustion" engine,[71] and after he had attained financial security through the success of *The Lord of the Rings*, he annotated one of his large tax checks with the words "Not a penny for Concorde."[72] Lewis did not read a daily newspaper and in his inaugural lecture at Cambridge, he described himself as one of the last of the species of "Old Western men," by which he meant those formed by, and at home in, the literature of premodern Europe.

Nevertheless, their sense of being out of place in history was not simple nostalgia or reactionary antimodernism. Lewis, who thought of himself as a type of historian, argued that one of the primary reasons for historical study was to liberate people from the past, and he observed that no one was "less enslaved to the past than historians."[73] At bottom their fondness for the past had an epistemological motivation; it was driven by a desire to expose and contest what Lewis called "chronological snobbery" or "the uncritical acceptance of the intellectual climate common to our own age and the assumption that whatever has gone out of date is on that account discredited."[74]

This sense of living on the wrong side of a historical rupture was most systematically worked out by Lewis in his inaugural lecture as Professor of Medieval and Renaissance Literature at Cambridge, a chair created to lure him from Oxford in 1954.[75] The address gave Lewis occasion to consider which moments in history could be classified as profound historical breaks. He explained that he had "come to regard the greatest of all divisions in the history of the West that which divides the present from, say, the age of Jane Austen and Scott."[76] This opinion was based on his sense of the impact of four major cultural shifts: the advent of modern mass politics, the unprecedented increase in the opacity of modern art, the decline of Christianity, and, above all, the dominance of machines. The idea that permanence was really stagnation, the fact that "primitive" had become a pejorative, and the assumption that "latest" was synonym for "best" all testified that "a new archetypal image" had been stamped on the human mind:

> It is the image of old machines being superseded by new and better ones. For in the world of machines the new most often really is better and the primitive really is the clumsy.... [A]ssuredly that approach

to life which has left these footprints on our language is the thing that separates us most sharply from our ancestors and whose absence would strike us as most alien if we could return to their world. Conversely, our assumption that everything is provisional and soon to be superseded...would most shock and bewilder them if they could visit ours.[77]

Though medieval and Renaissance Europe would seem like an alien world to residents of the twentieth century, it could be explained and demystified by those who understood it. Lewis thought his scholarly vocation was to be a "spokesman of Old Western Culture" who crossed back over the historical rupture and then returned with the knowledge that lay on its far side. Similarly, he used his mythic fiction to resurrect and convey ideas from Old Western Culture as a way of questioning and subverting modern assumptions.

The modern assumption that Lewis and Tolkien challenged above all was the unquestioning acceptance of science's increasing cultural authority. They wanted to make the case that scientific knowledge had limits while at the same time showing that myth conveyed particular kinds of truths that science could not.[78] In his Lang lecture, Tolkien tried to reassure his audience that an appetite for mythic fiction should neither "blunt the appetite for, nor obscure the perception of, scientific verity." He therefore acknowledged the value and importance of scientific reasoning, while urging that scientific knowledge must be balanced by the metaphysical truths that were uniquely delivered by myths: "legends and myths are largely made of 'truth', and indeed present aspects of it that can only be received in this mode."[79] Lewis was likewise frustrated that his attempts to point out the misuses of science were often interpreted as outright hostility, once rhetorically throwing up his hands and acknowledging, "Nothing I can say will prevent some people from describing this lecture as an attack on science."[80]

The problem they saw, then, was not science but rather the misuse of science. At a time when the cultural and academic stature of science was increasing, they were concerned that it not dominate other forms of knowledge and erode ethics. As Lewis explained to a correspondent who had inquired about university reform, "One must not...distort or suppress the sciences. It is rather...a question of reducing them to their proper place."[81] This proper place could be maintained by an awareness that science was, at bottom, "hypotheses (all provisional) about the *measurable* aspects of *physical* reality."[82] Lewis and Tolkien feared that advancements in humanity's ability to control nature would lead to the elimination of all ethics. As Lewis wrote to the novelist Arthur C. Clarke, "Technology is *per se* neutral: but a race devoted to the increase of its own power by technology with complete indifference to ethics *does* seem to me a cancer in the universe."[83] Despite the fact that a critique of science was part of their project, Tolkien and Lewis had a limited understanding of modern science. Those who knew Lewis have commented on his apparent ignorance of contemporary science.[84] Tolkien liked to read science fiction, but seems to have had no interest in science as such.[85]

Nevertheless, they were both willing to speculate extensively about a future dominated by science, particularly Lewis, as evidenced by the Riddell Memorial Lectures he delivered at the University of Durham in 1943. He argued that this possible future would be characterized by the dominance of technocrats, by "the rule of the Conditioners over the conditioned human material," resulting in a "world of post-humanity."[86] Lewis traced the power-seeking tendencies of modern science to the historical conditions under which science emerged, hand-in-hand with magic in the sixteenth and seventeenth centuries. Drawing on his work as a scholar of this era he contended that "The serious magical endeavour and the serious scientific endeavour are twins: one was sickly and died, the other strong and throve. But they were twins. They were born of the same impulse." The common impulse was the desire "to subdue reality to the wishes of men."[87] Lewis dramatized this link between magic and science in the third volume of his Space Trilogy, in which a government bureaucracy, the National Institute of Coordinated Experiments, pursues a nihilistic, totalitarian agenda using methods that make no distinction between science and magic.[88] But he thought this dystopian future could be averted:

> It might be going too far to say that the modern scientific movement was tainted from its birth: but I think it would be true to say that it was born in an unhealthy neighborhood and at an inauspicious hour. Its triumphs may have been too rapid and purchased at too high a price: reconsideration, and something like repentance, may be required.[89]

Lewis and Tolkien believed that this reconsideration could be prompted by the mythic fiction they produced, which aimed to present the necessity of a realm of moral principles beyond science.

Lewis, Tolkien, and the politics of literary seriousness

Lewis and Tolkien's convictions about the privileged epistemic status of myth compelled them to confront other cultural groups who offered rival understandings of myth. First and foremost, it was necessary for them to challenge the work of nineteenth- and twentieth-century anthropologists who held that myth was an artifact of a particular stage of human cultural evolution, a primitive, prescientific form of human thought. They countered this by trying to remove the wedge that anthropologists had driven between myth and supposedly higher forms of thought, and by challenging the unquestioned presumption of modern cultural superiority on which anthropological theories of myth rested.

Lewis, by nature a controversialist, was eager to engage with anthropological theories of myth. His conversion set him against the anthropological skepticism about myth that he had previously embraced, even though he continued to accept that anthropology could shed light on the cultural conditions in which particular myths emerged. For instance, he accepted the argument of the Ritualists that most myth emerged as explanations of a ritual.[90] And he saw some merit in the Jungian explanation of myth that focused on archetypes produced by the collective unconscious.[91] But ultimately Lewis turned the methods of his discipline on the anthropologists themselves, arguing that the very proliferation of theories about myth only testified to its indisputable power—they were latter-day quests, with the goal not a Grail but an explanation of myth's power.

Because much of Lewis's scholarship was in a field (medieval and Renaissance literature) that attracted anthropologically driven myth and ritual criticism, he had good reason to ask whether anthropology really was of benefit to the study of literature. Though he freely acknowledged that anthropologists might well shed light on some aspects of myth, he remained skeptical about how valuable such knowledge was for the understanding of literature. He pointed out that myth and ritual scholars seemed motivated by the idea of uncovering hidden ritual origins of a work of literature. Their work gave the impression "that they have surprised a long-kept secret, that there are depths below the surface, that something which the uninitiated might pass over as a triviality is big with meaning."[92] They were, he argued, inventing around themselves a quest story that gave them an experience mirroring that which the myth itself was intended to invoke. As he wrote to a correspondent, "Their quest for Pagan ritual is itself another romantic quest and gives just the same sort of pleasures as the romances they think they are explaining. The same holds for the Jungians."[93] The would-be debunkers of mythic stories unknowingly succumbed to the power of myth themselves. Lewis's critique of the myth and ritual scholars was thus intended to safeguard the imaginative power of mythic literature against reductionist explanations.[94]

In defending their conception of mythic fiction Lewis and Tolkien were also compelled to challenge competing views of literature. Much has been written about how a conception of myth was central to a specifically Christian worldview developed by Lewis and Tolkien, but these accounts have often failed to notice how myth was central to their long-running critique of the British literary establishment and their response to changes in how literature was read and used. Both resisted the Leavisite idea of literature as a substitute for religion and the notion that literature's chief role was to provide relevant social commentary on contemporary problems.[95] They were suspicious as well of the impenetrability of modernist literature and its tendency to use myth as a mere literary gambit. In short, they reacted against the belief that the modern world required a particular kind of "serious" literature, and they made their argument against this position in part by drawing attention to the literary function of myth. Their defense of myth was part of a revolt against a literary establishment that elevated serious literature while denigrating popular literature.

Lewis and Tolkien's attempt to distinguish themselves from the modernists and the Leavisites can be seen as an intervention in what could be called the politics of literary seriousness. By choosing to write the sort of fiction they did and by linking that fiction to a particular theory of myth, Lewis and Tolkien were involving themselves in an ongoing debate of the cultural role of literature in twentieth-century Britain. Both writers were aware, not least because of their success as authors of popular fiction, of the ever-growing size and significance of an educated mass reading public. They clearly recognized that any attempt to shape the culture would require reaching many of these readers, and they were convinced that neither the view of literature advanced by the modernists nor that advocated by the Leavisites could satisfy the modern reading public.[96] Modernist literature was simply too obscure, and Leavisite strictures threatened to transform reading into a joyless morality lesson, when the real value of literature was that "it admits us to experiences other than our own."[97] And in any case, the defenders of "serious" literature were working with a wrongheaded, question-begging notion of what really counted as serious. In a 1952 essay defending mythopoeic literature Lewis contended:

> [M]ost 'popular' fiction, if only it embodies a real myth, is so very much more serious than what is generally called 'serious' literature. For it deals with the permanent and the inevitable, whereas an hour's shelling, or perhaps a ten-mile walk, or even a dose of salts, might annihilate many of the problems in which the characters of a refined and subtle novel are entangled.[98]

It was a view with which Tolkien would have entirely agreed. Thus, when Lewis remarked to Tolkien that there should be more of the stories they liked to read, he did not only mean more mythic fantasy literature; he also meant there should be more fiction of broad appeal that did not pose as "serious" literature. And when Lewis and Tolkien defended reading for pleasure, it did not reflect merely a sentimental attachment to the stories they had read during childhood; it was part of a broader effort to defend the tastes of a public that was embracing their work. In a 1943 essay Lewis explained that he believed in democracy not because he thought everyone was fit to rule, but because no one was.[99] His approach to criticism was similarly demotic: one need look no further than Leavis to conclude that no one was qualified to police literary taste by defining an approved canon of serious literature.

In his last major critical work, Lewis argued that the critical demand that serious fiction must be "true to life" was unreasonable when examined closely. Lewis acknowledged that "The dominant taste at present demands realism of content,"[100] but he insisted that this standard both relied on a highly selective understanding of "realism" and excluded much unquestionably important literature. He made a distinction between two independent types of realism: presentational realism, "the art of bringing something close to us, making it palpable and vivid, by sharply observed or sharply imagined detail," and "realism of content," which demands that fiction be "probable or 'true to life.'"[101] The second sense of realism was, in Lewis's opinion, unduly influential in contemporary criticism:

> No one that I know of has indeed laid down in so many words that a fiction cannot be fit for adult and civilized reading unless it represents life as we have all found it to be, or probably shall find it to be, in experience. But some such assumption seems to lurk tacitly in the background of much criticism and literary discussion. We feel it in

the widespread neglect or disparagement of the romantic, the idyllic, and the fantastic, and the readiness to stigmatise instances of these as escapism.... We notice also that "truth to life" is held to have a claim on literature that overrides all other considerations.[102]

The demand for realism was thus rigged against the fantastic or mythical. Such a view failed to acknowledge that fantastic stories could also be "true to life" in their own way while simply excluding from the realm of serious literature most of what was written prior to the nineteenth century. The demand for realism of content could simply not accommodate an entire range of fictions, from the story of Oedipus to science fiction to *The Canterbury Tales*, not to mention the stories produced by Lewis and Tolkien themselves. In making his argument, Lewis was drawing on the ideas Tolkien had formulated in his Lang lecture; he was addressing from a different angle the charge of escapism that Tolkien had then attempted to rebut.[103] Their attack on prevailing critical assumptions was not simply an intervention in a debate about literary taste in which the stakes had to do with critical authority. Rather, their arguments were an intellectual move necessitated by the need to defend the kind of fiction they produced. Tolkien and Lewis's challenge to critical standards was in aid of their larger attempt to establish mythic fiction as a genre that did unique epistemic work.

Conclusion: Mythic fiction for the masses

Tolkien and Lewis had begun their endeavor to produce a body of mythic fiction when Lewis observed that there were not enough stories of the sort they wanted to read. As it turned out, many others wanted to read the same sort of stories as well, though this does not of course mean that readers were embracing the notion of myth that Tolkien and Lewis advocated. Sales figures and poll results both attest to the cultural influence of their fiction. In 1964 Tolkien's publisher reported that sales of *The Lord of the Rings* had topped 186,850 volumes.[104] In 1996 the British bookseller Waterstone's, in cooperation with the BBC Channel 4 program *Book Choice*, conducted a poll to identify the 100 greatest books of the century. Tolkien's *Lord of the Rings* topped the list, with *The Hobbit* finishing in 19th place. Subsequent polls by the *Daily Telegraph*, the Folio Society, the television program *Bookworm*, and Mori confirmed the popularity of Tolkien's *Lord of the Rings*: the book came first in all of them but the Mori poll, in which it came second.[105] In the Waterstone's–BBC poll, Lewis's novel *The Lion, the Witch and the Wardrobe* came in 21st.[106] In part this is because one of the key themes of their fiction—a critique of the modern desire to exercise control through science and technology, which was often linked in their work with anti-imperialist, anti-establishment, and environmentalist themes—resonated with many postwar Britons.[107]

Though it is difficult to conclude that Tolkien and Lewis succeeded in rehabilitating the epistemic value of myth, it can be concluded that they succeeded in clearing a cultural space for fictions of fantasy and enchantment, while establishing a set of literary conventions that have proved remarkably influential and popular. Lewis's Narnia novels revived and reworked an older British genre of adventure novels centered on schoolchildren and inspired a host of imitators. Tolkien's *Lord of the Rings* essentially invented the genre of fantasy fiction, one of the most commercially successful genres in the modern publishing industry. More directly relevant for this study, Lewis's "space trilogy" of science fiction novels served as examples for the "New Wave" science fiction writers who attempted to transform science fiction into a serious genre of literature in the 1960s.[108]

In the end, there was a deep, and perhaps productive, tension in Lewis and Tolkien's understanding of myth as it related to the mythic fiction they produced. On the one hand, they took a very elevated view of their oeuvre by arguing that the myths they produced communicated deeply important truths, and, on the other, they repeatedly emphasized that literature should be consumed for pleasure rather than for improvement.[109] There were thus two poles to their intervention in the politics of literary significance: a serious pole built around the notion that the kind of fiction they produced had a key cultural role to play in mediating perennial truths through a contemporary mythic format, and a more frivolous pole centered on the idea that literature should be read for enjoyment and not as a substitute for religion. They thus held, somewhat paradoxically, that myth was an epistemic category of great metaphysical import, and that attempts to substitute literature for metaphysics were wrongheaded. Nevertheless, their campaign on behalf of myth and mythic fiction intersected serendipitously with a growing reaction against prevailing definitions of what constituted serious literature. Lewis and Tolkien thus helped initiate a shift in literary opinion that would culminate during the 1960s in a widespread revolt by many leading writers against the so-called "social" novel. Key figures in this revolt were the "New Wave" writers examined in the following chapter, who would develop their own strategy for using myth to secure meaning in a modern age.

5
Coping with the Catastrophe: J.G. Ballard, the New Wave, and Mythic Science Fiction

Introduction

In 1973 a manuscript reviewer for a major British publisher sat horrified by what she was reading. As she turned the pages she grew increasingly disturbed by the tale of a group of Londoners who are sexually fascinated by car crashes. The wife of a prominent psychiatrist, she was certain the manuscript was the product of a mind that was utterly deranged. What she was reading was not a novel at all; it was evidence of hopeless psychopathology. She returned the manuscript with the recommendation: "This author is beyond psychiatric help. DO NOT PUBLISH."[1]

The author of the work, a young writer with a devoted cult following, was James Graham Ballard, who had made his name as a writer of short stories and novels that straddled the boundary between science fiction and serious literature. When he learned about the reader's report he was elated, because to him the diagnosis of insanity was proof of a total artistic success. He had intended the book to be profoundly disturbing so that its readers would be forced to confront ominous undercurrents of violence in their own culture. The publisher, Jonathan Cape, did not suppress the book as the reviewer had recommended. Knowing that a novel by Ballard would sell, and a controversial one even more so, it published the book under the title *Crash*, and its controversial reception quickly transformed Ballard's moderate fame into something more like infamy. But stirring up controversy had not been Ballard's goal. As with his other fictions, he conceived of the book as a contemporary myth which, by exposing worrying cultural trends, would enable people to cope with them. It was coping rather than controversy that Ballard aimed to achieve with what he called his "myths of the near future."

Why Ballard believed that his fiction functioned as myth in this way is the question that drives this chapter, which seeks to place Ballard's work in a new context by examining his use of myth as means of forging meaning for modernity. Ballard rose to prominence in the 1960s as writer associated with the British "New Wave" of science fiction writers, a group that included Michael Moorcock and Brian Aldiss. These writers sought to reorient science fiction as a genre, turning it away from clichéd conventions and toward relevant social critique. Though the fiction of the New Wave, and of Ballard in particular, has been the subject of illuminating and fine-grained analysis by literary scholars, comparatively little attention has been devoted to examining their work in the broader context of Britain's twentieth-century cultural history. With Ballard's recent death refocusing attention on his life and work, the time is perhaps ripe to consider how he and other members of the New Wave can be understood in relation to the broader context of postwar British history.

This chapter argues that the concept of myth was central to the work of Ballard and other New Wave writers and that their goal was to produce mythic science fiction that enabled readers to cope psychologically with the pressures of modern life. For the New Wave writers science fiction was contemporary myth, a source of meaning in a perplexing world. To advance this argument, the chapter places their work in the context of both the transformation of British society in the postwar period, and the prevalence of mythic thinking in twentieth-century British culture. While the New Wave in general will be examined, Ballard's thought from the early 1960s to the early 1980s will be the primary concern, because he proved to be the most prominent and influential writer to emerge from the New Wave.

We have seen in previous chapters that the turn to myth was justified by claims that it gave access to deeper truths than historical or scientific explanation, and that it offered a unique means of coping with the psychological pressures of modernity. It was the psychological aspects of myth that attracted Ballard's attention. Because Ballard saw the modern world as profoundly threatening to the individual psyche, it is not surprising that myth's capacity to provide psychic relief was a central theme of his work. His assessment of the modern world tended to emphasize the alienating effect of modern urban life, the emotional estrangement produced by modern mass media and communications, and the advance of technocracy. He argued that living in the environment he called "the modern technological landscape" produced deep psychological turmoil in the individual. By mediating between the outer world of the modern technological landscape and the inner world of the psyche, myth could help individuals cope with and find meaning for their lives. Precisely what Ballard meant by this and how he came to believe it becomes clearer when his work is understood as part of a unique literary movement that emerged in Britain during the 1960s.

Which way to inner space?: The rise of the New Wave

A key context for understanding Ballard's views on the mythic nature of fiction is his association with the group of writers known as the British New Wave. These writers shared a conviction that science fiction was the literary genre best suited to analyzing the contemporary world. Yet at the same time, they sought to redirect the genre by abandoning trite, pulp-science fiction conventions and developing science fiction's potential as an experimental form of writing. In Britain, the New Wave's most prominent members were Ballard, Moorcock and Aldiss, all of whom went on to build reputations as leading contemporary novelists. These three did not share all of the same literary inclinations, yet each of them believed science fiction was the only form of literature capable of addressing the problems of life in a society increasingly shaped by modern science, technology, and media.[2]

The New Wave in Britain initially coalesced in 1964 when Michael Moorcock took over editorship of the magazine *New Worlds*. In an attempt to cultivate a highbrow, avant garde sensibility, he immediately began a concerted effort to improve the quality of writing in *New Worlds* and to this end solicited ambitious, experimental contributions. The tone of the magazine was set by aggressive editorials and articles, mainly written by Moorcock and Ballard, that took aim at the literary establishment, obsolete traditions and social institutions, and scientific orthodoxy while touting a self-proclaimed *New Worlds*-led popular literary renaissance. As Moorcock proclaimed in the first issue of *New Worlds* that he edited, "A *popular* literary renaissance is around the corner. Together, we can accelerate that renaissance."[3] According to Moorcock and Ballard, this renaissance would be produced by grafting experimental literary techniques onto a form of science fiction that had cultural relevance and mass appeal. This amalgam, a new breed of science fiction, was summed up in their frequent use of the terms "speculative fiction" or "speculative fantasy" as substitutes for "science fiction." The New Wave was characterized by a distinct air of rebellion against American cultural hegemony, because the popular literary renaissance proclaimed in the pages of *New Worlds* could only be achieved by overthrowing the genre conventions that defined traditional science fiction, and these were largely American conventions. Part of *New Worlds*'s appeal, though, was that it tempered its revolutionary zeal with a sense of humor. For instance, the artist Eduardo Paolozzi, a friend of several of the New Wave writers, was listed on the *New Worlds* masthead as "Aeronautics Advisor."[4]

The New Wave positioned itself as an outsider, populist movement in opposition to a complacent literary establishment that did not engage with contemporary life and was content to reproduce versions of the nineteenth-century "social novel." Driven by a concern that contemporary British literature was too elitist and was not adequately addressing current concerns, *New Worlds*, and by extension the New Wave, sought to combine literary experimentalism with literary populism. There was thus a tension, if not a contradiction, at the heart of the New Wave movement. New Wave writers claimed that a strength of science fiction was its status as popular genre. Yet at the same time there was an element of cultural uplift in their project because they sought to replace certain science fiction conventions with experimental literary methods.[5] There are good reasons to take the New Wave writers' revolutionary rhetoric with a grain of salt, for it contained not a little savvy self-promotion. It is ironic that, after *New Worlds*'s distributor went bankrupt, the magazine was kept afloat in the late 1960s by a grant from the Arts Council arranged largely by Aldiss and a sympathetic Angus Wilson.[6] The movement that positioned itself against the literary mainstream was helped along by its patronage.

In the end, the initial success and popularity of *New Worlds* under Moorcock was mitigated by publishing and distribution difficulties. Moorcock did improve the sales of *New Worlds* after he became editor, and was able to keep many of the old subscribers while attracting new ones. And his talent for publicity attracted some media attention that increased newsstand sales. But not all of the attention that *New Worlds* attracted was beneficial or welcome. In 1968 the magazine serialized Norman Spinrad's novella *Bug Jack Barron*, which contained its share of obscenities and graphic sexual content. This prompted questions in Parliament, with the Minister of Arts being asked to explain why taxpayers' money was being spent on such a publication. After the *Bug Jack Barron* episode, W.H. Smith and John Menzies quit stocking the magazine on grounds of "obscenity and libel," even though all the characters in the Spinrad serial were fictitious. This was a fatal blow to *New Worlds*'s circulation, which was not meant to be "another Arts Council-supported little magazine" and hence depended on newsstand sales.[7] Though W.H. Smith eventually relented after a few months and took the magazine back in the face of critical publicity, its circulation never recovered. Moorcock and friends continued to publish *New Worlds* as a monthly for subscribers until April 1970, and then as an irregular publication throughout the 1970s.

Nevertheless, the fate of the New Wave was not tied to the fate of *New Worlds*. Though *New Worlds* faltered, the careers of the core New Wave writers did not. Aldiss, Moorcock, and Ballard only gained in popularity as novelists from the 1960s. In addition, by the late 1970s they were sought after as columnists and reviewers for a range of widely circulated publications, including *Time Out*, the *TLS*, the *New Statesman*, *New Society*, *Books and Bookmen*, *Vogue*, *The Guardian*, and later *The Times*, *The Telegraph*, *The Observer* and *The Independent*.

The New Wave writers had several reasons for seeing science fiction as a promising vehicle for their literary movement. To begin with, it was an undeniably popular genre with a ready-made readership. But beyond that, it was a genre that operated below the radar of the influential literary critics, who, with a few exceptions, deemed it unworthy of their attention. It was therefore a genre that allowed for more freedom of experimentation. As Moorcock put it, "Sf was attractive because it was overlooked by the critics and it could be written unselfconsciously.... There was no sense of having someone looking over your shoulder."[8] This conviction went hand in hand with their belief that the nineteenth-century style social novel had become obsolete and detached from everyday life. It simply was not up to the task of analyzing mid-twentieth-century life, whereas science fiction was uniquely equipped to do so. For instance, New Wave writers rejected the Angry Young Men as being preoccupied with insular social concerns. From the perspective of the New Wave, the ironic truth about the fiction of the Angry Young Men was that it was "worn-out, cliché-ridden, laborious, seemingly the tail-end of a literary movement which had begun in the twenties and petered out by the forties."[9] In contrast, Ballard declared, "[O]nly science fiction is fully equipped to become the literature of tomorrow, and it is the only medium with an adequate vocabulary of ideas and situations."[10] Ballard's words capture the New Wave writers' conviction that the most important forces shaping twentieth-century Britain were not politics or economics but science, technology and the media. Their belief that the mainstream novel was not adequately addressing these forces led them to science fiction as an alternative literary vehicle for their concerns.

But if science fiction was the only genre properly suited to describing and analyzing contemporary life, it also needed to be modified in order to serve this purpose in a relevant way. Science fiction conventions and tropes made the genre an effective medium of cultural critique, but only if these were appropriately modified to fit contemporary conditions. For instance, science fiction's traditional interest in the future could be adapted and put to good use. Whereas science fiction usually exhibited a fascination with predicting the achievements of science in the distant future, New Wave writers often projected current trends merely into the *near* future. This allowed for analysis of contemporary trends through a focus on their latent content. New Wave writers thus used the future not as prophecy but as a metaphor for the present; the future was used to interrogate contemporary reality. In addition, science fiction's traditional fascination with science and technology could be modified by New Wave writers, who were deeply concerned about how Britain was being transformed by these forces. But whereas science fiction writers were typically optimistic and celebratory about scientific and technological advances, the New Wave viewed such changes with a critical and ironic eye. This perspective was evident, for example, in their fascination with the concept of entropy as a metaphor for social and psychic disintegration. Finally, in New Wave writing science fiction's customary interest in alien planets and outer space was absent, replaced by a interest in the "alien" suburban landscapes of contemporary Britain and in what Ballard termed "inner space," or the psychological tensions produced by modernity. But Ballard urged that if writers wanted to explore this territory it was not more stories about outer space but rather an "*inner* space-suit which is needed, and it is up to science fiction to build it!"[11]

The nature of the catastrophe: The New Wave in historical context

This concern with psychological well-being in the contemporary world was a hallmark of how the New Wave movement responded to changes in British society and culture that were becoming apparent in the 1960s. Indeed, a hypersensitivity to these changes and their psychological implications was a basic feature of New Wave sensibility. Aldiss argued that because Britain had changed so dramatically—losing an empire in a matter of decades, for example—British writers tended to be more comfortable with and attuned to change than American writers.[12] Changes like the rise of mass media and advertising in a newly affluent consumer society, psychedelic drug culture, changing sexual mores, the increasingly technological modern landscape, the Cold War, the dying gasps of British imperialism and the first stirrings of a new American imperialism all reverberate throughout New Wave fiction. Their understanding of these dramatic changes reflected their understanding of the twentieth century as a whole, which they saw as an epoch of violence, disruption, and apocalypse.

The views of the New Wave writers were both typical and atypical of a generation shaped by the Second World War and the rapid social changes of the 1950s and 1960s. The political ethos of the New Wave tended toward an anti-authoritarian libertarianism. Ballard claimed that his politics were formed largely by his youth in Shanghai and coming of age in a detention camp, experiences that taught him to "detest barbed wire, whether of the real or figurative variety," a sentiment the other New Wave writers would have certainly endorsed.[13] For the most part, they had little interest in party politics and favored a vaguely defined populist democratic socialism, in some cases, as with Moorcock, tinged with anarchism.[14] Concerns about racial intolerance, environmental degradation, and overpopulation featured prominently in their work. The New Wave project, however, entailed an implicit critique of the narrowness of politics in postwar Britain, because it assumed that existing political categories and values could not address the changes being brought about by science and technology. As Ballard explained, "the modern communications landscape creates a different system of needs and obligations."[15] He meant that traditional British politics, driven by class interests, had become obsolete. This critique of politics was also a shrewd bid for cultural authority. By defining politics as irrelevant while simultaneously arguing that their brand of science fiction fulfilled an indispensable cultural function as the authentic literature of the late twentieth century, the New Wave writers sought to position themselves as uniquely equipped to confront the changes shaping Britain.

A suspicion of authorities and powerful elites also ran through their work. The targets of this suspicion included conservatives who resisted change and defended elite privilege, proselytizing Marxists who sought to enforce an ideological orthodoxy, the self-satisfied British middle class, American cultural hegemony and militarism, government ministers, international corporations, and, above all, scientists. New Wave writers frequently portrayed scientists as obsessed and voyeuristic, overcome by deviant subconscious impulses and tending toward insanity. The scientists imagined by the New Wave mask perverse obsessions with a façade of objective expertise and use the context and apparatus of the laboratory to gratify those obsessions. Typically, they are in the service of big business or big government. Whereas in traditional science fiction the scientist was represented as a hero, in New Wave science fiction the scientist became an often repugnant character. This debunking of the scientist's authority reflected the New Wave assumption that science had failed to realize its potential as a liberating, revolutionary social force. Instead it had been diverted to serve the needs of governments and corporations.

Interestingly, this same theme of liberatory potential giving way to authoritarianism was evident in the New Wave writers' view of America. Most of them grew up admiring a country that seemed "a bastion of freedom and continued revolution." To them America seemed a less socially rigid and class-bound society than Britain. Consequently, "It was a sad thing to see that image crumble after the [Second World] war."[16] The Vietnam War turned this idealization of America into disillusionment and was one reason they rejected the benign, optimistic vision of the future offered in much American science fiction. The American writer Norman Spinrad was in a unique position to observe this process of disillusionment. Spinrad, who knew many of the New Wave writers and published in *New Worlds* under Moorcock's editorship, noted:

> I was in Europe during a piece of the Viet Nam War...the war had created a lot of European anti-Americanism, which of course was to be expected. But the tenor of it was peculiar. The real gut-feeling had little to with the plight of the Vietnamese. It was a feeling of sorrow, of loss, of betrayal. Europeans felt diminished by what America was doing, abandoned by the "Leader of the Free World," let down by something they had believed in.[17]

American power had arguably saved the lives of Moorcock, Ballard, and Aldiss in the Second World War; certainly all three were thankful for American intervention in the war. Moorcock had dodged bombs in the Blitz and feared a German invasion, Ballard and his family had been on the verge of execution by the Japanese in China, and Aldiss had been poised to invade Japan with his army division. Because American intervention prevented all such possibilities from materializing it was easy for them to take a positive view of American power. Vietnam shattered these feelings and put the New Wave writers on guard against an America whose power seemed to be transforming from benign to imperialistic.

Strangely, commentators on the New Wave writers have not yet shown much interest in the critique of imperialism that is present in their work, a theme that is tied to their views of American power. Ballard and Aldiss in particular had direct experience of imperialism, and the conflict between competing imperialist projects, in their formative years. Ballard's father was directly involved with commercial ventures in China, and Ballard and his family later became victims of Japanese imperialism. Aldiss served with the British army in Burma during the Second World War, when he saw how British imperialism had oppressed colonized peoples.[18] And during the war he had ample opportunity to observe the brutality of Japanese imperialism. This experience of imperialism translated into a suspicion of American power that was confirmed by the Vietnam War. American invasions of Britain and Europe would become a common trope in New Wave fiction. For instance, Ballard prefaced his 1977 short story "Theatre of War" with the comment that, in the event of a class war in Britain, "I take it for granted that despite its unhappy experience in South East Asia the intervention of the United States to defend its military and economic investments would be even more certain that it was in Viet Nam."[19] New Wave treatments of imperialism often depicted the entropic dissipation of imperial projects, suggesting that such endeavors were ultimately doomed, the twentieth-century American imperial project no less than the nineteenth-century British one.

The atomic bomb was another central metaphor in New Wave fiction. New Wave writers agreed that the use of atomic weapons at Hiroshima and Nagasaki marked the beginning of a new historical era, but they refrained from opposing all use of nuclear weapons and technology. Their feelings about the atomic bomb and nuclear power were complex and ambivalent. Both Ballard and Aldiss were convinced that the atom bomb had saved their lives by ending the Second World War. In Ballard's case this meant that the Japanese did not have time to carry out their plan of transferring the inhabitants of his internment camp to the countryside where they could be executed in secrecy. In Aldiss's case this meant his division did not have to invade Japan: "When the Bomb was dropped, my division was in India.... So I had good reason to rejoice in the flattening of Hiroshima and Nagasaki. My bacon was saved."[20] But Aldiss's words should not be seen as an indication that the New Wave writers took the dawn of the nuclear age lightly; they clearly recognized the seriousness of the bomb's implications. The bomb became one more metaphor for the threats posed by modern science. As Patrick Parrinder has explained, the New Wave writers "began to exploit post-nuclear nightmares as a way of questioning the scientific enterprise as a whole."[21]

Perhaps the best known example is Ballard's acclaimed short story "The Terminal Beach," in which a former military pilot named Traven is driven by unconscious motives to the island of Eniwetok. There, in a "wilderness of weapons, aisles, towers, and blockhouses," he begins a quest for psychological fulfillment.[22] As the story progresses it becomes clear that the death-haunted atomic wasteland of Eniwetok is a metaphor for the automobile-dominated technological landscape of modernity in which Traven's wife and son met their death. The apocalyptic technological destruction represented by Eniwetok is a symbol for the prosaic technological destruction that takes places daily on highways.

This apocalypticism was behind two words, used as labels for the times, that recurred throughout the writings of Ballard and the New Wave: "catastrophe" and "disaster." The implication of the words was that modernity, and in particular the twentieth century, was a catastrophe that has *already* happened and *continues* to happen, constantly amplified in new ways. Aldiss once remarked that he really had no faith other than "belief in Catastrophe."[23] And it was no coincidence that Ballard's first four novels were all disaster stories. The modern catastrophe could not be reversed, but it could be confronted, analyzed, and described. The question, "What is the exact nature of the catastrophe?" echoed throughout New Wave writing as an unofficial slogan, and the attempt to answer it was central to the New Wave project.[24] Ballard placed the catastrophic disruption around 1945, since which time "the specters of mass psychosis stride across the communications landscape (the specters of the atom bomb, of the Nazi death camps, of the misuse of science, and so forth)."[25] The 1960s in a sense amplified the catastrophe, because it was then that modern media began to emerge and saturate the psyche with images of these "specters." Aldiss and Moorcock echoed this view of a historical rupture in 1945, the real meaning of which only became apparent in the 1960s.[26] When asked about the nature of the catastrophe in an interview, Ballard explained with reference to his experimental novel *The Atrocity Exhibition*:

> Well, it is happening. Even the stories in *The Atrocity Exhibition* are disaster stories of a kind. The book is about the communications explosion of the '60's. From my point of view, the '60's started in 1963 with the assassination of President Kennedy—his death and Vietnam presided over the whole of the '60's. Those two events, transmitted through television and mass communications, overshadowed the whole decade—a sort of institutionalized disaster area.[27]

The New Wave writers thought that a unique feature of the twentieth century was that its traumatic, violent, man-made catastrophes were rapidly absorbed into the "mass communications landscape" where—amplified by advertisers, mass-merchandisers, and media programmers—they fed society's latent desire for images of destruction and brutality.

New Wave anxiety about "the catastrophe" and its representation in the media was thus linked with an anxiety about the erosion of personal identity by numerous impersonal forces. New Wave writers admired Freud for his analysis of how the psyche could be destabilized from within by unconscious mental processes and for the way he exposed the limits of human rationality; Freud's *Civilization and its Discontents* was a key text for the New Wave writers.[28] They also admired Jung for his warnings about how the modern psyche had become unbalanced through reliance on science and for his emphasis on the psychological importance of literature and mythology; his *Modern Man in Search of a Soul* was another influential text in the New Wave movement.[29] In addition, they followed contemporary developments in psychology such as the work of R.D. Laing, who argued that mental illness was a psychological coping mechanism that could ultimately be therapeutic. Both Aldiss and Ballard were friends of Christopher Evans, a psychologist and computer scientist at the National Physical Laboratory whose research on dreaming had an obvious appeal for writers who were interested in the role of the unconscious. Their interest in psychology, combined with their analysis of the social and cultural changes occurring around them, resulted in a conviction that the self was threatened with erosion as never before. This "consciousness of [personal] mutability" was described in a 1967 *New Worlds* editorial which concluded: "The social sciences, imperfect as they still are, indicate this much at least: that a man's character (and soon, perhaps, his physical person) is as artificial and arbitrary as any artifact of his culture." But instead of turning away from this threatening present, the New Wave writers decided to confront it and deal with it on its own terms:

> [L]iterary art has characteristically lagged behind in dealing with these elements of modern life, even sometimes in recognizing them. When our best writers have recognized them, it has too often been to renounce them to a past that is viewed as somehow more congenial and "humanistic". Lawrence's primitivism and Eliot's orthodoxy represent two popular alternatives to an acceptance of the present world.

The editorial went on to explain how *New Worlds* would confront the present unflinchingly, rather than seeking the comforts of an idealized past. The passage, with its references to the importance of imagination, is indicative of surrealism's influence on the New Wave movement:

> We all stand in need of the "new sensibility" that can enable us to handle experiences and ideas for which nothing in our past lives has prepared us, and this sensibility can be won only by an act of sustained and informed imagination. It is to be hoped that this magazine can provide, in some degree, imaginative works that will fulfill this need.[30]

New Wave writers thus framed their speculative fiction as literature of coping that would help readers deal with their experience of modernity. And the key to speculative fiction's efficacy in this role was its mythic component.

The New Wave writers viewed science fiction as a contemporary form of myth which, when crafted well, mediated between the threatening outer world and the inner world of the psyche. By doing this it helped its readers cope with the "catastrophe" of modernity. The New Wave writer Thomas Disch declared: "As mythmakers, science fiction writers have a double task, the first aspect of which is to make humanly relevant—literally, to humanize—the formidable landscapes of the atomic era."[31] In taking this view, the New Wave writers were in part building on an existing British tradition of viewing science fiction as myth that went back at least to the 1930s. This understanding had been articulated first by science fiction novelist, critic, and erstwhile academic Olaf Stapledon, and later by C.S. Lewis, J.B. Priestley, and Raymond Williams.[32] The best science fiction possessed what Aldiss called "a myth-making quality" in the service of a serious literary purpose rather than escapist entertainment.[33] It allowed writers to draw on "both ancient and modern myth-ingredients," thereby creating a powerful form of contemporary fiction.[34] When they spoke of the writing process and their working methods, they often mentioned their attempts to make "direct use of mythic material" or build a "mythological stratum" into their works, often by drawing on Jung's theory of archetypes.[35] Disch called this "the second task of sf writers as mythmakers...the custodial work of keeping the inherited body of myths alive."[36] Accordingly, the leading New Wave writers wrote stories or novels that were titled or subtitled as myths, that retold well-known myths, or that made heavy use of mythic allusions.[37] They also constructed a literary genealogy for themselves that reflected this emphasis on the mythic dimension of science fiction. They claimed that they stood in a long tradition of serious writers who exemplified science fiction at its mythic best. This tradition ran from Mary Shelley and H.G. Wells, through Olaf Stapledon and Aldous Huxley, to recent practitioners like William S. Burroughs. Their view of science fiction as contemporary myth also drew inspiration from influential critics of the 1950s such as Priestley, Lewis, and Williams who spoke of science fiction as a form of myth. New Wave writers described both themselves and the writers who stood in this tradition as "myth makers" and "mythographers."[38]

Chronicling the death of affect: The life and work of J.G. Ballard

The New Wave writer who developed the most nuanced and comprehensive view of myth was J.G. Ballard. Ballard spoke of his short stories and novels as "myths of the near future" and saw myth as a necessary means of comprehending and coping with the changes that were shaping postwar Britain.[39] His myths of the near future chronicled what he termed "the death of affect," or the deadening of normal emotional response that followed in modernity's wake. Because of its concern with such troubling aspects of modernity, Ballard acknowledged that his work was driven by "a great sense of urgency" and had a strong "cautionary element."[40] But despite this cautionary tone, Ballard's fiction was not antimodern protest literature. He accepted the modern world, dominated by science and technology, as a given, but he set himself the task of examining how that world generated unprecedented pressures on the individual psyche. His ability to do so in an often prophetic way earned him a reputation as "the Sage of Shepperton," and he is immortalized in the Collins English Dictionary with the entry "Ballardian."[41]

Ballard's background gave him an outsider's perspective on British culture, along with a fund of experience and a conceptual vocabulary that were ideally suited to articulating his concerns in fiction. Born in 1930, he spent his childhood in Shanghai. His father worked for a Manchester-based textile firm and had been posted to Shanghai to serve as managing director of the subsidiary there. Ballard was fascinated by Shanghai, which he later called the first "media city," "purpose-built by the west as a test-metropolis of the future. London in the 1960s had been the second, with the same confusions of image and reality, the same overheating."[42] The years he spent in Shanghai echo throughout Ballard's fiction, because it was there that he came face to face with the apocalyptic nature of the twentieth century. During the Second World War he spent three years in a Japanese internment camp with his family, an experience he later fictionalized in his novels *Empire of the Sun* and *The Kindness of Women*.

Ballard first came to the U.K. in 1946. He entered Cambridge, where he studied medicine while entertaining thoughts of becoming a writer. He eventually gave up the study of medicine when he realized such a career would leave him insufficient time to write. He then spent a year studying English literature at King's College, followed by brief jobs in advertising and encyclopedia sales. Fascinated by flying and by the new supersonic jets that were being developed, he next spent a few years training to be a pilot in the Royal Air Force (RAF). This also turned out to be a dead end, though it was during RAF training in Canada that he first became intrigued with science fiction. By the late 1950s Ballard found himself editing the journal *Chemistry and Industry* while trying his hand at writing science fiction of his own. This position immersed Ballard in the world of scientific publications, which came to his office by the dozens. Reading these gave him an understanding of science's influence in the modern world and helped him develop the unique pseudo-scientific style and vocabulary for which he became known. He was subsequently able to keep this scientific knowledge current through his friendship with Evans, who weekly sent Ballard the contents of his wastepaper basket, the detritus of the world of ephemeral scientific publications. Eventually he began to envision the possibility of making a living as a writer, and had clear ideas about his subject matter and preferred style:

> I began writing in the mid-Fifties. Enormous changes were going on in England at that time, largely brought about by science and technology—the beginnings of television, package holidays, mass merchandising, the first supermarkets. A new landscape was being created. The so-called mainstream novel wasn't really looking at the present day. The only form of fiction which was trying to make head or tail of what was going on in our world was science fiction.[43]

Or, as he said elsewhere, "science fiction is a response to science and technology as perceived by the inhabitants of the consumer goods society."[44]

The social effects of new technologies and the increasing cultural authority of science thus provided the backdrop for Ballard's fictional project. In his view, the increasing influence of science and technology was at best an ambiguous development, and trusting technological innovation to cure Britain's social and economic ills was naive. Ballard maintained that his speculative fiction was skeptical that "science and technology can solve all problems," and unconvinced of "the magic of science and the moral authority of science."[45] By his own admission, Ballard was far from being a Luddite;[46] in fact, he was fascinated with new technological and scientific developments. But his concern was how the technological and scientific landscape of modernity changed the individual.

This is one reason why so many of Ballard's stories and novels are set in the suburbs of London around Heathrow Airport, near his home in Shepperton. This was a landscape of motorways, billboards, highway interchanges, reservoirs, airports, large retail outlets, all-night cafes, multistory car parks, and high-rise tenements. As an environment "bounded by a continuous artificial horizon," it epitomized what modernity meant to Ballard.[47] He was fascinated by the unobserved ways in which this urban space threatened the stability of individuals and the relationships they formed. As one critic has written of Ballard's technique, "The ordinary, normally unexamined world of the everyday is defamiliarised and shown to be the source of threats to personal and social existence."[48] One of Ballard's shorthand phrases for this threatening world was "the modern technological landscape," by which he meant the dominance of a scientific outlook, the modern urban environment, the mass media, and the constant proliferation of new technologies.

In Ballard's view, the artificial landscape of modernity contained hidden "logics"; it embodied sets of assumptions that both reflected and altered the psyches of individuals who lived within it. These logics could be decoded to reveal the inner nature of modern society. His fiction from the 1960s on was in part driven by the anxiety that the technological landscape of modernity might uncover and stimulate violent impulses submerged deep in the psyche. One of the primary themes of Ballard's work was the "irrational violence of modern society," the significance of which went largely unnoticed. This was in part an effect of modern communications and media: "We're all spectators (often bored ones) at tragedies like Vietnam. Real violence, frequently life, as it occurs, becomes a part of a huge entertainments industry."[49] Consequently, disturbing varieties of violence, made possible by science and technology and made palatable by the modern media landscape, figured prominently in his work. One of his most controversial works, *The Atrocity Exhibition*, suggests that iconic personalities like Marilyn

Monroe, the Kennedys, and Ronald Reagan function as mythic figures in contemporary culture. Their deaths, whether real or imagined, may have a purgative function "just as there used to be in ancient ritual murders, and always has been in the death of charismatic figures like Christ."[50] This situation was compounded by the fact that, while the media fed atavistic impulses by trivializing and normalizing violence, modern technology increasingly offered people the possibility of freely pursuing these impulses.

Ballard summed up the breakdown of the modern psyche under the heading "the death of affect." By this he meant a deadening of natural emotional responses and sympathy for others, which resulted from a modern environment that undermined human relationships and from the media's monotonous repetition of images of violence. Because of the way it distorted human relationships and liberated suppressed violent impulses, he saw the death of affect as "the most terrifying casualty of the century."[51]

Given these views, it makes sense that Ballard was intensely interested in psychology and particularly in Freud's ideas. While at Cambridge he read as much Freud as possible and even considered becoming a psychiatrist. Ballard believed that some of Freud's key insights could be adapted to help explain the pressures that the individual psyche was subjected to in a world dominated by technology. It is tempting to see Ballard's project as a translation of Freud's *Civilization and its Discontents* into a fiction for the late twentieth century. He shared Freud's pessimism about healthy psychological development. Just as Freud saw the psyche as constantly threatened with the possibility of regression, so Ballard worried about how the individual psyche was forced to continually confront pressures toward atavistic degeneration. Hence his insistence that contemporary fiction should explore "*inner space*, that psychological domain ... where the inner world of the mind and the outer world of reality meet and fuse."[52] Accordingly, New Wave writers used the psychiatrist as a stock character. The psychiatrist was the natural explorer of inner space, the analog of traditional science fiction's astronaut.

According to New Wave writers, the mainstream "social" novel assumed that identity was shaped primarily in and through social conventions and interpersonal relationships. But in a modern technological landscape this was no longer true: individual identity was primarily shaped through immersion in a sea of information and images delivered by the mass media, and by inhabiting an urban landscape that radically reconfigured traditional social relationships. This explained why the mainstream novel, so influential in the nineteenth century, had declined precipitously in influence. As Ballard put it, "The social novel is reaching fewer and fewer readers, for the clear reason that social relationships are no longer as important as the individual's relationship with the technological landscape of the late twentieth century."[53] In this new context Freud's insights were more relevant than ever, because modernity uncovered and stimulated a variety of disturbing, submerged psychological drives.

Ballard's views on the relationship between the psyche and the modern technological landscape can be clarified by examining his analysis of the meaning of automobiles and automobile accidents. The car crash figured prominently in three of his novels from the early- to mid-1970s, *The Atrocity Exhibition*, *Crash*, and *Concrete Island*, and continued to be a recurring image in his subsequent fiction. For Ballard the automobile and the automobile crash were keys to decoding the dark subconscious impulses that were unmasked and stimulated by the modern technological landscape. He felt that the twentieth century was summed up by the image of a man in a car, driving on a concrete highway to an unknown destination. This image was "a focal point for an immense range of social, economic, and psychological pressures" because

> Almost every aspect of modern life is there, both for good and for ill—our sense of speed. Drama, and aggression, the worlds of advertising and consumer goods, engineering and mass manufacture, and the shared experience of moving together through an elaborately signaled landscape.... Here we see, all too clearly, the speed and violence of our age, its strange love affair with the machine and, conceivably, with its own death and destruction.[54]

Accepting the freedom offered by the automobile also entailed accepting widespread death and violence in form of the car crash. At the very least, then, the annual toll of crash casualties amounted to "a huge institutionalised disaster," a "pandemic cataclysm institutionalized in all industrial societies that kills hundreds of thousands of people each year and injures millions."[55] Ballard wondered if unconcerned acceptance of this death and violence concealed deeper psychological impulses.

In an introduction written for the French edition of *Crash*, Ballard opined that Freud's *Civilization and its Discontents* was a more relevant text for the times than the theories of Marshall McLuhan, because the diseases of the psyche described by Freud had culminated in the contemporary death affect. *Crash* was thus "a cataclysmic novel of the present day," an exploration of a world in which the death of affect made it possible to "pursue our own psychopathology as a game."[56] He explained that in the novel the car was used "as a total metaphor for man's life in today's society" in order to issue "a warning against that brutal, erotic, and overlit realm that beckons more and more persuasively to us from the margins of the technological landscape."[57] *Crash* was a warning, but not of the moralizing variety. It warned by exposing the latent meaning of automobile culture. It was certainly not the sort of warning issued by Ralph Nader, whom Ballard dismissed as consumer society's first populist demagogue.[58] According to Ballard, Nader offered a simplistic, obsessive mix of anxiety and guilt in response to modern technology, which did not help people cope with technological modernity at all. Instead people needed contemporary myths, like *Crash*, that helped them deal with the psychological pressures of contemporary experience. Ballard felt that in attempting to uncover the meaning of the car crash, one came up against the limits of rationality: "It's a mistake to adopt a purely rational attitude towards events like the car crash."[59] Myth could break through these limits and reveal the latent meaning behind them, thereby serving an indispensable role for those seeking to cope with the catastrophe.

Myths of the near future: Ballard as mythographer of modernity

Throughout his career as a writer Ballard viewed his fiction as a form of contemporary myth. Myth is the concept that holds together his key ideas like "inner space" and "speculative fiction," as well as his varied obsessions about and analyses of the twentieth century. Ballard's views on the mythic function of his fiction remained remarkably consistent throughout his career. His theory of myth was unique and drew from eclectic influences including, as already noted, both Freud and Jung. Freud impressed upon Ballard how myths manifested psychological tensions and conflicts. Furthermore, Ballard's conception of how his myths functioned bears some resemblance to Freud's talking cure. Both enable psychological coping by bringing the hidden or suppressed to light so that it can be confronted. Though Ballard was more drawn to Freudian than to Jungian psychoanalysis, he was influenced by Jung's account of how myth can reveal otherwise inaccessible dimensions of the psyche.[60]

But Ballard's understanding of myth drew on more than psychological theory. One of the books that deeply impressed Ballard when he was just beginning to write was Robert Graves's idiosyncratic theory of myth-making, *The White Goddess*.[61] From Graves Ballard seems to have gained an appreciation of the persistence of a myth-making impulse in European culture. Despite the distinctiveness of Ballard's understanding of myth, he shared with other British mythic thinkers several assumptions about the cultural importance of myth. These included the belief that all cultures produce myths regardless of how advanced they were, a belief that ideally myth had a beneficial cultural role, a sense that a turn to myth was the natural antidote to the dominance of scientific discourse, and a conviction that modernity made reliance on myth more vital than ever before.

The problem Ballard faced was how to construct a form of contemporary myth that was relevant and effective. Neither the past, nor political programs, nor the mainstream novel were really up to the task of helping people cope with the twentieth century; the pace of change had made these irrelevant. But change was precisely what science fiction was adept at handling; therefore it was the leading candidate to serve as a modern mythology in Ballard's view: "S-f has been one of the few forms of modern fiction explicitly concerned with change—social, technological, and environmental—and certainly the only fiction to invent society's myths."[62] Science fiction's concern with change was therefore important in two ways. On the one hand, by confronting change head on science fiction engaged subject matter that was by definition highly significant and relevant. On the other hand, science fiction dealt with this change by mythologizing it, by using it as the basis for new myths that made sense of the change for those who were threatened by it:

> [S]cience fiction... in fact constitutes the strongest literary tradition of the twentieth century, and may well be its authentic literature. Within its pages, as in our lives, archaic myth and scientific apocalypse collide and fuse.... [I]t has tried to respond to the most significant events of our time—the threat of nuclear war, over-population, the computer revolution, the possibilities and abuses of medical science, the ecological dangers to our planet, the consumer society as benign tyranny—topics that haunt our minds but are scarcely considered by the mainstream novel.[63]

Science fiction thus produced myths that mediated between the inner world of the psyche and a rapidly changing external reality.

Ballard thought that the pace of change driven by science and technology had actually altered the cultural function of myth. Myth no longer looked backward out of a concern to explain where a culture had come from, as with the classical Greek myths. Instead it looked forward out of a concern to discover where the culture was going. Ballard argued that the first writer to demonstrate how science fiction could be fashioned into a twentieth-century mythology was William S. Burroughs. He acclaimed Burroughs as the "first mythographer of the twentieth century," because by adapting certain science fiction conventions he had been able to create "the first authentic mythology" of the present era of catastrophe.[64] But all too few writers showed a similar ability or willingness to take inspiration from Burroughs.

Building on his understanding of psychoanalysis, Ballard argued that myth-making was a fundamental human activity and a central purpose of effective and relevant contemporary literature. He held that individuals naturally construct their own mythologies as coping mechanisms that allow the inner self to deal with a threatening external world: "Each of us builds the mythology of our own lives out of the materials that surround us in our everyday streets."[65] This view also characterized his own work, which he spoke of as an attempt to mythologize his experience through writing.[66] Furthermore, he often described his characters as "mythologizing" their experience in order to cope with and make sense of it.[67] Hence, he offered "stories of psychic fulfillment"[68] that showed how people could cope with the "threatening possibilities offered by modern science and technology."[69] The imaginative writer's role, then, was to perform the normal process of private mythologizing more extensively, analytically and publicly, in an effort to help others make sense of the landscape of modernity. Thus, the best contemporary writers functioned as mythographers.

Consequently, Ballard described his stories and novels as "myths of the near future" and as "predictive mythologies" that used the near future to interpret the present. Doing so revealed the threats to the individual psyche that were latent or unobserved in the contemporary world and equipped readers to cope with them:

> The title *Myths of the Near Future* exactly sums up what I think a lot of present writers, musicians ... filmmakers, painters ... are concerned with: the mythologies of the future. Not myths which will one day *replace* the classical legends of ancient Greece, but *predictive mythologies*; those which in a sense provide an operating formula by which we can deal with our passage through consciousness.... These are mythologies that you can actually live by: how to cope with the modern urban landscape.... I'm interested in what I think

of as a radically new set of mythologies that *aren't* concerned with the past.[70]

He elaborated on how his mythologies were intended to function: "I construct my emergency kit—the latest short story or the novel I'm working on at the present—an emergency assemblage with which I try to cope with the situation in which I find myself. I offer it to anybody else I feel is in the same boat."[71] Thus, Ballard's description of his writings as "stories of psychic fulfillment" was true in two senses: not only did his characters seek psychic fulfillment, but, if the stories did their work as myths of the near future, his readers would find it as well.

Underlying Ballard's conception of myth was a belief that it offered unique access to reality at a time when "reality" had become almost entirely fictionalized due to the metastasis of the mass media landscape. And Ballard believed that, because of the size of the country, the network of national newspapers and television stations, and the sheer volume of advertising and media images, the British were "the people most dominated by the media landscape; the most dominated the world has ever known."[72] He concluded that by the mid-1960s reality had become dominated by fictions, by which he meant "anything invented to serve someone's imaginative ends, or aims." The media landscape overflowed with "movies, television, and constant advertising. Politics is a branch of advertising, the whole thing is a hothouse of fictions." In a Britain in which reality itself had become an enormous fiction, the fiction writer's role was virtually superfluous. Consequently, the writer's vocation needed to be radically reconceptualized: "the writer's job is no longer to put the fiction in, the fiction's already *there*; the writer's job is to put the reality in."[73]

Ballard's understanding of myth was also linked to his belief that history was deficient as a guide to life in the contemporary world. His views on the mythic function of science fiction were closely linked to his understanding of time and history. Ballard argued that history had become irrelevant because it did not really explain the present and therefore could provide no real guidance about how to cope with it. In actuality, he argued, "the future provides a better key to the present than does the past."[74] This was because the "latent content" of contemporary reality could only be revealed by projecting current trends and conditions into the near future in order to comprehend their meaning. Hence his myths of the near future, which were "concerned with seeing the present in terms of the immediate future rather than the past."[75] Ballard explained that "classical mythologies ... tended to be concerned with explaining origins ... I think the sort of mythologies I'm interested in ... are concerned with ends rather than with beginnings."[76] The future had simply become a better source of guidance than the past, necessitating a new type of myth-making.

According to Ballard, inhabitants of the modern technological landscape experienced time in a fundamentally different way than their nineteenth-century predecessors. The Victorians had experienced time linearly and had explained the world in those terms. This diachronic epistemic perspective was exemplified in the Victorian novel, in which a moralizing, omniscient author portrayed characters and their relationships in terms of change over time. But Ballard contended that life in the contemporary world was far different: "We live in quantified non-linear terms.... We don't live our lives in linear terms in the sense that the Victorians did."[77] Time in the modern world was experienced synchronically as a continuous present, in which individuals struggled to cope with the images offered by the media and in which technology continually offered new ways of changing one's identity or lifestyle.

In such a world, the influence of even the recent past on people was radically mitigated. Individuals did not see the past as relevant to their experience because they somehow realized that the social conditions of their existence were not inherited, but were provided externally by the nature of modern science and technology.[78] In 1970 he diagnosed a rejection and loss of interest in the past: "Look at most people and you will find that they have declared a moratorium on the past; they are just not interested. One is constantly meeting people who have only a hazy idea of their parents—who have changed their lifestyles since their childhood in every possible way."[79] In these new conditions the Victorian-style novel, with its "retrospective bias," was totally inadequate.[80] What was needed instead was "a mythology that starts now, this moment in time, and runs forward."[81]

Just as history offered no means of coping with the catastrophe, so also politics was of little avail in Ballard's estimation. The post-human world portrayed in Ballard's fiction is also a post-political world. Andrzej Gasiorek has pointed out, "Politics is sidelined in Ballard's texts because it is seen to have little purchase on the economic, technological and social circuits that incessantly decode and recode twentieth-century life."[82] By the early 1960s Ballard had concluded that politics had become little more than a branch of advertising. Rather than ameliorating the pressures of contemporary life, it contributed to them as one more dimension of the mass communication landscape. The difference between politicians and entertainment icons had become negligible, as

Ballard had recognized when he predicted Ronald Reagan's rise to the presidency in his collage novel *The Atrocity Exhibition* (1970). Politics had been subsumed by the image-driven communications landscape.

This led Ballard to suggest in some of his fictions that true psychic fulfillment could only be achieved by an individual who was somehow placed outside of this landscape. This manifested in his work as a recurring theme of primitivism. His stories and novels often depicted characters who, either through isolation in a hostile or desolate environment, exposure to a man-made disaster, or sudden separation from modern urban life, are removed from social, cultural, and political networks. Thus left to confront their own psyches and the possibility of primitive regression, they discover within a more authentic, more psychologically integrated self. Ballard's novel *Concrete Island*, for example, offered a contemporary retelling of the "myth" of Robinson Crusoe. After crashing his car, the protagonist Maitland is marooned on a piece of waste ground between converging highway embankments. Because he is injured he cannot climb to safety or signal for help effectively, but being cut off from the continual pressures of London life enables him to achieve a new kind of psychic fulfillment that prepares him to return to civilization on his own terms. Myths of primitive existence thus became vehicles for Ballard's critique of the communications landscape.

Ballard offered his mythologies as antidotes to what he saw as a host of false mythologies circulated by the mass communications landscape. These false mythologies included the notion of space travel, the dream of a society perfected by science, and the vision of a better life offered by advertising.[83] Though there is no evidence that Ballard had read Roland Barthes's *Mythologies*, there were some points of contact between their respective conceptions of myth.[84] Both spoke of how the culture was an incessant propagator of myths. But they had very different conceptions of where these myths originated. Barthes aimed to expose how myths embedded in popular culture served the interest of the advertisers or reinforced bourgeois ideology. As such, the myths he identified were false—or at least obscured important realities—and served to reinforce the status quo. Ballard could have agreed that the media propagated numerous false mythologies that served various interests, but he would not have shared Barthes's understanding of the political implications of this. Where Barthes's theory of myth had distinct Marxist overtones, Ballard's instead had Freudian resonances. False mythologies were not part of an ideological apparatus, but were ultimately products of the subconscious that fed only partially recognized desires. The difference between these and the mythologies Ballard crafted was that his were helpful because they were true. We have seen that Ballard conceived of the writer as a truth-teller, as someone whose role it was "to put the reality back in" to everyday experience. Ballard thus distinguished between the false myths of the media landscape and the myths he crafted, which aimed to expose the true nature of contemporary reality.

Conclusion

By the early 1970s Ballard was widely read, published, and translated, and highly sought after as a reviewer, columnist, and interview subject. Though he consistently spoke of his work as science fiction, he gained a reputation that extended well beyond the boundaries of that genre. From the beginning there was a strong populist dimension to the New Wave project, and this was further evidenced in Ballard's concerted attempts to present his work and views in venues that would reach the widest possible readership. His primary means of doing this was through interviews, which he agreed to with astonishing frequency; indeed, it is likely that Ballard was one of the most interviewed major writers of the twentieth century.[85] As John Baxter has observed:

> Few figures in British public life could be depended on so confidently for a forceful opinion and a cogent quote. London journalist Jason Cowley recalled that "a shout used to echo through the newsroom at moments of great national trauma, the death of Princess Diana, say, or a terrorist outrage—'Call J.G. Ballard.' "[86]

Where these interviews appeared gives us some indication of who was reading Ballard and of the sort of audience he wanted to reach. Alongside interviews in highbrow publications like *Paris Review* or *Books and Bookmen* are interviews in obscure fanzines (*Cypher*, *Vector*), journals of science fiction criticism (*Foundation*, *Thrust*), underground publications (*Friends*, *Search and Destroy*), London weeklies (*Time Out*, *New Musical Express*), and large format glossy magazines (*Vogue*, *Rolling Stone*). The number of magazine and newspaper interviews from the 1960s through the 1980s totals more than 80, and this does not include his numerous radio, television, and book interviews. Ballard also disseminated his views through numerous book reviews and non-fiction essays, which, as Roger Luckhurst has pointed out, he was able to use "as a surreptitious way of continuing his fiction by other means and gaining a wider audience for his polemics."[87] This outreach to a popular readership underscores the cultural influence of Ballard's fiction and views.

Ballard's fiction, and New Wave fiction more generally, should be seen as a literature of skepticism about modernity rather than a literature of protest against it. Indeed, it may be best to describe Ballard's fiction as a literature of coping, given his consistent emphasis on the psychological effects of modernity and his repeated insistence that his fiction was intended to help readers deal with these effects. Like other mythic thinkers of the century, he did not advocate a return to a simpler past, nor did he believe that this was possible. And he was at odds with the response to modernity offered by many of the political groups and countercultural protest movements prevalent in Britain during the 1960s and 1970s. He had little sympathy for protest movements like the Campaign for Nuclear Disarmament (CND) and he thought that the New Left was "out of touch."[88] His view was that, by vilifying politicians and policy makers, such groups missed the point entirely. Ballard suggested that political elites were not to blame for the troubling aspects of modernity because these aspects were the realization of humanity's unconscious psychopathic impulses, impulses that were both brought to light and abetted by modern science, technology, mass communications, and urban life.

Though critical of many consequences of twentieth-century science and technology, Ballard's fiction was not anti-science and technology. Instead, its underlying concern was the psychological impact of modernity, especially the "death of affect." Thus the ultimate point of Ballard's of fiction was not to protest against the catastrophe of modernity, but rather to analyze it with a view toward developing coping strategies. That is why, as Colin Greenland has noted, the role of Ballard's protagonists "is to accept the disaster and acclimatize to the new environment."[89] Ballard knew he and his readers could not undo the catastrophe, but they could come to terms with it. New Wave fiction advertised itself as a new literature for the present and future. Its advocates touted it as the only truly "modern" form of literature, not only because it used the idiom of science fiction, but also because it explored the meaning and significance of characteristically modern experiences. Moorcock was fond of pointing out that writers like Virginia Woolf did not deserve the title "modern" whereas Ballard did, precisely because he was able "to recognize a genuine modern concern" and frame a fiction that came to grips with it.[90] On these terms, then, Ballard's myth-making can be seen as a fundamentally modern project. His myths of the near future offered readers the possibility of making meaning for modernity.

Adding the story of the New Wave's mythic science fiction to the narrative of twentieth-century British history both sharpens and complicates our understanding of British modernity. The New Wave project is a reminder that the categories of the two cultures debate can obscure the complexity of how Britons experienced the scientific and technological aspects of postwar modernity. The science versus humanities model does not help us contextualize and make sense of the New Wave project. The New Wave writers never identified themselves as advocates of the humanities and made no attempt to argue that the humanities had a central cultural function. Neither did they take up the cudgels on behalf of technocratic progress. Instead, they argued that mythic science fiction had a cultural importance that was necessitated by the nature of modernity. The work of Ballard and the New Wave is a telling instance of how a search for meaning in modernity led to a constructive embrace of mythic thinking instead of the humanities, traditional religion, or an idealization of the past.

Finally, when the fiction of Ballard and the New Wave is understood as an attempt to craft myths that spoke meaningfully to twentieth-century experience, connections to a range of seeming unrelated figures come into view. Affinities that on the surface seem improbable suddenly become comprehensible. For example, Lewis and Tolkien understood themselves as using myth to respond to a modernity disfigured by misuse of science and technology, though they did so with different motivations and at a different historical moment than the New Wave. Nevertheless, the New Wave writers recognized that they were doing something that resembled what Lewis and Tolkien had done. Thus, though Aldiss did not share Lewis's religious presuppositions, he saw Lewis as a fellow writer of mythic science fiction and was elated when he had the chance to discuss science fiction with Lewis in 1962.[91] Though he had sought and received personal encouragement from Lewis and Tolkien when he first began writing, Moorcock later felt it necessary to distance his work from Tolkien's on the grounds that *The Lord of the Rings* was "Winnie-the-Pooh posing as epic," that is, more escapist rural romance than potent myth.[92] Moorcock recognized Tolkien as a fellow producer of myths, but thought *The Lord of the Rings* was the wrong kind of myth because it refrained from engaging contemporary life in a relevant way. The New Wave writers recognized that they were not the only British writers to produce mythic fiction, but deemed their own form of mythic science fiction the best means of coping with the catastrophe of the late twentieth century.

6
Myth and the Quest for Psychological Wholeness: C.G. Jung as Spiritual Sage

Introduction

Readers leafing through the *Manchester Guardian* on 26 July 1955 might have been somewhat surprised to find a leader noting the eightieth birthday of Carl Gustav Jung. The editors of the paper saw the occasion as a fitting opportunity to consider the Swiss thinker's intellectual legacy and continuing relevance: "to-day is not an occasion for paying lip-service to a celebrated thinker. It is a time to take note of his works, especially those which may help to get ourselves out of the fantastic social and political muddles we have got ourselves into." The leader went on to emphasize the breadth of Jung's thought, noting how his early work in psychoanalysis gave way to "intellectual excursions [that] reach far beyond the consulting-room." Unlike Freud, "who belonged essentially to the nineteenth century," Jung's intellectual excursions marked him as fundamentally "a twentieth-century figure" with abiding significance.[1]

The *Manchester Guardian* was not the only forum that took note of Jung's eightieth birthday. The BBC also paid homage with features on both radio and television, further reinforcing an already established perception of Jung as a living prophet who dispensed much-needed wisdom, often through an emphasis on humanity's need for myth. As one writer later recalled:

At 80 Jung was the modern high priest of a psychotherapeutic tradition reaching far back into ancient mythology—a sage, almost an oracle.... Many famous men and women came from all over the world to pay homage as they might to a holy man, or to pose questions which he alone, they believed, was equipped to answer.

The same writer noted that even though Jung "recoiled from the term mystic," he could not avoid being seen as one by many. He was a man who "woke the world," and his posthumous influence "seem[ed] to widen" in direct proportion to the level of criticism he received.[2] To many, Jung seemed to be equal parts pioneering scientist, trusted sage, and celebrity.

When Jung died about five years later, many of the obituaries echoed the praise that had been expressed on his eightieth birthday. The *Times* obituary for Jung noted the widespread feeling "that he had light to throw on problems which were the concern of all thinking people."[3] The *Guardian* obituary ventured the judgment that: "When the heated disputes about him die down he will doubtless emerge as a remarkable thinker who has deeply influenced not only our theories of symbolism but also our conceptions of the spiritual life of man."[4] The next day the same paper again emphasized Jung's role as a kind of spiritual sage who reminded his readers of the importance of "spiritual experience."[5] As we will see, this role as a sage in matters spiritual was a key aspect of Jung's persona in Britain.

These encomiums and eulogies are evidence of Jung's remarkable but underappreciated influence on British intellectual and cultural life in the second half of the twentieth century. That influence is remarkable for at least two reasons. The first is the *nature* of Jung's influence: during the postwar period he enjoyed widespread respect and sage-like status in a way few other writers or intellectuals did. For decades, Jung was regarded in Britain as a unique fount of spiritual counsel, offering wisdom on both perennial and specifically modern problems. Jung's reputation in Britain as a spiritual sage was established as early as the 1930s, when his approach to psychology was recognized as more open to spiritual questions than Freud's. Already in 1935 a reviewer for the *Manchester Guardian* was praising Jung for acknowledging "spiritual values as neither Freud nor Adler do" and for appreciating "that the problem of the modern man is essentially a religious one."[6] Jung's treatment of the spiritual problems faced by moderns involved an investigation of the meaning and significance of myth, and his views on the subject resonated throughout twentieth-century British culture.[7]

This view of Jung as a spiritual sage became stronger and more widespread in ensuing decades, and comparisons with Freud and Adler diminished as the Swiss psychiatrist's thought came to be considered on its own terms. And the marks of this consideration appeared not only in highbrow journals and reviews such as *Encounter* or the *Times Literary Supplement*, but also in venues with much wider circulation, such as

The Guardian and even the *Daily Mail*—not to mention radio and television. The widespread view of Jung as a fount of spiritual insight was undiminished by his death in 1961. Indeed, Andrew Von Hendy has pointed to the 1960s as a moment when intellectual respect for Jung was at its height.[8] Media interest in Jung showed little sign of abating even by the 1980s.

The second reason Jung's influence is remarkable is that, in many ways, he was a very unlikely candidate to achieve such stature in Britain. Although he neither lived nor worked in Britain, this did not prevent him achieving fame there. Indeed, few non-British thinkers enjoyed as much prominence and respect in Britain as did Jung between, say, 1945 and 1980. In addition, Jung was seen in Britain not as a specialist intellectual whose authority came solely from his professional expertise, but rather as a thinker who offered an integrated vision of life in the style of the great Victorian sages. Jung certainly did invoke his professional authority when speaking to contemporary issues, but it is also clear that he was seen as a figure of profound moral and spiritual authority. So how did a seeming outsider and anachronism like Jung, the so-called "Sage of Zurich," come to exert such influence in postwar British culture?

This chapter will offer an answer to that question. Focusing on the period after the Second World War, I argue that Jung's significance as a spiritual sage in Britain can be explained by considering three main factors. The first of these was Jung's lifelong affection for England and its culture. This fondness for England meant that Jung visited the country numerous times, took a particular interest in making a name for himself there, and was anxious that "ordinary people" there understand his writings. His strong desire to make himself understood enabled him to promote his ideas abroad even in the midst of transition to the age of mass media. The second factor was that the writers, reviewers, and intellectuals who shaped the contours of Jung's reception in Britain tended to emphasize the spiritual aspects of his work, including his ideas about myth, even when they had reservations about those aspects. The third and most important factor, however, was compatibility between key themes of Jung's thought and key concerns of a broad constituency within the British public.

In particular, Jung was very much concerned with the problem of making meaning in the modern world, and he confronted this problem in a way that convinced many meaning could indeed be found. Jung implicitly agreed with Auden about the existence and seriousness of "the modern problem," but he also held that individuals could solve this problem if they committed themselves to the quest to achieve the state of psychological integration that he called individuation. A key aspect of this process was embracing the importance of myth, and Jung's explanation of this importance was one of the most influential facets of his thought. Jung's popularity was thus above all due to the fact that many craved meaning and spiritual significance, which his work seemed to offer.[9]

Jung and Britain: A brief overview

In 1904 Carl Jung made a journey to Britain with the intention of improving his English. His visit, the first of many, lasted for two months and it confirmed him as a lifelong Anglophile. Jung not only improved his English, he became a devotee of the language. Indeed, as Deirdre Bair notes, Jung would eventually come to prefer expressing his ideas in English, which he believed offered "more precise, direct, and focused terminology" than German.[10] He simultaneously developed a deep respect for the English culture. In particular, he became enamored of what he took to be the self-reliant individualism that characterized the English way of life.[11]

Yet in 1904 there were few indications that Jung's love of England would be reciprocated. Not yet 30, Jung was at the very start of his career and had only published his dissertation the previous year. Moreover, his chosen field of psychiatry was by no means well established by the early years of the twentieth century. But, over the next few decades, both Jung's stature and that of his chosen profession would rise, resulting in many more opportunities for him to visit his favorite foreign country. Jung's visits served to both establish his reputation in England and cement his affection for the country. With each trip Jung won new students and devotees and drew the attention of prominent writers and intellectuals, some of whom became advocates of his theories.

The outbreak of the First World War put a temporary stop to Jung's visits, but not to his interest in the country and its culture. During the War Jung served for a time as the commandant of a prisoner of war camp in Switzerland, and he was deeply impressed by the British officers under his charge, which strengthened his Anglophilia.[12] Also, some of his writings began to be translated into English for the first time. After the War, Jung's visits to England resumed and he even began to affect an English style of dress.[13]

Certainly by the 1930s Jung was recognized in Britain as a psychological authority of some eminence. He gained added prominence due to his willingness to comment on the momentous political events of that decade and analyze some of the key figures behind those events, such as Hitler and Mussolini. At the same time, in the 1930s Britons first began to appreciate that Jung's psychological theories had significant implications for questions of religious belief. When L.W. Grensted delivered the prestigious Bampton Lectures at the University of Oxford in 1930, he chose as his topic "the implications of recent psychology for religious belief and practice" and devoted considerable attention to Jung. It was an early instance of what would be sustained interest by British theologians in Jung's thought. It is no coincidence that this was also the decade when much ink was spilled in Britain about the religious implications of the new physics. There was much discussion in Britain during these years about the relationship between science of all types and religion.[14]

Jung's examination of spiritual questions went hand in hand with an examination of the meaning and purpose of myth, an aspect of his thought that contributed to its positive reception in Britain. A culture already marked by a profound interest in myth was understandably receptive toward a thinker like Jung who had much to say on the subject.

There were, to be sure, those who were critical of Jung and his views on myth. R.G. Collingwood, for one, was distinctly unimpressed with him. The intellectually omnivorous Collingwood was already interested in Jung by 1923, when he reviewed an English translation of Jung's *Psychological Types: or, The Psychology of Individuation* for the *Oxford Magazine*. In the mid-1930s Collingwood began composing a manuscript on folktale and magic. This project necessitated a wide-ranging survey of scholarship on myth, which led him in turn to Jung's ideas. He noted how many of Jung's views on myth seemed to recapitulate those of Max Müller, and this was not meant as a compliment: "One feels as if Max Müller had come to life again, having forgot nothing but his scholarship and learnt nothing but a smattering of psycho-analysis."[15] In Collingwood's view, Jung's understanding of myth had two main flaws: it was reductionist and it was historically ignorant. He explained, "[T]he two characteristics of Jung's thought are the tendency to suppress distinctions like that between myth and dream, so as to falsely simplify problems, and the tendency to create pseudo-history so as to give fictitious explanations of origins."[16]

Prior to the Second World War, however, few who considered Jung's theory of myth were willing to be so critical. Those who were fascinated by myth were much more likely to see Jung as at least an erstwhile ally in the quest to explain its power. Some even saw in Jung's theory of myth a philosopher's stone that could entirely transform methods of investigation in some academic disciplines. For example, the science of psychology in general, and Jung's insights in particular, became fertile sources of ideas on the relationship between myth and literature. Beginning in the 1930s, some literary critics turned to Jungian psychology for insights that could be used to interpret recurrent patterns, themes, and imagery in literature. The two most influential figures in this regard were the psychologist-critic Maud Bodkin and the Shakespearean scholar G. Wilson Knight. Bodkin's *Archetypal Patterns in Poetry* viewed archetypal symbols as a crucial means for the poet to achieve psychological fulfillment, a process that readers could share vicariously through their interpretation of the work.[17]

By the 1940s, Jung's advocates included some of the most prominent intellectuals in Britain, such as H.G. Wells and Herbert Read. The outbreak of the Second World War, however, understandably led to diminished interest in Jung for a time. But the end of the postwar era of austerity led to a general cultural revival in Britain, and interest in Jung seems to have revived at the same time. This postwar interest gathered momentum in the mid-1950s, as indicated by the widespread notice taken of Jung's eightieth birthday, and became a widespread phenomenon during the 1960s. Jung's roster of high-profile admirers in Britain continued to expand, with figures such as J.B. Priestley and Arnold Toynbee, among many others, acknowledging intellectual debts to the Swiss thinker.

Jung's death did little to diminish his prominence in Britain. Interest in his life and work continued apace, reinvigorated every few years by a new book, a new television program, or a new revelation by a celebrity or public figure that he or she was a fan. The most conspicuous of these instances occurred in the early 1980s, when Prince Charles revealed his interest in Jung.[18] In a review of a new book on Jung in 1990, Nicholas de Jong pointed to a "growth of interest in Jung," but it would perhaps be more accurate to say that interest in Jung never really abated.[19]

Indeed, in many ways the 1970s were a high point of Jung's popularity in Britain. It was in these years that his image as a countercultural guru was solidified.[20] Liverpool was one center of interest in Jung during these years. It even became the site of a short-lived Jung festival, which took its inspiration from Jung's famous dream of Liverpool as "the pool of life."[21] Much of the British coverage of Jung in this decade emphasized the spiritual or religious dimensions of his thought, including his ideas regarding myth. Having sketched the broad outlines of Jung's relationship with Britain, and before examining more deeply his role as a spiritual sage in the postwar period, it is necessary to clarify his understanding of myth and its spiritual dimensions. In Jung's view, those living in the modern world had a deep, though often unrecognized, need for myth as source of spiritual meaning. His pragmatic emphasis on finding meaning through myth would prove to be one of the keys to his influence in postwar Britain.

Jung and myth

One of the most assiduous, reliable, and equitable interpreters of Jung's thought in postwar Britain was the psychiatrist Anthony Storr. One of Storr's strengths was his ability to keep all aspects of Jung's work in view; he avoided reducing a complex and sometimes confusing body of doctrine to a few postulates and resisted the urge to dismiss out of hand even some of Jung's more implausible and abstruse notions. Storr recognized that Jung was motivated by both a strong scientific impulse to explain the human psyche, and a profound religious concern for the spiritual predicament of his contemporaries. Storr noted in 1962 how this latter aspect of Jung's thought had become more prominent as the years passed:

> Jung, in his later work, devoted more and more attention to what he called the process of individuation.... Individuation might be defined as the final realization of a man's uniqueness as a person. It was a search for integration and wholeness, and could therefore be compared to a religious quest for salvation, although the symbols in which the process was expressed were seldom those of an orthodox creed.[22]

As this summary suggests, in Jung's thought the quest to achieve psychological health could be treated as a matter of religious import. At the same time, religious experiences tended to be valued by Jung insofar as they promoted psychological health and wholeness. Sonu Shamdasani has observed how Jung's view of religious experiences was characterized by an underlying pragmatism:

> Ultimately, the criterion to which he appealed to validate religious experiences ... was pragmatic: "And if such experiences help to make life healthier, more beautiful, more complete and satisfactory to yourself and to those you love, you may safely say: 'This was the grace of God.'"[23]

Jung's pragmatic approach to religious questions was a consistent feature of his public pronouncements and published views on the subject, and was a salient characteristic of his postwar public persona.

This religious pragmatism was a key factor in Jung's appeal in the postwar period. Jung talked about the religious life as a quest to find meaning at a time when the phenomenon of mass society threatened the individual's ability to achieve psychological wholeness. In the last years of his life, Jung talked in increasingly personal and revealing terms about his own lifelong efforts to forge meaning for himself. His reflections on his life, his work, and the contemporary world were recorded over a period of several years by his secretary Aniela Jaffé (supplemented by sections actually written by Jung himself) and published in English in 1961 as *Memories, Dreams, Reflections*. The book sold briskly in Britain and its sales "far outstripped any other work by Jung."[24]

The reasons for the book's popularity are not difficult to comprehend. *Memories, Dreams, Reflections* offered the autobiographical reminiscences of the great sage, his spiritual and intellectual last will and testament. The book's subject matter was right for the moment, and the manner of its composition seemed to underscore its significance. It was in fact published posthumously, with an introduction by Jaffé describing the book's genesis and the urgency Jung felt to complete it before his death. But the book's popularity owes something as well to its presentation of Jung's life as a quest for psychological wholeness. And it is certainly significant, especially when considering the resonance of *Memories, Dreams, Reflections* in Britain, that Jung did not see his life quest in generic terms, but specifically as a Grail quest. Jung explained how he finally unlocked the meaning of a dream in which a knight appeared to him:

> The stories of the Grail had been of the greatest importance to me ever since I read them, at the age of fifteen, for the first time. I had an inkling that a great secret still lay hidden behind those stories. Therefore it seemed quite natural to me that the dream should conjure up the world of the Knights of the Grail and their quest—for that was, in the deepest sense, my own world.... My whole being was seeking for something still unknown which might confer meaning upon the banality of life.[25]

Years later, at another turning point in his life in the late 1930s, Jung experienced another vivid dream in which the Grail featured as the central symbol.[26] This leads him to reflect on the persistence of myths and their capacity to offer meaning despite the mass of stultifying modern scholarship that had grown up around them:

> Some ten years before, I had discovered that in many places in England the myth of the Grail was still a living thing, in spite of all the scholarship that has accumulated around this tradition.... Myths which day has forgotten continue to be told by night, and powerful figures which consciousness has reduced to banality and ridiculous triviality are recognized again by poets and prophetically revived; therefore they can also be recognized "in changed form" by the thoughtful person. The great ones of the past have not died, as we think, they have merely changed their names.[27]

Jung was also fascinated by, and sometimes identified himself with, the figure of Merlin, whom he took to be an archetype of the Wise Old Man.[28]

In addition to the leitmotif of Jung's search for meaning as a Grail quest, the book is rife with reflections on the nature and necessity of myth. Jung's understanding of myth cannot be reduced to what is found in *Memories, Dreams, and Reflections*, but since the book contains his final and most widely disseminated views on the subject, and because those views are generally representative of his thinking, they are worth considering here. Jung was comfortable thinking about myth and drawing on it to give meaning to his life. He believed, however, that most of his contemporaries had difficulty thinking with myth because "Rationalism and doctrinairism are the disease of our time; they pretend to know all the answers." An unfortunate consequence of this was that "the mythic side of man is given short shrift nowadays. He can no longer create fables."[29] Jung consistently refused to take a position on the reality of life after death, but he thought it possible that myths might offer clues about the afterlife. It was certain, however, that myths were necessary, because they could promote psychological health and because they kept alive an enchantment that counterbalanced the excessive rationalism of the modern world.[30] In the end what myth offered was meaning:

> The need for mythic statements is satisfied when we frame a view of the world which adequately explains the meaning of human existence in the cosmos, a view which springs from our psychic wholeness, from the cooperation between conscious and unconscious. Meaninglessness inhibits fullness of life and is therefore equivalent to illness. Meaning makes a great many things endurable—perhaps

everything. No science will ever replace myth, and a myth cannot be made out of any science.[31]

The cooperation between conscious and unconscious that Jung refers to here is the process of individuation. The universal themes, motifs, and character types in world mythology testified to the existence of archetypes, which had their ultimate origin in the collective unconscious. The process of individuation entailed, in part, becoming conscious of which archetypes are subconsciously at work in an individual's psyche (as evidenced, typically, by their appearance in dreams).[32] Myth, then, was something to be embraced, but for fundamentally pragmatic reasons. *Memories, Dreams, and Reflections* did not offer a comprehensive or cogent *explanation* of myth's importance, but it certainly gave the *impression* that myth was deeply important as a means of making sense of life. The autobiographical work revealed a Jung who was willing to confront religious and metaphysical questions in deeply personal ways, but without abandoning the pragmatism that had always characterized his views on such issues.

Jung's treatment of myth thus combined the pragmatic and the grandiose in a way that was deeply compelling to many in postwar Britain. As will be seen below, many of those who took inspiration from Jung noted his ability to dignify the individual's quest for meaning while at the same time treating that quest as eminently, though by no means easily, achievable. The Swiss sage seemed to many to possess an ability to hold the spiritual and the scientific in productive tension in a way that seemed to elude many British thinkers of the period.

The construction of a spiritual sage: A survey of Jung's reception in postwar Britain

Jung's work resonated in Britain because key themes and emphases in his thought meshed perfectly with concerns and tensions that defined British cultural life in the middle decades of the twentieth century. Though British commentators on Jung often contended that the overall structure and content of his thought could be confusing and even contradictory, certain key Jungian ideas found a ready audience in Britain. In particular, Jung's popularity during these years seemed to depend above all on his opposition to scientific materialism and the respectful attention he devoted to the spiritual dimension of human life. As one commentator noted: "His increasing popularity coincided with a new climate in wide areas of intellectual and public life.... In this mental and spiritual climate Jung's deep roots in myth, religion, and alchemy were widely attractive and his appeal over-ran the generation boundaries."[33]

In 1973, journalist and cultural commentator Roy Perrot concisely summarized the elements of Jung's thought that attracted attention in Britain. Reviewing a new book on Jung's thought by Storr, Perrot attempted to define "the relevance of Jung." He described Jung as "not the scientist, but the phenomenally intuitive child who made himself at home in that awesome landscape [of the unconscious], seeing there the healing power of archetypal mythology, the sources of religious feeling, and all the elements which rat-racing Western man had cast out." Perrot concluded that Jung was a "sage" whose relevance depended on his notion that the psychological growth of the ordinary person was a process with religious, mythic significance. This was a message that those preoccupied with the quotidian concerns of modern life needed, and wanted, to hear:

> Busy western man goes home to his sleeping pill and nightcap, and dreams of lost luggage and trains annoyingly missed. Jung says that, instead, there is a dream of a more moving Ulyssean kind of journey struggling to get out.[34]

Instead of being embarrassed by the religious dimension of Jung's thought, Perrot urged, it was important to acknowledge and embrace it as a salve for the modern soul.

Perrot's recognition that "busy western man" had good reasons to be attracted by Jung's thought would have pleased Jung had he still been alive. In the summer of 1960 the English journalist Gordon Young visited Jung in order to conduct an interview. Jung's eighty-fifth birthday was fast approaching and, as had been the case five years earlier, newspapers were in search of material to mark the occasion.[35] When asked how he was planning to spend his birthday, Jung replied that he intended to keep away from visitors, "Especially the highbrows. Most of them don't have the remotest idea what I am talking about." He then continued, "Do you know who reads my books? Not the academic people, oh no, they think they know everything already. It's ordinary people.... And why do they do it? Because there's a deep need for spiritual guidance—almost any sort of spiritual guidance."[36] In the last years of his life, Jung became increasingly concerned with reaching these non-specialist, ordinary readers, partly due to the flood of positive correspondence he received from viewers in England who had seen his BBC interview with journalist John Freeman.[37]

Though somewhat hyperbolic, Jung's assessment of his readership did contain a measure of truth. There had long been a significant under-current of uncertainty and suspicion in the British intelligentsia's view of Jung, a view that often contrasted sharply with the wide readership he enjoyed in Britain. Philip Toynbee captured some of the "highbrow" attitude toward Jung when he noted:

> In this country Jung has never quite achieved intellectual respectabil-ity. He has been regarded as a wayward mystagogue who traduced the rigorous and empirical doctrine of Freud in favor of a sort of occult romp through the history of the human psyche.[38]

Nevertheless, even the writers who were most critical of Jung leavened their criticism with acknowledgment of his achievements, influence, and readiness to strike out into new intellectual territory. And even though Jung often was frustrated by what he perceived as the failure of "highbrows" to take his work seriously, when the reception of his works is actually examined in detail it becomes apparent that highbrows generally viewed his thought quite sympathetically.

Setting aside devoted Jungians who saw it as their goal to dis-seminate faithfully Jung's ideas, British commentators on Jung's life and work can be divided into five categories that had differing but overlapping opinions. This taxonomy ranged from scientifically trained specialist commentators at one end of the spectrum to ordi-nary journalists at the other. Though the review pages of Britain's newspapers and journals could register reservations about particular aspects of Jung's thought, the picture that emerges is of a gener-ally positive and sympathetic reception. In the remainder of this section I intend to sketch briefly the outlines of these five cate-gories, focusing on ideal types who can be taken as representative. The amount of attention paid to Jung in the British press was certainly much greater than the necessarily limited examples that follow would indicate.

In the first category were professional psychologists or psychiatrists such as Anthony Storr and Oliver Louis Zangwill, both of whom frequently wrote on Jung for the *Times Literary Supplement*. Under-standably, such writers tended to focus on Jung's contributions to psychological science, often emphasizing how Jung's greatest contribu-tions to the field of psychiatry were those that he made early in his career, before he developed his theory of the collective unconscious. Even as these writers sought to keep their focus squarely on the scientific relevance of Jung's work, however, they often inadvertently helped to burnish his reputation as a spiritual sage.

A typical example of this tendency was Storr's 1962 review of *The Psychology of Jung* by Avis M. Dry. Dry's book was one of the first book-length assessments of Jung's thought to be published in England after his death. The review's title, "Commonsense About Jung," encapsulated Storr's opinion of the book: he saw it as a lucid, thorough, and fair-minded evaluation of Jung that was a welcome change from typical writing about a thinker who "[i]n exposition ... has been almost as ill-served by his followers as his enemies." There was a pressing need for Dry's book because "in spite of the comparative neglect of Jung by psychiatrists, and in spite of the difficulty of determining his actual meaning, the wise old man of Zurich has exerted a widespread influence." In considering Jung's legacy, Storr noted the significance of his work on word association, schizophrenia, and psychological types. Though less sanguine about the value of Jung's more spiritually inclined later work, Storr did not deny that it had explanatory value. He noted, for instance, that "Jung's interpretation of the alchemists' search for the philosopher's stone as a spiritual quest makes sense out of an activity which had previously been dismissed as meaningless."[39]

Zangwill's views on Jung often echoed Storr's: the less "scientific" Jung's writings became, the less patience Zangwill had for them. At the same time, he was unwilling to completely dismiss Jung's more philosophical work. Reviewing a new anthology of some of Jung's writings in 1954, he concluded:

> In fact, the whole thing amounts to little more than an assembly of comments on diverse human issues, some profound, some silly and nearly all dogmatic, which have about as much to do with science as ordinarily understood as have Rousseau's *Confessions*. None the less, something of Jung's remarkable quality of mind shines through these snippets, and the volume should make strong appeal to those who come to psychology in search of faith rather than unending empirical quest.[40]

The response of professional psychologists or psychiatrists to Jung in the postwar period was more nuanced than one might expect. Though such writers saw greater value in Jung's early scientific work, they did not ignore or dismiss his later work. Moreover, they tended to acknowledge that Jung offered much that might satisfy the spiritual concerns of many Britons.

In the second category we can place non-specialists who were sympathetic to the spiritual dimensions of Jung's thought, while at the same time skeptical of some of its implications. Some of the most prominent exemplars of this type were the novelist and writer Philip Toynbee, the poet-critic Kathleen Raine, and the philosopher Stuart Hampshire. Even though Jung probably had writers such as these in mind when he railed about highbrows who willfully misunderstood him, they almost certainly did more to enhance his reputation in Britain than weaken it. Though quite willing to criticize and challenge Jung, they were equally willing to acknowledge him as a profound, creative, and highly relevant thinker. Indeed, the evaluations of Jung offered by writers in this second category could sound remarkably like the opinions of specialists in the first category.

Raine was by no means hostile to the spiritual themes in Jung's work. She had a lifelong interest in spirituality, an interest that culminated in her work as a cofounder of the Temenos Academy, an organization devoted to the study of creative spirituality. Moreover, she was convinced that there was an urgent and widespread, albeit inchoate, spiritual yearning in postwar Britain. She recognized that Jung appealed powerfully to those who felt such a yearning: "Dr. Jung speaks with the authority and conviction of his professional insight into the mind of an age whose great longing is for some new heavenly marriage that shall produce a new divine child to save us from impending apocalypse."[41] At the same time, Raine identified a potentially irreconcilable tension between the scientific and the spiritual in Jung's thought:

> Jungian psychology has always had inherent in it a tendency to move away altogether from its points of attachment with mental pathology, and to become a sort of cult, comparable to initiation into the Mysteries of the classical world. Instead of patients seeking health, we have initiates seeking illumination. Whether this will prove to be the weakness or the strength of Jungianism, the future will show.[42]

Though Raine acknowledged that Jung's work answered a felt spiritual need in Britain, she stopped short of proclaiming it a panacea. Jung's thinking, in her view, had distinct shortcomings, which were evident when he turned his attention to the exegesis of particular myths. When he tried to play the role of the literary critic, he tended to evince a distinct indifference to both textual and historical particularity.[43] Raine thus complained about the same reductionism that Collingwood had noticed in the 1930s. Jung was on firmer ground, she argued, when explaining humanity's need for myth rather than analyzing particular myths. It was "the great Jungian contribution to psychology to have pointed out the reality and value of the archetypal world, as against the Freudian view that the unconscious contains nothing very good." Jung's understanding of archetypes and their power equipped him with a sensitivity to the human need for myth. He was thus able to appreciate sympathetically religious concepts that simply baffled others: "No one to whom mythological thought means anything can fail to recognize the strength of the arguments with which he defends the recent dogma of the Assumption of the Virgin."[44] For Raine, then, Jung was not inerrant, but at the same time his relevance and stature as a spiritual sage were beyond dispute.

Toynbee, who had frequent opportunity to engage with Jung's work in his position as a leading reviewer for *The Observer*, held a similar opinion. Though he certainly understood Jung's appeal and popularity, he was also a perceptive critic of the psychologist's sometimes gnomic pronouncements. Early in his career Toynbee was a passionate supporter of Jung's theories, but by the 1960s and 1970s he had become somewhat more circumspect. Though he no longer considered himself a Jungian, he was happy to admit that "something of Jung's brilliant imagination has penetrated my own," and he credited both Freud and Jung with creating "the equivalent of new and startling theologies for our time."[45] Toynbee took for granted that Jung's theories had been deeply influential and he welcomed responsible attempts to popularize for "a new and wide public many of the mysteries of symbol and archetype which had remained veiled to them before."[46] He also noted that the way Jung approached the issue of myth bore some resemblance to another pioneer in the study of that subject: "The way Jung dealt with the image- and myth-creating minds of many different races and religions was much the same as Frazer's eclectic way with world-wide religious practices and overt beliefs."[47]

In the mid-1970s, however, Toynbee began to move hesitantly toward embrace of the Christian faith, and it was during this period that he had the opportunity to review Laurens van der Post's book on Jung.[48] Whereas van der Post (and many others) saw Jung as an ally of religion, Toynbee was convinced that, "properly understood," Jung's work

amounted to a fairly formidable attack on Christianity and almost every other world religion—certainly far more formidable than Freud's comparatively naïve attempt to explain away religious beliefs in terms of his own mythology of the mind. For what Jung was trying to show was that all religious belief about a transcendent reality can be reduced to certain myths and images which developed inside the mind, without any necessary stimulus from outside it.[49]

In the end, Toynbee attributed Jung's remarkable influence to the fact that he was neither scientist, nor religious prophet, nor charlatan, but rather "a philosopher, in the traditional...sense of the word, and that he was a man of genuine poetical imagination."[50]

In short, these writers applauded Jung for asking the right questions and investigating the right issues even though they did not always concur with his findings. Their assessments of Jung, though sometimes critical, therefore reinforced a perception of Jung as a spiritually oriented thinker.

This perception was also reinforced by the third category of writers on Jung, which comprised theologians and religious thinkers. Storr noted how members of this group seemed "uncertain whether they are dealing with a defender of the faith or with a particularly dangerous form of heretic."[51] The attempt to answer this question occasioned a steady stream of books from theologians during the 1950s and 1960s. Perhaps the most able and perceptive of such writers was the Dominican priest Father Victor White, who hoped to find a way to reconcile analytical psychology with Christian theology and established a friendship with Jung to that end.[52] But White was only the most significant example of a common type. Other theological interlocutors in Britain were H.L. Philp, who both corresponded and collaborated with Jung, and David Cox.[53] The fact that professional specialists in matters spiritual saw Jung as a figure to be reckoned with did much to create and reinforce his image as a spiritual sage.

The fourth category was occupied by the enthusiastic Jung boosters who saw him as *the* great modern thinker, not least for his insights regarding religion. This group included the writers Priestley and van der Post. Both of these men established friendships with Jung and expressed frustration with theologians for failing to appreciate the revolutionary fact that Jung's religious insights were grounded in objective, empirical scientific research.[54] According to van der Post, this failure was "[t]he great theological scandal of our time."[55] Writing in the *Times Literary Supplement* in 1954 Priestley contended that Jung, through his explorations of the psyche, "has arrived at religious experience as the fundamental experience, at the final mystery of the numinous, by way of his own therapeutic practice, by way of science. He has in fact come closer to bridging the great gap of our time than any other thinker."[56]

If anything, van der Post was more fulsome in his praise, citing Jung as "a man who is a turning point in the history of the world," and "the greatest anti-establishment figure the world has seen since the renaissance."[57] Van der Post enjoyed a long friendship with Jung and was a key figure in sustaining his reputation in Britain. He wrote and presented a three-part BBC television series on Jung in 1971 and a few years later published the popular *Jung and the Story of Our Time*, which emphasized the spiritual dimension of Jung's thought. He agreed with Priestley that Jung's greatest contribution was to place religious belief on an empirical foundation. In van der Post's view, Jung's greatest contribution to twentieth-century thought was to achieve a breakthrough in how to conceptualize God:

> And Jung's contribution is simply this; he established, scientifically, that God is no longer a wishful, remote super-reality somewhere out in the blue of the universe, and His great intermediary, the Son of Man, was not just a single, never to be repeated historical event. On the contrary both are immense, recurrent and daily transforming activities in the soul of each one of us.[58]

Thinkers in this fourth category thus accepted Jung's repeated insistence that he was not a speculative thinker, but rather an empirically rigorous scientist. The great genius of Jung, in their view, was his ability to bridge seamlessly the worlds of science and religion in way that made religious belief a possibility for modern people.

The fifth group of commentators on Jung was composed of all those whose contributions were more anonymous or ephemeral. This included the anonymous writers of editorials and profiles, as well as anonymous or little-known interviewers of Jung. The material produced by such writers, such as the birthday notices and obituaries cited at the beginning of this chapter, tended to reflect the key themes highlighted by writers in the other four categories.

Jung thus drew the interest of a wide variety of commentators, yet the degree to which the opinions of these disparate commentators converged is remarkable. When the output of these five categories is considered as a whole, what is striking is the overwhelmingly positive view of Jung that emerges along with a consistent portrayal of him as a pioneer in the examination of religious experience and the spiritual dimension of life. Even the professional psychologists and more critical reviewers leavened their criticisms with a significant measure of praise and acknowledged Jung's contributions to understanding the spiritual dimensions of the psyche. Robert Ellwood has pointed to the period from the 1950s through the 1970s as a time marked by a "general tendency to adulate Jung as one of the world's wise men."[59] In light of the views of Jung considered above, it becomes evident how such a persona was constructed, reinforced, and disseminated in Britain.

Conspicuously absent from discussion and even criticism of Jung in Britain was any sustained consideration of his supposed anti-Semitism. This topic had been debated on the Continent since at least the late 1930s, but it was not a significant factor in Jung's reception in Britain. On the contrary, Jung was consistently portrayed as a prophetic critic of the Nazi regime, rather than as someone who may have been complicit in Nazi persecution of Jews.[60] When "controversial" aspects of his life and thought were mentioned, this usually meant his falling out with Freud, his relationships with women (including his unfaithfulness to his wife), and his unorthodox interpretations of Christian theology.[61] His break with Freud, however, was seen as understandable and even justified, his marital failings were seen as a private matter, and his religious opinions, however provocative, were in the end those of a layperson. Lacking any serious moral or political blemishes, then, Jung's image as a sage could be burnished to a high sheen.

The emphasis on the spiritual relevance of Jung's thought was not limited to print media, but was also a prominent feature of how Jung was presented on radio and television. These forms of media allowed him to reach a broader audience of ordinary people—the very people that he claimed understood him best and gave him a fair hearing. In 1965 *The Observer* asked its readers to nominate the most memorable television programs they had seen. The paper received a deluge of replies, but a handful of programs clearly emerged at the front of the pack as most memorable. One of those was a televised interview with Jung conducted by Freeman for the BBC program *Face to Face* in 1959.[62] This wide-ranging interview generated a tremendous response and is still viewed today, having been given new life on the internet.

The interview with Freeman was Jung's last television appearance in Britain during his lifetime, but programs about him remained common on television and radio throughout the 1970s. The most significant of these was undoubtedly van der Post's three-part program on Jung's life and work, which aired on the BBC in 1971 and was frequently rerun afterwards. Van der Post's program marked the beginning of a golden decade for Jung on radio and television, when programs about him were common. These ranged from "The Healing Nightmare," a radio drama about Jung's personal psychological crisis that aired in 1977, to more straightforward profiles of the man and his thought. Not only did these programs sustain interest in Jung and introduce many to his thought, they also reinforced his image as a sage and prophet. Articles about Jung often noted his sage-like appearance and manner, and when he began to appear on television, viewers could see that this was indeed the case.[63] Simply put, Jung looked and even acted the part, making it much easier for viewers to regard his pronouncements as deliverances of wisdom from a modern prophet.

Putting Jung's appeal in context: Three cultural controversies

In order to more clearly illustrate Jung's prominence in postwar British culture, this section considers his thought in relation to three key intellectual and cultural controversies of the postwar period. These controversies revealed key fault lines within British culture, brought to the surface elements of public concern that had been little noticed, crystallized bodies of opinion that hitherto had been ill-defined, and testified to the depth of the "modern problem" identified by Auden. These controversies were the reaction to the rise of analytic philosophy, the two cultures controversy, and the storm surrounding the publication of the book *Honest to God* by Church of England bishop John Robinson.

Each of these controversies gives insight into how Jung's thought was able to gain purchase in Britain, for each illustrates expectations and desires in the British public that Jung's thought at least partially satisfied. The controversy over philosophy revealed an expectation that philosophers should provide metaphysical and moral guidance. The two cultures controversy revealed a yearning for cultural unity and an integration of scientific and non-scientific knowledge. And the *Honest to God* controversy revealed a desire to maintain some kind of pseudo-Christian religious belief in the modern world.

In the first half of the twentieth century, professional philosophy in Britain underwent a profound transformation that has come to be known as the "analytic revolution." The result of this shift was that a new style of philosophy, called analytic philosophy, superseded and marginalized the neo-Hegelian idealist philosophy that had dominated the late Victorian and Edwardian eras. Taking science as their model, analytic philosophers rejected the philosophical system building and metaphysical speculation that they believed characterized idealist philosophy. Instead, they contended that philosophy's proper subject matter was actually very circumscribed. According to analytic philosophers, philosophy was concerned only with examining the meaning of propositions by means of a rigorous method known as the analytic method—hence the name "analytic philosophy."

When, in the mid- to late 1950s, the British public became aware of what had happened in the philosophical profession, they were not happy about it. During the Victorian era and the early decades of the twentieth century, the British public had become accustomed to philosophers offering moral counsel and guidance about "big questions." But these were precisely the kind of questions that the analytic philosophers had abandoned.

The reaction to the rise of analytic philosophy revealed significant public discontent with this shift, to the point that the new breed of philosophers were even accused of corrupting university students with an amoral brand of philosophy.[64] Analytic philosophers were very aware of the negative reaction to their work and they worried about it. Speaking on the BBC Third Programme in 1961, Cambridge philosopher Renford Bambrough noted the educated public's low opinion of analytic philosophy and its practitioners: "The philosophers of today...are accused both of wasting time on trivial word games and of undermining moral standards.... Philosophy is said to be isolated and specialized, out of touch with the general educated public and with specialists in other fields."[65] In the 1950s and 1960s analytic philosophers spent a considerable portion of their time worrying about how to improve their public image while remaining true to the dictates of their strict analytic method.

The reaction of the British public to the rise of analytic philosophy provides a valuable context that can help us understand why Jung enjoyed such prominence in Britain. Britons who were disappointed that philosophers no longer provided the kind of guidance they once had could find just that sort of guidance offered by Jung. Here was a thinker who was unafraid to offer bold metaphysical claims, who was eager to make spiritual pronouncements, and who entirely disregarded the boundaries between fields of knowledge in his search for material to support his theories. Whereas professional philosophers in Britain had abandoned metaphysical system building in favor of atomizing analysis, Jung appeared to be a grand unifier of knowledge who was able to survey disparate data from psychology, history, mythology, and comparative religion and weave it into a coherent—or at least compelling—whole.[66] This indicates the significance of Toynbee's assessment, cited above, that Jung was in the end "a philosopher in the traditional sense of the word." Jung was a philosopher of a type that had become all but extinct, but his approach to philosophy was one that many ordinary people appreciated and wanted to survive.

During the postwar period universities increasingly became the centers of intellectual life in Britain, and this process went hand in hand with increasing academic specialization—as the controversy over analytic philosophy showed. Anxieties surrounding this increasing specialization were also revealed in another controversy of the late 1950s and 1960s, the so-called two cultures controversy. Understanding the key issues in this controversy can help us understand why the holistic view of life offered by Jung held considerable appeal for many in postwar Britain.

The two cultures controversy began when in 1959 the physicist and novelist C.P. Snow delivered a Rede Lecture called *The two cultures and the Scientific Revolution*, which was subsequently published in the journal *Encounter* and in book form. In the lecture Snow diagnosed and lamented what he saw as a growing divide and "a gulf of mutual incomprehension" between the two cultures of the sciences and humanities.[67] Snow's lecture was an immediate sensation and it generated intense discussion and debate. This debate was given added impetus in 1962 when the literary critic F.R. Leavis delivered his own lecture excoriating Snow in a manner unheard of in British intellectual life. Leavis's lecture was subsequently published in *The Spectator*, occasioning a flood of correspondence to the journal and prolonging the debate over Snow's thesis.[68]

One of the key themes to emerge in the two cultures controversy was a widespread sense of regret for lost cultural unity. In fact, even though Snow and Leavis were completely at odds with each other on the key issues in the controversy, they both lamented a bygone era of cultural unity, though they disagreed about how and why this unity had been shattered. Snow argued that the English educational system in effect institutionalized the two cultures divide by marginalizing the sciences while unfairly privileging the humanities and classics. As a result, Britain's leaders were denied the balanced preparation and breadth of perspective needed to survive in a modern scientific world that, Snow firmly believed, was morally superior to the preindustrial world it had replaced. Leavis, on the other hand, looked back longingly to a preindustrial era when cultural unity had prevailed and when materialism had not yet eradicated other moral values.[69]

However, Jung's work and public persona in Britain exemplified how the gap between the two cultures could be bridged. Jung, in short, personified the integration of the sciences and the humanities. Though Jung was widely perceived as a spiritual sage in postwar Britain, he was also perceived as a sage with considerable scientific credentials.

This fact was often emphasized in descriptions of Jung by writers and media members. Van der Post and Raine have already been quoted to this effect above, but even an unapologetic denizen of the scientific culture like Storr could note that part of Jung's significance was his capacity to reconcile the two cultures by forging links between psychology and religion:

> Jung demonstrated, both in his life and in his writing, that some kind of reconciliation between...opposites is possible, even if it requires an esoteric religion to achieve this. The psychology of religion is still unfashionable; but it is obvious that some persons who are deeply disturbed in mind become less so if they succeed in attaining a unifying point of view; and there are many who might spend their lives in mental hospitals were it not that in theosophy, spiritualism or some other esoteric belief they have found a system which...seems to make sense out of life. The healing power of such beliefs is a subject scarcely investigated by psychologists.[70]

In short, Jung seemed to posses the ability to translate scientific findings into spiritual insights that were highly relevant to life in the modern world.

In a front-page article in *The Observer* on March 17, 1963, John Robinson, Bishop of Woolwich, informed his readers that "Our Image of God Must Go." The article was followed two days later by his book *Honest to God*, which rapidly sparked a public controversy.[71] Robinson's book gave the impression that a bishop in the Church of England was very publicly denying the traditional Christian doctrine of God, perhaps to the point of atheism. *Honest to God* generated a heated debate that played out in theological journals, letters and columns in the daily newspapers, hastily written pamphlets, book-length rebuttals, and discussions on both radio and television.

Robinson's book encapsulated a dilemma felt by many twentieth-century Britons, the horns of which were a de facto acceptance of a scientific, modern worldview and a yearning for some metaphysical meaning beyond the truths offered by science. Robinson was attempting to reconcile these conflicting motivations—by way of engaging with the thought of Rudolf Bultmann, Paul Tillich and Dietrich Bonhoeffer. A key theme of the book was the need to worry less about adherence to "traditional orthodox supernaturalism" and to focus instead on refashioning Christianity so that it worked for ordinary modern people. Robinson emphasized "meaningfulness" (i.e., reframing Christianity in a way that made it meaningful and helpful for modern people) at the expense of "truth" (i.e., defining and defending a body of dogma).

The controversy surrounding *Honest to God* points to the complex nature of religious belief in postwar Britain. The sociologist of religion Grace Davie has described the religious condition of postwar Britain as an era of "believing without belonging." It is an apt phrase to characterize a society marked by "the persistence of the sacred . . . despite the undeniable decline in churchgoing."[72] Many people in postwar Britain continued to believe in some components of traditional Christianity even as they increasingly eschewed involvement with religious institutions. Davie has subsequently described a shift in the tone of northern European religion from an "ethic of obligation" to an "ethic of consumption."[73] Under an ethic of obligation, according to Davie, modes of life are primarily imposed or inherited, whereas under an ethic of consumption, modes of life are primarily a matter of personal choice.

Jung's views on religion echo themes present in *Honest to God* and reflect trends identified by Davie. At roughly the same time that Robinson was de-emphasizing the category of truth in favor of meaningfulness and helpfulness, Jung was telling an interviewer from England:

> One should not be deterred by the rather silly objection that nobody knows whether these old universal ideas—God immortality, freedom of the will, and so on—are "true" or not. Truth is the wrong criterion here. One can only ask whether they are helpful or not, whether man is better off and feels his life more complete, more meaningful and more satisfactory with or without them.[74]

These words again illustrate the pragmatism that characterized Jung's approach to religious questions, but they also indicate a tension in his thought. He could be an insightful commentator on modernity and a trenchant critic of the materialism and consumerism that were such significant aspects of modern life. Yet it is hard to avoid the conclusion that his views on religion meshed seamlessly with consumerist attitudes, perhaps contributing (along with contemporaries like Robinson) to the shift toward the ethic of consumption identified by Davie.

Conclusion

A few months after Jung's death, Storr offered a prediction: "His influence on man's conception of his own nature has been extensive, and will probably increase as his ideas become more generally understood."[75]

At least with regard to the professional study of psychology, this must be judged a failed prediction. In 2001 the British Psychological Society produced a hefty tome entitled *Psychology in Britain: Historical Essays and Personal Reflections.*[76] The book, which runs to more than 400 pages, comprises 26 essays, by historians and practitioners, on psychology in Britain since the late nineteenth century. The personal reflections by practitioners in the volume focus on precisely the period examined in this chapter. It is telling, therefore, that Jung merits but three brief mentions; his appeal was much greater with the general public, it would seem, than with his professional peers.

The primary reason for this appeal was Jung's ability to confront "the modern problem" and offer answers that many found compelling. Significantly, his answers acknowledged the importance of myth and offered an explanation of its persistence, prevalence, and power. In a culture shaped by an increasingly individualistic approach to religion, no longer offered metaphysical guidance by its philosophers, and faced with a seeming divorce between the humanities and the sciences, Jung's thought, with its pragmatic treatment of religious questions and willingness to hold the spiritual and the scientific in tension, seemed indeed to supply resources for making meaning in modernity.

It is generally known that Jung became something of a countercultural icon in the second half of the twentieth century and was seen by many as a spiritual guru. Indeed, the caricature of Jung as a fuzzy-minded modern mystic—or "wayward mystagogue" to use Philip Toynbee's phrase again—was at least partially established prior to his death. This caricature, however, has certainly inhibited a proper appreciation of Jung's role as a spiritual sage in postwar Britain. Perceptions of Jung as a spiritual sage for modern times were not confined to the countercultural fringes, but were instead fairly widespread and mainstream. In his landmark study *The Modern Construction of Myth*, Andrew Von Hendy points to the middle decades of the twentieth century as a key moment in the popularization of mythic thinking. It was during this period that that talented popularizers proliferated, writers "who disseminate to large middle-class audiences versions [of myth] that promise what amounts to gnostic enlightenment. For the first time myth becomes the conceptual property of millions of people searching for spiritual guidance."[77] Jung's prominence in postwar Britain can be seen as one manifestation of this trend.

7
Minding the Myth-Kitty: Myth, Cultural Authority, and the Evolution of English Studies

Introduction

In 1975, the literary critic William Righter surveyed the British literary scene with a view to explaining the prevalence of myth talk in literary discourse. Righter averred that myth's appeal to literary intellectuals was powerful and complex: "'[M]yth' has become a kind of intellectual shorthand which has gained acceptance as standing for an elusive, almost unanalysable amalgam of beliefs, attitudes and feelings. The very unapproachability of the content of myth has created the utility of the term and guaranteed its widespread usefulness."[1] This assessment of the myth question as "almost unanalysable" serves as a daunting, though apposite, introduction to the complexity of the issue. And though Righter was certainly correct that "the unapproachability of the content of myth" had much to do with the term's appeal, it is now apparent that "unapproachability" was not the only factor that assured the prevalence of mythic thinking among literary critics in postwar Britain.

To fully explain the prevalence of mythic thinking in critical discourse, we must examine how professional literary critics sought to justify their discipline in an era characterized by the increasing hegemony of science and scientific discourse. The explanation for critical interest in myth can be found in the struggles between academic disciplines that characterized the 1960s. Literary critics' ambivalence and defensiveness toward science gave impetus to the attempt by the nascent field of English studies to find a discourse of its own that was authoritative without being scientific. Their response to the intellectual hegemony of science took various forms, including a growing interest in new hermeneutic theories of interpretation and language. Christopher Norris has noted that "the chief result [of the 1960s hermeneutical turn in literary criticism] was to encourage a less defensive, indeed a more self-assertive attitude which rejected any notion of physical science as a paradigm or method or a privileged truth-telling discourse."[2] This justification of critical discourse as a valid disciplinary method was combined with an effort to defend the discipline's subject matter itself. Many critics contended that literature had unique epistemic value as a way of knowing that gave access to deeper truths than science. This effort to justify the critical study of literature had been underway at least since I.A. Richards's *Science and Poetry* appeared in 1926, but it was given new urgency during the university expansion of the 1960s when disciplines struggled to claim places in the new educational institutions that were being formed. In such a context the argument that myth—a concept rich with connotations of transcendence, significance, profound truth, and timeless relevance—was somehow a crucial element of literature was a rhetorical weapon too appealing to ignore. By positioning themselves as the interpreters of the mythic significance of literature, British literary critics could claim access to truths that were somehow more real, and even more relevant, than the deliverances of science.

These factors combined to produce a surge of interest in mythic thinking among British critics, beginning in the 1950s, peaking in the 1960s and continuing into the 1970s. Looking back on this period of criticism, the novelist and critic A.S. Byatt took for granted the fact that anyone who studied literature then would have been immersed in discussions of how myth offered resources for coping with modern life.[3] The British literary figures who were at the forefront of theorizing about the relationship between literature and myth included some of the most significant critics of the post-Second World War period, such as Byatt herself, Paul West, John Holloway, David Daiches, Graham Hough, Frank Kermode, and Raymond Williams.

In addition to the effort to define a non-scientific critical discourse, two other related concerns were central to postwar myth-oriented criticism: a wish to delineate the relationship between myth and literature generally and the connections between myth and narrative specifically; and an aspiration to use the concept of myth in a measured, culturally relevant way that would avoid being dismissed as mere willful irrationalism or reactionary antimodernity. Thus, myth-oriented criticism was related both to criticism's increasing focus on the nature and function of narrative and to its attempts to justify itself as a discipline that, because it was uniquely equipped to respond to modernity, had cultural relevance beyond academia.

Critical interest in myth, which had emerged alongside the first stirrings of theoretical interest among literary critics, began to recede in the 1970s as French theory in particular became more established in Britain. The growth of theory was one of the main causes for the ebb of myth-oriented criticism, for it held out much greater promise as an analytic method that could serve the institutional and cultural needs of literary critics. Critical interest in myth was thus a halfway house on the road to a broader embrace of theory.

This chapter, then, approaches mythic thinking by British literary critics as an important episode in the evolution of English studies and literary criticism. It does so by examining a group of British literary critics who were loosely linked by their belief that critics should abandon the rarefied agenda of modernist criticism in favor of a socially relevant criticism that helped to foster connections between author and reader. This led them to myth. I refer to these as "myth-minded" or "myth-oriented" critics in order to distinguish them from the North American myth critics. I argue that the rise of myth-oriented criticism can be understood as a transitional phase in the evolution of English studies from a discipline that conceived of itself as the transmitter of essential values and cultural heritage to one who purpose was the production of knowledge by means of critical progress and innovation.[4] The work of the myth-oriented critics reflected this shift toward a discipline whose goal was no longer to preserve the cultural heritage, but rather to foster dissent and effect social change. In their case dissent took the form of resisting science's claims to be the sole source of valid knowledge, and their program for social change took the form of mitigating what they saw as modernity's dehumanizing tendencies.

The rise of American myth criticism

In seeking to develop a socially relevant criticism, British myth-oriented critics were consciously setting themselves apart from certain North American critics who had developed a sub-genre of literary study known as myth criticism. This type of criticism enjoyed tremendous popularity in North America during the 1950s and 1960s, but most British critics viewed it with misgiving. In their desire to achieve some form of "transcendence" American critics were simply too willing to see myth everywhere in literature, or so many British critics believed. The result was a criticism that had lost touch with real concerns. Because British myth-oriented criticism was in part formed in reaction to North American myth criticism, it is necessary here to survey that movement.

Numerous commentators on the history of literary criticism have noted that the interpretation of literature in terms of recurring archetypes and perennial themes became increasingly popular following the Second World War.[5] What had been largely the preserve of psycho-analysts and anthropologists before the war was in the postwar years brought "to the centre of intellectual discussion" by literary critics.[6] In the 1940s various North American critics began to interpret literary works in terms of the primeval myths and archetypal patterns they believed were present in all literature. This method came to be known as "myth criticism" or the "myth-and-symbol movement." One of the early and most prominent advocates of this so-called "myth criticism" was Richard Chase, whose 1949 *Quest for Myth* in many ways inaugurated the movement. The 1940s saw a proliferation of this genre of criticism with special issues of journals devoted to the subject and young critics on the make like Chase, Leslie Fiedler, and Francis Fergusson throwing their weight behind the movement.[7] By the end of the decade a backlash could be detected, with respected critics like Stanley Edgar Hyman and Philip Rahv expressing dissenting opinions.[8] However, myth criticism was reinvigorated and transformed in the 1950s through the influence of the Canadian critic Northrop Frye, whose *Anatomy of Criticism* (1957) seemed to many of his peers to raise the genre to new heights.[9]

Frye's bold intention was to provide a taxonomy for the classification of all types of literature and criticism. To this end, he created a scheme for classifying literature according to such factors as mode, theme, type of symbolism, narrative structure and so forth. Myth occupied a central place in this scheme. Following Aristotle, Frye suggested that of the five modes of western fiction the highest was the mythic mode. In his analysis of literary symbolism he argued that the highest kind of meaning is that found in holy scriptures and mythopoeic works. Of the four basic narrative patterns—comedy, romance, tragedy, and irony/satire— all were at bottom reflections of a larger "quest-myth." The ultimate goal of the critic, then, was to reveal the archetypal form that all literary works imitated. Thus, the overwhelming significance of myth is an inescapable aspect of Frye's system. Frye, in Chris Baldick's assessment, "subordinated all other critical approaches to the master code of myth criticism."[10] His work showed British critics that myth criticism could be taken seriously, indeed that it had to be taken seriously.

Nevertheless, Frye's influence, as well as the influence of myth criticism more broadly, was much stronger in the United States than in Britain, partly because of the differing literary traditions of the two countries. Righter noted that the overtly symbolical or allegorical mode of nineteenth-century American literature virtually invited myth criticism.[11] David Daiches observed that American novelists structured their works by creating "symbolic landscapes" whereas English novelists worked against the backdrop of "a fully differentiated class-patterned social scene."[12] The British novelist-critic Paul West suggested that the prevalence of myth criticism in America was attributable to the nation's unique social and historical circumstances, but he did not dismiss the movement as merely an American quirk. Rather, he argued that American myth criticism's palpable yearning for values like "consolation" and "transcendence" exemplified a typical reaction by intellectuals to modernity. "What the Myth critics appear to seek," observed West, "is a kind of philosopher's stone which turns all conflict into golden myth."[13]

The British background

It was some of these same concerns about modernity that motivated British critics to take an active interest in myth. Reflecting on recent critical trends in the early 1970s, David Daiches observed: "Interest in myth has gone further in America than it has in England, but the interest has become fairly widespread even on this side of the Atlantic."[14] In Britain, however, thinking about the relation of myth and literature had shaped Frazer's *Golden Bough* and the work of the Cambridge Ritualists.[15] Some Ritualist assumptions were readily transferrable to the study of literature, such as the notion that myth offered more comprehensive access to reality than did modern knowledge. One observer noted the appeal of the notion

> that the literature of Western civilization can be understood and evaluated by establishing its connection with, or similarity to, the religious rituals of an assumed world-wide primitive society and primitive mind, the last being an important idea, since it is assumed that the primitive or unspecialized mind has a greater contact with, a more complete view of, total reality than the modern mind.[16]

Of course, the modernists had reinforced and further disseminated such ideas with their interest in mythic structures.

Inspired in large part by Frazer, the poet Robert Graves made his own erudite but idiosyncratic forays into myth and ritual criticism with such works as *The White Goddess* (1947), his own Penguin collection of

The Greek Myths (1955), and even popular novels like *The Golden Fleece* (1944). But it was not just the authority of figures like Eliot and Graves that established the prevalence of myth and ritual criticism: the authority of science helped establish the approach as well. As Brian Coates observes, "The quasi-scientific dictates of the Cambridge Ritualists gave their work an appealing appearance of system, then badly needed by the new English Tripos; this is how 'myth' became an accepted element in the new literary schematic."[17] Thus, in addition to North American myth criticism, British critics by the 1950s had a wealth of scholarship on myth from various fields at their disposal. This was not always seen as beneficial: Frank Kermode, one of the leading myth-minded critics of the 1960s, saw this body of theory as so vast and disparate as to be "unmanageable."[18] Nevertheless, critics could not help but draw on it, and Kermode, as we will see, was no exception.

Thus, critical interest in myth did not remain confined to American critics; by the end of the 1950s British critics seemed increasingly interested as well. In the view of Cambridge's M.J.C. Hodgart, this was not a development to be welcomed. Hodgart wrote several articles tracking the development of mythic thought for journals like *The Twentieth Century*, the *New Statesman*, and the *Spectator* in the 1950s and 1960s. His views are worth examining briefly not only because they provide a window into the rise of myth criticism, but also because he offered a detailed historical explanation of why mythic thinking had gained such purchase in literary circles.

In a 1955 piece in *The Twentieth Century*, Hodgart attributed the rise of literary interest in myth to multiple factors. It resulted from causes both ancient and recent, both cultural and intellectual; it revealed interests both perennial and merely fashionable. It was clear to Hodgart that the emerging interest in myth combined ideas from various fields of inquiry. But the way in which the ideas were combined troubled him: he lamented the tendency of literary intellectuals to borrow ideas about myth cavalierly from other disciplines, in ways that seemed self-serving and shallow. In the proliferation of literary talk about myth he detected a desire to fabricate a consoling but undemanding religion:

> Its main features are familiar enough: there is an inclination to take myth seriously as embodying intuitions of truths about the human situation and not merely as entertaining fictions; there is general interest in certain kinds of anthropology and psychology (Jung is now more the vogue than the materialist Freud), and the terms 'archetype', 'ritual', 'fertility rite', and 'poetic myth' have wide

currency in the literary weeklies, implying a certain modish hostility to philosophical materialism and rationalism.[19]

Hodgart interpreted the emerging interest in myth as but the latest reemergence of the occultism that "is a permanent minority strand in Western culture."[20] This strand tended to reappear whenever the authority of the church declined, the difference with the current situation being that it was "the church of science" that had lost adherents. Yet in Hodgart's view there was something distinctive about the new occultism in that it was characterized by "less talk about magic and more about myth. The reason for this lies partly in the immense prestige enjoyed by a group of Cambridge dons between forty and fifty years ago, the greatest of whom was Sir James Frazer." But Frazer's influence was curious because "Frazer was a classic Victorian rationalist and it is ironical that his work should have had so fertilizing an effect on contemporary trends of irrational thinking."[21] In the end, Hodgart's main worry was that mythic thinking would encourage either a widespread antimodern irrationalism or an empty, pseudo-religious escapism. In his opinion, the vast body of myth was there for writers to reshape for their own "purely literary" purposes, not to be reshaped into a fabricated belief system.[22] Hodgart's views amounted to a narrative of the emergence of myth criticism that British myth-minded critics would rely on throughout the 1960s and into the 1970s.

A new kind of criticism

Hodgart was a frequent contributor to *Essays in Criticism*, a journal launched in 1951 that quickly came to occupy a prominent place among British critical journals. Chris Baldick has identified the early 1950s as a turning point in British criticism, because it was then that a group of British critics began to react against the dominance of the New Critics and the *Scrutiny* school of criticism. Some of these critics coalesced around *Essays in Criticism*, started by Oxford's F.W. Bateson. It was from this loose group that several of the young myth-minded critics would emerge in the late 1950s and 1960s.

In an early editorial manifesto of 1953, "The Function of Criticism at the Present time," Bateson outlined the journal's mission. Its very title, like the title of the manifesto itself, were clues: both were borrowed from the work of Matthew Arnold. Bateson's aim was to reinvigorate an Arnoldian style of criticism updated for modern purposes—that is, a criticism that combined textual scholarship and concern with social relevance, that sought to connect the literary world with the social world, and that balanced concern for both "literary meaning in the ordinary sense and the social context in which meaning alone acquires value."[23] What was so evidently needed, in Bateson's view, was "a balance ... of literary and sociological criticism, in which one mode may serve as the complement and the corrective of the other."[24] Twelve years later Bateson could claim that "The Arnoldian ideal of scholarship and criticism ... is still the star to which *Essays in Criticism's* waggon is hitched."[25] This general desire for a professional, socially relevant criticism was shared by the myth-minded critics examined below, most of whom contributed to *Essays in Criticism* during their careers.

The work of these myth-minded critics must also be understood in the context of broader changes that were taking place within the discipline in the 1960s and 1970s. Most studies of literary criticism in twentieth-century Britain agree that at some point in the 1960s the field began to be transformed by that collection of critical techniques that have come to be known as "theory." Chris Baldick dates its arrival to 1968 and notes that it was not a harmonious movement, but rather "was a variegated cargo of literary and linguistic theories of continental European origin."[26] Chronologies of theory's emergence vary, with some scholars locating its advent in the late 1960s and others the early 1970s. Raman Selden identifies "the period between the mid-1960s and the present day as the age of theory,"[27] while Christopher Norris notes "a growing awareness among Anglophone critics" of hermeneutic theory "from the early 1960s on."[28] Frank Kermode remembered "the late 1960s and early 1970s" as the period which saw the advent of "the new approaches to literary theory that a quarter century later have so altered every aspect of the subject," and elsewhere recalled ruefully how his 1967 *The Sense of an Ending* looked in light of the appearance of structuralism: "I remember feeling rather dismally that quite a lot of work had gone into a book which became antediluvian almost on publication."[29]

Perhaps the conflicting chronologies of theory's rise in Britain can best be reconciled by conceding that there was a growing awareness of Continental theory throughout the1960s, but that the "age of theory" did not dawn until the end of the decade. Until that point criticism was characterized by theoretical ventures and experimentation that revealed an increasing interest in the workings of narrative. It was in the 1960s that critics began to ask how narrative thought was different than, for example, scientific thought. In fact, Kermode defined the critical enterprise itself in essentially narrative terms: the modern critic's task was "making sense of the ways we make sense of the world."[30] The move to explicate the workings of narrative necessitated an explanation of myth as one particularly significant type or element of narrative. This increasing interest in narrative theory was one way that critics sought to justify their discipline. Science was one way of making sense of the world, but narrative was another, and literary critics increasingly claimed that they were uniquely qualified to explain how narrative worked.

Thus, the idea that narrative forms were uniquely valuable ways of making sense of life came to be a central critical concern, and literary interest in myth during the 1960s and into the 1970s was in part a function of this shift. This myth-narrative connection was perhaps expressed most concisely by Paul West. Criticizing the French "anti-novelists" for their failure to offer any interpretation of the inchoate flux of experience he contended that "interpretation is really the effect of myth. Myth is the universal pattern that confers meaning on all kinds of experiences."[31] Thus, the reason why anti-novels failed as fiction was their lack of a mythological element to give form and meaning to experience. West's assumption that at the heart of fiction was a dialectic between the mythic and the mimetic, between myth and the realistic representation of experience, was shared, to varying degrees, by all the myth-minded critics examined here. Their attempts to explain the nature of this dialectic led them to explain as well why myth remained for the common reader a powerful means of finding meaning in modernity.

Compared to American myth criticism, British attempts to theorize the relationship between myth and literature were more cautious, more circumspect, more concerned with showing how mythic literature was socially relevant rather than with making sweeping defenses of the possibilities of transcendence offered by myth. David Daiches was among the British critics most interested in investigating the relationship between myth and literature, but he felt that American inquiries in this area were prone to go too far. American myth criticism, he noted, "has produced much that is illuminating, much that is provocative, and a fair amount that is wholly absurd."[32] West had a similar view of American myth criticism's shortcomings. West's main criticism of the American myth critics was that their search for myth could "only too easily end up in a grandiose cerebrality" and "sheer escapism."[33] Their explanation of how myth reconciled and transcended conflicts within works of literature was never translated into explanations of how it could help individuals reconcile and transcend the conflicts they encountered in their lives. The myth critics sought to reveal in literature a common myth "that enables us to live intelligently in the presence of a suggested pattern. Such a pattern we can invoke in trouble, and use to develop a sense of belonging and identity."[34] In the end, West concluded, "Myth criticism... offers an external pattern, but authenticates without reference to society."[35] It was just this sort of escapism and disconnection from actual social concerns that the British critics sought to avoid in their theorizing about myth. For them the relationship between myth, literature and society was a problem to be solved. They accepted that literature was somehow grounded in myth; this seemed to them undeniable. Their aim, then, was to describe the nature of literature's relationship to myth and explain why this was significant for the average reader.

The British myth-minded critics also felt it necessary to distance themselves from the modernists. Because they were seeking a critical idiom more attuned to the needs of the common reader, the myth-minded critics dissented from the entire modernist revolution in literature. They argued that the modernist abandonment of ordinary discourse had effectively severed literature from the average reader.[36] More specifically, they viewed modernist strictures about a "mythical method" as too grandiose, too constraining, and too evidently constructed to serve the modernist critical agenda. Finally, modernists like W.B. Yeats, D.H. Lawrence, and Eliot came under suspicion for having made the error of believing too deeply in their own self-created myths.

Even though literary critics of the 1960s and 1970s were reluctant to grant myth the level of importance that earlier, modernist-influenced writers and critics had, they nevertheless continued to suggest that myth was a literary form of special significance. Though the myth-minded critics were uncomfortable with the use of myth as a blunt rhetorical weapon against science and modernity, they continued to grant myth a special status in their increasingly sophisticated critical approaches. Compared with much earlier British myth criticism or with North American myth criticism, their concept of myth was more cautious and attenuated. They sought to explain myth's significance in credible critical language, without foreclosing the possibility that writers might use myth as a form of narrative that had a unique potential to speak to modern needs. Writing in 1970, Graham Hough captured their motivations well in suggesting that British literary critics had "two real needs": "One is for a clearer methodology, a method capable of giving a genuine sense of direction to intellectual development. The other is for a far closer engagement with social reality, with the history that still surrounds us, not with the history that exists over against us as an accomplished past."[37] The sections that follow will attempt to show how these motivations took shape in the thought of specific myth-minded critics who directly addressed the issue of myth's relation to literature.

David Daiches

By the 1960s David Daiches was one of the most prominent and respected critics in Britain. A Scot by birth, he became known for his breadth of scholarship. His studies of leading Scottish and English literary figures were well-received, but he was equally comfortable writing about American novelists and poets. One of the recurring themes of his criticism is the problem of the place of imaginative literature in the modern world. Like other myth-minded critics, he was deeply concerned that imaginative literature be relevant to the concerns of the average individual, and his thoughts on the relationship between myth and literature were shaped by this concern.

This was a theme he addressed in a lecture on "Myth, Metaphor, and Poetry" given to the Royal Society of Literature in 1961. Here Daiches framed his thoughts on myth and literature in terms of the confrontation between the literary and scientific cultures. He began by suggesting that critical interest in myth resulted from "[t]he modern concern with the differentiating qualities of the literary use of language and the modern insistence that poetic discourse is different in kind from factual or scientific communication."[38] This concern to define the distinctiveness of poetic language, by which Daiches meant the language of imaginative literature in general, "led literary critics to ponder over the nature of myth and its relation to poetic ways of knowing and creating."[39] In other words, "interest in myth has been pressed on literary critics by their need to emphasize the basic difference between—to put it crudely—poetry and science."[40] In Daiches's view this effort to distinguish literary "ways of knowing" from scientific ways had been going on since the late nineteenth century, but the emergence of anthropological and psychological theories of myth meant that the project was being carried out with ever-increasing sophistication. But without knowing it, Daiches was describing a telling historical irony. On the one hand he was convinced that modern literary criticism was more reliant on the knowledge produced by anthropology and psychology than ever before, that is, more scientifically grounded than ever before. Yet at the same time he contended that "Modern literary criticism is on the whole more committed to an affiliation of poetry, myth, and religion than the criticism of any other age has been."[41]

Daiches's thoughts on the relation of myth to literature were part of an attempt to articulate how literature works as narrative and conveys truth about human experience. Working from the assumption that imaginative literature had epistemic value as a non-scientific way of knowing, Daiches sought to show how myth, when properly integrated into imaginative literature, offered access to deep truths about human experience. The key questions were:

> Does myth represent a way of apprehending or interpreting reality, and a related use of the imagination and method of handling language, which is identical with or significantly analogous to the way in which the literary artist functions?... Is there necessarily an element of myth in all great works of imaginative literature? If so, how can we define that element and how will our definition give us a greater insight into the nature of knowing?[42]

In answering these questions, Daiches presumed that myth was a way of interpreting experience whose legitimacy, because of its very universality, did not need to be justified. That is, myth's explanatory usefulness was really beyond question because it had been used by all cultures at all times. This was what theorists from Malinowski to Cassirer—both cited by Daiches—had shown, overturning the arguments of the Victorian anthropologists that myth was merely a feature of primitive societies. It was thus time-honored and, because culturally transcendent, seemingly an innate aspect of human nature, a necessary manifestation of the human need to make meaning.

In his attempt to explain just how myth gave meaning to experience, Daiches posited that myth is essentially a symbolic mode of discourse that imposes meaning on reality. This was very significant because symbolic discourse was necessary for expressing what he called "implicated truths" about reality. Daiches acknowledged the phrase was imperfect, but explained: "by it I mean a truth which reflects human hopes, fears, yearnings, aspirations, intuition—one could extend the list indefinitely."[43] This led him to a tentative definition of myth: "Can we perhaps say that myth (whatever else it may be) is symbolic discourse aimed at achieving human involvement in a neutral universe?"[44] Poetry was also a symbolic discourse that aimed at telling implicated truths, but in a different way than myth, for "myth aims at mutual implication between man and nature while poetry aims at implicating man in the history of human experience."[45]

But this left unanswered the question of what role myth should play in literature. Daiches's notion of the implicated truths offered by poetry provided the connection, for in his view poetry was only doing its job of telling implicated truths if those truths were *relevant* to the reader's experience. This was the point of contact with myth, for all individuals experienced specific hopes, fears and aspirations, and myth's very subject matter was "the elemental hopes, fears, aspirations of mankind." The poet's task was therefore to update this mythical material and render it relevant, "to counterpoint the patterns of his own culture with those primitive elements in such a way as to give those primitive elements new life, new modernity."[46] Thus, Daiches arrives at the conclusion that novelists and poets had a responsibility to use myth in a way that was relevant to modern experience:

> We make poetic contact with our human past by metaphor; a myth used metaphorically is, if it is properly handled, a myth used after its literal belief has passed away in order to explore areas of feeling and awareness to which that myth can still be made relevant. And the relevance is not simple; it is complex and suggestive, revealing that ... the primitive mind is still with us but so changed, or so hidden, that a revelation of it, and the relating of it to our present ways of thinking and feeling, startles us into a new awareness of the human dimension.[47]

Daiches' lecture was not intended to provide a theory of myth, but it did make a provocative case that myth, when properly integrated into relevant imaginative literature, offered substantial resources for coping with and finding meaning in modernity. This was a notion that would be explored in greater detail by some of his contemporaries.

John Holloway

The idea that myth had importance as a resource in a disenchanted modern world was also explored by the poet-critic John Holloway. Born in London in 1920, Holloway was of roughly the same generation as Daiches and Hough and almost the same age as Kermode. In 1966 C.P. Snow was referring to Holloway as "one of the three or four most distinguished critics of his generation in England."[48] By this time Holloway had also been publishing poetry for ten years.

One of Holloway's primary concerns as a critic was defending imaginative literature as a valid discourse in its own right. Against some who argued that only science was equipped to provide useful knowledge about reality, Holloway asserted that literature need not abandon its claims to offer unique knowledge about experience. Targeting scientific apologists like the Nobel laureate Sir Peter Medawar, he vigorously defended this position throughout the 1960s in periodicals like *Encounter, Critical Quarterly, The Listener* and the *Times Literary Supplement*, as well as through the talks he frequently gave on the BBC.[49] Typical Holloway essays on this theme could be found under such titles as "Poetry for the Technologist" and "Our Contracting Universities." Such pieces reveal his sense of urgency about the need to secure for a literature a place in the evolving university system. Holloway felt that imaginative literature must be understood as an invaluable component of any university education that could be considered adequate. He worried, however, that new proposals to reform the university system took no account of literature's importance. Responding to the Robbins Report, Holloway observed, "the idea seems chiefly to be, teach more science so as to have more technologists."[50] Holloway conceded that the value of literature was not necessarily as obvious as the value of a technological achievement, but it did not follow that literature was therefore less important, for what it offered were resources for coping with modernity.

Holloway's concern with defending imaginative literature as a discourse with its own value clearly shaped his thoughts on myth's relation to literature. In 1960 Holloway participated in a conference at the University of Bristol on the topic of "Metaphor and Symbol." Taking part in the conference were other noted writers on the subject of myth, such as philosopher Philip Wheelwright, critic Owen Barfield, and theologian F.W. Dillistone.[51] Holloway used this opportunity to work out his thoughts on "The Concept of Myth in Literature."

In his lecture, Holloway considered how the anthropological study of myth could be used by literary critics to develop a more comprehensive understanding of imaginative literature. By considering the contributions of various branches of anthropology, Holloway sought to build a case that myth and great imaginative literature were analogous in significant ways. To do this he considered the views of myth offered by three branches of anthropology. One view was represented by the "armchair" anthropology of Max Müller and J.G. Frazer, which held that myths were essentially primitive forms of explanation. Yet Holloway noted that a recent revolution in anthropology had displaced this older view of myth. The new understanding was advanced by functionalist anthropologists such as Malinowski and Radcliffe-Brown, who by means of fieldwork observed how myth actually functioned in primitive societies. They found that myth's "function is not so much to answer a question about the world... as to contribute to, or sustain, some reality now current in the society."[52] In Holloway's opinion both views contained insights that were helpful to the literary critic who wanted to understand the power of literature:

> But in the literary field there is no reason whatever to suppose that if we attempt to exploit this newer viewpoint of anthropology with regard to myth, and consider some of our great imaginative works as sources of power and influence rather than information, as great sustainers and moulders of cultural life of the community or the individual, we are therefore bound entirely to repudiate the view which sees them as expressing 'meanings', or suggesting answers to fundamental questions about the nature of man or human life.[53]

But Holloway did not end his survey of anthropological theory there. He next turned to the myth and ritual school of anthropologists, and asked whether their work could bring to light "aspects of imaginative works which might otherwise elude critical observation."[54] Holloway did not argue that works of imaginative literature are rituals in disguise, but rather suggested that many of the great literary masterpieces functioned within modern culture in a way similar to the role played by ritual in primitive cultures. With this premise in place, the function of "the great imaginative masterpiece" was no longer so mysterious:

> Its irreplaceable value as part of the cultural heritage, its explosive and disturbing power, its remoteness and total difference in kind from anything offered by cognitive thinking or in particular by science, its ability to contact the deepest parts of our nature, and the well-known fact that encountering it can be a decisive experience and mark a stage in our lives, now fall easily into place.[55]

Modern individuals no longer took part in rituals that enacted an underlying myth in which they believed. This role of myth and ritual was now filled by imaginative literature, which both ordered and expanded the reader's experience in a powerful way; like myth, literature "has a *mana* of its own."[56] He concluded: "The work's essential interest will be to have added a great new item to the furniture of the world, to have become a thing, a fount of experience. It is precious to individuals because of the great experience which it offers them, and to society because... it thus enhances the life, and the capacity for life of society's members."[57]

Holloway would continue to develop this line of thought throughout his career, arguing repeatedly for the relevance and importance of imaginative literature in a modern world. Because of its quasi-mythical power and its capacity to expand experience, imaginative literature was directly relevant to the concerns of those coping with modernity. Hence, literature should not be studied for its own sake; it must be studied in a way that "speaks potently to those many in a large-scale enterprise whose concern for our own time and its general problems is stronger than... a taste for reading old books.... [I]t must evoke and greatly foster such an interest in our own contemporaneity even in those who lack it."[58] On a practical level, this meant that literature could be a source of strategies for resisting "the ethos of endless growth," or encouraging "guardianship of the biosphere."[59] Yet in his critical writings Holloway was never able to make clear precisely how literature, performing the function of myth and ritual, could help readers give meaning to their experience of modernity.

Graham Hough

Graham Hough was a prominent British critic who went further than either Daiches or Holloway in examining how poets and novelists could manage the tension between myth and experience in their work. Born in 1908, Hough produced much of his criticism while at Cambridge between 1955 and 1977, and much of his early work appeared in Bateson's *Essays in Criticism*. His criticism was shaped by many of the same concerns as Daiches, Holloway, and Kermode's, not least among them the desire to develop a form of criticism that was free of Leavisite dogmatism.[60]

Hough still assumed in the 1960s that literary criticism was concerned with a fairly well-defined canon, yet he also felt the need for criticism to be relevant and capable of justifying its place in an expanding university system, a desire that went hand-in-hand with his willingness to criticize the elitism of literary education. Hough believed that it was impossible to ignore that "the texture of living experience" had been transformed into something so rapidly changing that much pre-twentieth-century English literature seemed simply irrelevant to many.[61] This situation necessitated a more practical, demotic criticism free of the "vague odour of old port and oak panelling" that pervaded Leavisite literary education. Hough had little use for the *Scrutiny* brand of criticism, which too often resembled "an orgy of approval and disapproval."[62] Hough's acerbic judgment on the Leavisites was that

> They start from a set of attitudes, derived from inherited moral, social environment and fragments of a surviving religious faith. They then make a careful selection of the literary tradition that will confirm these attitudes; and finally announce in triumph that literature has validated whatever they believed to start with.[63]

The worst consequence of such criticism was that it robbed literature of its unique ability to expand the reader's experience: "We cannot expect much from a mentor who can never surprise us, never shock us, never induce us to change our mind. As long as literature is used in this way its guidance will be a nullity and an illusion."[64] If literature was to serve its proper function as a gateway to "the whole of man's imaginative experience," then it was necessary to maintain contact with a diversity of literary works. By doing so,

> we shall continually be meeting minds that work on entirely different premises from our own. We shall be confronting beliefs that we find impossible, emotions that we have never entertained, experiences that the contemporary world gives us no inkling of. And we shall be continually forced to realize that they are a part of our human inheritance, that our citizenship of a rather ramshackle, probably declining, continually threatened twentieth-century welfare state is only part of a wider citizenship that is ultimately more real. Literature can do very little to alter the brute facts of power and history. Its capacities in this respect have been generally exaggerated; for this we need to call on other energies; and no amount of literary culture can excuse us from employing them. But it can knock a window in the subtopian fall-out shelter to which contemporary politics and economics seem bent on condemning us. With its aid we have continually before us a view of other possibilities.[65]

In short, literature offered possibilities for coping with modern life, a view of imaginative literature's importance that is remarkably like Holloway's. For Hough literary critics played a key role in allowing literature to do its work, because "the business of criticism is to insert [the literature of the past] into the living fabric of the present."[66] The task was to convince those outside the field of literary criticism that critics fulfilled a vital function. Critics needed to dispel "the scandal of amateurism and indirection that still hangs around literary criticism in the judgement [sic] of philosophers, historians and natural scientists."[67]

Thus, throughout his career Hough was concerned with justifying the importance of imaginative literature and the role of the critic as an interpreter of it. If, as he argued, the critic "should be able to give some intelligible account of the relation of literature to the social order,"[68] then one of most pressing concerns for the modern critic was to explain the relationship between myth and imaginative literature and why that relationship was relevant to everyday experience. He took up this issue in *An Essay on Criticism* (1966), his most extended and comprehensive attempt to elucidate his critical approach.

Hough devoted two chapters of the work to an assessment of myth criticism as represented by the work of Northrop Frye combined with his own views on the relation between myth and literature. He was sympathetic to and impressed by Frye's achievement, but he had several reservations. One of his objections was that Frye's work was premised on the "discredited" anthropology of Frazer's *Golden Bough*. More fundamentally, Hough balked at Frye's argument that mythic patterns always dictate the structure of literary works, myth providing the form and experience the content. Hough essentially accepted Iris Murdoch's conception of the "journalistic" and "crystalline" poles of literature. On this view, proposed by Murdoch in a famous 1961 *Encounter* essay, the "journalistic" pole was the artist's desire to render accurately the contingent flux of experience, while the "crystalline" pole was the urge to impose on this flux a mythic pattern.[69] This view is implicit in Hough's suggestion that

> A juster view of the relation of myth to literature would be that myth represents one pole of literary creation; the other pole being experience, reality, 'nature', our sense of how things happen. Ever since literature became literature the two have existed in a state of dialectical tension—on the one side the archaic outlines of a relatively few persistent and unchanging stories, on the other the inexhaustible flux of experience.[70]

Hough believed that the great virtue of Frye's work was that it demonstrated convincingly "that myth is indeed an abiding element in literature."[71] However, myth did not provide the fundamental structure of all literary works as Frye supposed; myth did not provide a container that the artist then filled up with representational material. Instead, Hough argued, myth provided a body of material that each artist had to engage on his or her own terms, for his or her own purposes: "Mythic elements mingle and fuse with mimetic ones, and both are contained... in a form that is dictated by purely literary considerations.... Myth is not the geometry of literature; it is part of its material."[72]

Hough held that modern literature was particularly rife with mythical elements and he believed this was directly related to the decline of Christianity. Myth, he argued, unavoidably raised the question of belief. Until the nineteenth century the deployment of myth in western literature had always been in a sense controlled by the Christian myth, which actually was believed.[73] Insofar as other myths were used in literature they served as rich sources of imagery, metaphor and so on, not as objects of belief. But the decline of Christianity had only increased the profusion of mythic elements in literature, out of a search for some transcendent pattern that could provide meaning and structure in its place. This mythopoeic impulse in modern literature derived from a recognition that "there is no ecumenical religion" and from an awareness that "the psychologists and anthropologists have revealed systems of symbolism anterior to the accepted cultural structures." Echoing W.H. Auden's assessment of the "modern problem," Hough lamented how "The poet has all the myths of the world available to him; which also means that he has none—none that can impose itself as indubitably his own by simple right of inheritance."[74] As he described this modern predicament elsewhere:

> literature embodies current mythology and is powerful on that account. It always did, and it always was. What is peculiar is that the myths seem now to have no organized existence outside literature. They are not worked out, modified or checked by religion or a prevailing philosophy.... [L]iterature finds itself saddled with nothing less than the responsibility for providing patterns of conduct, feeling and imagination that used once to be in the keeping of institutional religion.[75]

Thus, though Hough acknowledged that literature had always drawn much of its power from myth, he worried that literature was becoming too invested with mythical significance, leading to a neglect of intellectual activities that were grounded in practical concerns.

What Hough found particularly intriguing was that the mythical elements in modern literature were being used for religious purposes, but without actually being believed in a religious sense. It was in addressing this phenomenon that myth criticism could prove especially useful:

> What we do learn after reading the mythological criticism of today is the enduring vitality of mythical structures *independent of belief.* We have been apt to think of certain recurring, more or less magical narrative patterns as part of religion and therefore objects of belief; and of certain others as parts of mythology and therefore mere decoration. It would seem that as far as literature is concerned this distinction cannot be drawn [emphasis in original].[76]

The question Hough kept asking was how individuals could give some sense of meaning to their lives in the absence of a system of religious belief. In struggling with this problem, the great authors and poets of the recent past had turned to myth:

> The one inevitable unifying force in the modern world is that of natural science; and since the poet is concerned with areas of experience that natural science does not touch, he is left to make his own myth, or to select one by arbitrary existentialist choice, from the vast uncodified museum, the limitless junk-shop of the past.[77]

The most that could be hoped for was that individual works of literature would employ myth as a way of coping with the modern problem in a way that opened up possibilities for the individual reader. And critics like Hough could facilitate this exchange between author and reader by illuminating the ways in which a text worked.

Frank Kermode

Hough's view that myth was one pole of the myth-experience dialectic at the heart of imaginative literature was shared substantially by Frank Kermode. This resemblance is unsurprising in light of the fact that each critic admired and built upon the other's work. Kermode was one of the keenest contemporary observers of the postwar trend toward mythic thinking. Because he understood the critic's task as "making sense of the ways we try to make sense of our lives" he was keenly interested in myth as one particularly important form of "making sense."[78] In other words,

Kermode came to an interest in myth through his interest in narrative theory.

Kermode's own views on myth were complex and developed throughout the decade as his own understanding of narrative theory grew more sophisticated. One of the dominant characteristics of his criticism was an abiding skepticism, a willingness to put all bold claims—whether methodological or metaphysical—to the test. He frequently expressed a suspicion of writers who seemed too committed to their own self-fashioned mythical systems and he often worried about the tendency of much modern literature to "regress" into myth, abandoning all effort to engage reality constructively. Yet despite this skepticism Kermode remained willing to grant myth an important and indeed necessary literary role. Myth was a form of narrative that he could not escape or dismiss, and his skepticism extended as well to those moderns who claimed to be able "to live in conditions of reality unprotected by myth."[79]

Kermode's interest in myth was most apparent between the late 1950s and the late 1960s, an interest evident in numerous reviews and articles of the period. Indeed, it is fair to say that during this period myth was Kermode's central critical concern. There is good reason to believe that he was first prompted to write on the topic by the emerging "two cultures" controversy. Within months after C.P. Snow delivered his famous Rede Lecture in May 1959, Kermode began to consider mythic thinking in light of the purported two cultures divide. In a series of pieces written around this time, he speculated about ways in which myth could be incorporated into modern thought without giving in entirely to the "cult" of mythical irrationalism or the "complex modern primitivism" that he believed to be so common in twentieth-century thought. In a *Spectator* review entitled "The Myth-Kitty," Kermode observed that his contemporaries "set great store by myth." This was attested not only by the fact that "our literary culture is saturated with mythological thinking," but also by an accumulating "unmanageable load of archaeological, anthropological and psychological theory about myth." Mythic thinking gained impetus from the fact that the modernists had given it their imprimatur:

> In the domain of myth we can short-circuit the intellect and liberate the imagination which the scientism of the world suppresses; and this is the central modern position. Myth deals in what is more real than intellect can accede to; it is a seamless garment to replace the tattered fragments worn by the modern mind.

In Kermode's view it was unfortunate that so much literary and artistic thinking about myth was crudely anti-science, driven by the belief that "if we seek the pre-logical and oppose the march of the intellect, we are the enemies of science...and the worshippers of myth." This, he contended, was deeply unsatisfactory:

> The need for a change of attitude, for a modification of this myth-science antithesis, is pressing. Mythology, as it was now understood, raises the whole question of belief. This would scarcely be so if it was thought of only as a breeding-ground of images; in fact it is too often the anti-intellectualist substitute for science.

Kermode offered no solution to the problem of how properly to integrate myth into the culture, but he concluded that writers like Kingsley Amis and Philip Larkin, who wanted no more mythological literature, would be disappointed because "The myth-kitty is inexhaustible; the ancient gods survive."[80]

Kermode used the nearly simultaneous appearance of Snow's lecture and David Jones's book *Epoch and Artist* as a further opportunity to examine how the mythic interests of literary intellectuals fed the suspicions of scientists about modern literary endeavor. Writing in *Encounter*, Kermode observed that "the cultural divide about which Sir Charles writes so well seems to me to reflect a grand modern antinomy that is well worth examining from a different viewpoint"—that of the literary intellectual.[81] Taking Jones as a typical example, Kermode sought to show why "primitivism" was so often at the core of a literary intellectual's thinking. He argued that "[t]he Romantic attack on intellect" had prepared the way for twentieth-century primitivism, of which mythic thinking was a prominent facet.[82] The Romantics, reacting to the materialist agenda of science, valued "primitive image-making powers" above development of the intellect.[83] This assumption remained "essential to the production of the kind of art most people are prepared to call important," creating a situation in which "mythical, imagistic, organicist thinking becomes as desirable for the artist as it is undesirable for the scientist; the first stands on the emblematic, myth-haunted mountain, the second on Peacock's intelligent pyramid."[84] An artist like Jones or Yeats, feeling acutely "that the artist has lost permanent access to a rich common 'mythus,'" might ransack various sources—"Welsh, Irish, Neo-Platonic, anthropological, and so forth"—to produce his own mythology, "his own *Vision*, his own answer to Darwin, Huxley, and their successors."[85] As he wrote elsewhere, "This is the programme of one of the 'two cultures'—the anti-scientific one, revolting from 'exteriority' and 'materialism.' " Such endeavors were motivated by a belief that "art has access to a truth not available to the intellect."[86]

Kermode had little patience with those writers, like Jones and Yeats, who professed actually to believe in their self-fashioned mythical systems. Yet he conceded that such systems were somehow aesthetically necessary in the twentieth century: "They are not required to be valid in themselves, but to provide contexts for the anti-intellectualism that modern art, for historical reasons, requires; its character is such that it *must* be in conflict with a scientific worldview to survive at all."[87] Within a year, however, Kermode was advancing a more measured view of myth's role in the two cultures divide. He concluded a consideration of Joseph Campbell's *The Masks of God* on a note of equanimity: "Perhaps we should be less disturbed that we have our physicist-hunters and artist-shamans; the division of labour is an old one, paleolithic at least. Mr. Golding caught it exactly in the Jack and Simon of *Lord of the Flies*. Perhaps the need is less to end it than to accept it. We need the hunter to go on living, the shaman to go on living according to the truth."[88]

What such comments make clear is that Kermode was convinced that myth was central to any serious literary endeavor of the time. As the 1960s progressed he wrote less directly about the cultural significance of mythic thinking and tried to approach this issue by investigating the specific role myth played in imaginative literature. Kermode pursued this line of inquiry by asking authors how they solved this problem for themselves, and he came to believe that all serious modern writers had to take a position on the importance of myth to their work. This conviction is evident in a series of interviews that Kermode conducted with seven leading English novelists in 1962. Kermode's primary concern in the interviews was to solicit each novelist's views on what he termed "the myth-fact relation."[89] The article version of the interviews proved to be a highly influential piece, appearing in at least three different journals and one edited collection.

Kermode confessed in *The Listener* that his interest in the subject was in part prompted by Iris Murdoch's 1961 *Encounter* essay "Against Dryness." In that essay Murdoch had argued that the great temptation for twentieth-century novelists "was to allow the myth to take over—to falsify human character and the fortuity of real life by an oversubtle attention to occult patterns of meaning and event."[90] In Murdoch's view this was a predictable response to the conditions of modern life: "The temptation of art…is to console. The modern writer, frightened of technology and (in England) abandoned by philosophy…attempts to console us by myths or by stories."[91] Yet, as Kermode pointed out, she did not reject the mythic dimension of literature, arguing instead for a fictional form somewhere between the "crystalline" mythic novel and the "journalistic" documentary novel. The novelists Kermode interviewed about their views on myth, reality and fiction were Murdoch, Graham Greene, Angus Wilson, Ivy Compton-Burnett, C.P. Snow, John Wain, and Muriel Spark. Though the writers did not share the same conception of myth, Kermode contended that they were linked by a desire to use it judiciously so as not to falsify experience and produce mere fables instead of novels. Each had to tread a narrow line between the mythic and the documentary, because too much emphasis on either pole could render a novel irrelevant to contemporary concerns.

The culmination of Kermode's interest in myth was his 1967 book *The Sense of an Ending: Studies in the Theory of Fiction*, based on the Mary Flexner Lectures he delivered at Bryn Mawr in 1965. A key point of the pioneering work was Kermode's distinction between fictions and myths: "Fictions are for finding things out, and they change as the needs of sense making change. Myths are the agents of stability, fictions the agents of change. Myths call for absolute, fictions for conditional assent."[92] One of Kermode's concerns was to show that "Fictions can degenerate into myths whenever they are not consciously held to be fictive."[93] It was thus necessary to hold myth in tension with the narrative form of explanation that we call fiction. Myth was seductive, and he wanted to caution against the temptation to retreat into it, an all too common reflex in modern thought. Kermode did not object to myth as such, but rather to the easy regress into myth, which replaced concern for the reality of contingent experience with belief in a consoling absolute. Such a flight from experience could not produce understanding of the world: "We know that if we want to find out about ourselves, make sense, we must avoid the regress into myth which has deceived poet, historian, and critic."[94]

Thus, though *The Sense of an Ending* approached the question of myth's relation to literature through a more sophisticated critical apparatus, many of Kermode's earlier views on myth remained intact. Just as he had earlier criticized the modernists who professed belief in their own self-created myths, so in *The Sense of an Ending* he criticized the misuse of myth, though not myth per se. He granted that "the novelist . . . has to allow for different versions of reality, including what some call mythical and some call absolute."[95] In other words, despite reservations about myth's seductive power, Kermode was unable to dispense with myth as a valuable aspect of literature. This was seen by John Bayley, who noted that Kermode's real concern was to discredit "false modernism," or the modernism that "tries to invent new myths"—precisely the offense that Kermode had claimed David Jones and Yeats committed.[96] The problem, then, was not myth itself, but myth believed in instead of integrated into fiction as a way of making sense of the world; myths were problematic when a writer submitted to them, but were illuminating when a writer used them creatively as subordinate elements in a larger work. In the end, Kermode could not abandon the category of myth as a literary technique for constructing meaning in modernity.

Taking stock in the 1970s

The work of the myth-minded critics contributed to a growing understanding that to live in modernity was to live surrounded by myth and firmly established myth as a central term of both literary and cultural analysis, though one whose meaning was not always clear. Critics of the 1970s, looking back at the work of the myth-minded critics, would realize that despite the prevalence of critical interest in myth the term remained troublingly vague. This engendered some anxiety among critics who were uneasy that their discipline was in such disagreement about so central a concept. The 1970s therefore saw various attempts to sum up critical opinion on the topic. Three key texts of the mid-1970s provide a cross-section of that decade's attempts to bring clarity to literary discussions of the fraught question of myth. These were William Righter's *Myth and Literature*, K.K. Ruthven's *Myth*, and, to a lesser extent, Williams's *Keywords*.

All three critics agreed that despite a lack of consensus about the precise meaning of myth for literary critics, it could not be dispensed with as a term of analysis. Ruthven thought that critics had no choice but to continue using the term, even though attempts to formulate a definition were pointless: "Nothing would be gained by formulating a brand-new synchronic definition of myth and insisting that everybody accept it."[97] Righter concurred: "It is easy to doubt that the working boundaries of such a concept may ever be drawn."[98] Similarly, reflecting on the myriad contemporary uses of myth, Williams acknowledged that "myth is now both a very significant and a very difficult word."[99] And precisely because they believed it was such a significant term, these critics sought to bring some resolution to the difficulty surrounding it. The response of each was not to frame a new, comprehensive definition, but rather to take the linguistic turn by "looking at the uses made of 'myth' in the modern literary imagination."[100]

They concluded that recent interest in myth was invariably political, in that the term was used to defend certain cultural interests. In particular, it was bound up with ongoing attempts to defend imaginative literature. Describing the focus of his study of myth, Righter explained: "Above all I am dealing with a modern situation and a modern word, representing a multiplicity of pressures and demands, themselves the keys to the senses of myth they have called into being."[101] Foremost among these pressures and demands was a need to defend imaginative literature. This was a point caught by Williams who, with the myth-minded critics obviously in mind, noted that myth "has become involved with the difficult modern senses of *imagination*, *creative* and *fiction*."[102] Similarly, Ruthven asked rhetorically, "Was it the very ambiguities of 'myth' which first attracted those engaged in the increasingly desperate endeavour of finding new ways of defending imaginative literature against enemies ancient and modern?"[103]

Yet, despite their awareness that "myth" was a term whose meaning was continually adapted to serve various interests, these critics could not dissolve the concept with their analysis.

[W]e have no direct experience of myth as such, but only of particular myths: and these, we discover, are obscure in origin, protean in form and ambiguous in meaning. Seemingly immune to rational explication, they nevertheless stimulate rational enquiry, which accounts for the diversity of conflicting explanations, none of which is ever comprehensive enough to explain myth away.[104]

Righter held out some hope that the theories of Lévi-Strauss might bring some clarity to discussion of myth and literature, but came to a similar conclusion that myth could not be explained away. He had no illusions about the concept, declaring: "We have found in it what we have sought, after our own fashion, and in whatever vocabulary happens to be our own made demands on something we have called 'myth', requiring it to answer in kind." Yet he was forced to admit the existence of "moments when the concept seems a necessary part of our thinking."[105] In the end, these critics of the 1970s seemed to concede that to live in modernity was to live with myth. The concept was simply too attractive to the imagination, too pregnant with meaning, too promising as a means of imposing literary order on the flux of modern experience and history; its persistence was overdetermined. Critics would have to continue to deal with the fact that, as Righter noted quoting Auden: " 'men have always lounged in myth', but perhaps in no time like the present."[106]

Conclusion

The myth-minded critics were not the only British critics of the period to be interested in myth, nor were they even the most enthusiastic about the potential of myth as a concept. Yet their work on the topic was more direct and developed than that of most of their contemporaries. The key move each made was not to conceive of myth as an all-consoling panacea for modernity's discontents—the mistake of the American myth critics—but rather to work out how myth fit within imaginative literature more broadly. Myth became for these critics a strategy for defending imaginative literature and, by extension, literary criticism as an explanation of that literature. Thus the work of the myth-minded critics was part of a larger project to develop a relevant and engaged critical discourse that encouraged relevant and engaged imaginative literature. These critics felt that literature must be of some use to ordinary readers, and one way it could be so was by mediating their experience of modernity, helping them cope with the fact that, to use Hough's words, "A culture dominated by the word is turning into a culture dominated by the number."[107] According to the myth-minded critics, a balanced use of myth could help literature to do this.

To open a volume of British literary criticism from the 1960s or 1970s is to find an anxious essay or chapter on "the function of criticism" or "the purpose of criticism." This reflects the fact that English studies is, as Josephine Guy has noted, "a discipline whose status has been contested more or less continuously since its inception in the late nineteenth century."[108] The primary reason for this is that its members have found it difficult to produce knowledge that meets "the twin criteria of specialisation and social utility which, by the late decades of the [nineteenth] century, had come to define and authorise professional knowledge as a whole."[109] Those who favor the former criteria have almost invariably compromised or sacrificed the latter, and vice versa. "Rarely," Guy observes, "do the extremes meet."[110] The debates surveyed in this chapter would tend to confirm her analysis. The myth-minded critics thought that myth would help them satisfy both criteria: elucidating myth's role in literature with recondite analytical techniques exemplified professional specialization, with the socially beneficial consequence that literature's potential to offer meaning and consolation would be unlocked.

During the 1960s British critics were developing increasingly sophisticated justifications for the importance of literature and their discipline. As literary criticism evolved into a more heavily theorized discipline, its increasing sophistication was in part manifested in an emerging interest in narrative theory. Critical interest in myth can be seen as one moment in this evolution, for an interest in how narrative worked led critics to ask how myth itself, as a form of narrative, worked. It is therefore unsurprising that some of the leading myth-minded critics would become some of the most theoretically literate British critics, making significant contributions in the field of narrative theory. Hough's essays in the late 1960s and 1970s showed an increasing interest in narrative theory and a growing admiration for the work of Barthes. Holloway would go on to write a pioneering work of narrative theory, *Narrative and Structure*, which was one of the first attempts at sustained engagement with structuralist theory by a British critic. Kermode's career revealed an even greater eagerness to make use of emerging theoretical tools for understanding literature. In the late 1960s and early 1970s he produced a number of works on narrative theory that redefined understanding of the topic in Britain.

The myth-minded critics could not be called naïve mythophiles; their treatment of myth was sober and measured rather than zealously enthusiastic. There were some who felt that the critics surveyed here did not take myth seriously enough. Bayley, for instance, charged that Kermode had slandered myth by citing anti-Semitism as an example of how myths call for "absolute assent."[111] Similarly, A.D. Moody criticized Hough for failing to acknowledge that myths "have their power from deep within our own experience, as well as from their common and permanent relevance."[112] For the critics surveyed here myth was under suspicion. The modernists had tried to restructure literature around myth. The North American myth critics had tried to reconfigure literary criticism around myth. These projects made myth suspect. Yet, despite their reservations, the myth-minded critics could not entirely escape the category of myth or dispense with it as a term of analysis. They acknowledged the literary importance of something they called myth and tried to offer an account of how it could secure meaning for modernity. They held that myth—if properly integrated into imaginative literature, if properly balanced with an equally necessary mimetic, documentary element—could aid readers in making sense of modern experience. But they were not simply interested in securing meaning: by positioning themselves as uniquely equipped to elucidate the mythic significance of literature, they also sought to secure a place for their discipline in an expanding university system when echoes of the two cultures debate were still audible. As we will see in the next chapter, they were not the only group to attempt such a move.

8
Making a Modern Faith: Myth in Twentieth-Century British Theology

Introduction

In a front-page article in *The Observer* on March 17, 1963, John Robinson, Bishop of Woolwich, summarized his recent theological ideas under the provocative headline "Our Image of God Must Go." Two days later appeared Robinson's book *Honest to God*, which presented his ideas in greater detail. As it turned out, the controversy generated by the *Observer* piece was ideal publicity for the book, which rapidly became the quickest-selling work of theology in history. By the end of the year more than 350,000 English copies were in print and within three years sales had reached almost one million. *Honest to God* outraged many, because the book gave the impression that a bishop in the Church of England was very publicly denying the Christian doctrine of God, in the opinion of many even to the point of atheism.[1] Immediately a heated debate emerged surrounding Robinson and his book, a debate that ranged from theological journals, to letters and columns in the daily newspapers, to hastily-written pamphlets critiquing Robinson, to discussion programs on both radio and television. The popularity of *Honest to God* established Robinson as the face of so-called "radical" theology in Britain even though much of his later work would be far more moderate and mainstream than his 1963 bestseller. Robinson's *Honest to God* was to popular theology what Colin Wilson's *The Outsider* had been to popular philosophy seven years earlier. And just as the media had labeled Wilson one of Britain's "Angry Young Men" it now christened Robinson the leader of a new radical theology.

Despite its shortcomings—noted by reviewers then and since[2]—the book was highly readable, and it resonated with the public like few other theological books of the twentieth century. The reason

Making a Modern Faith 177

was that Robinson's book encapsulated a dilemma felt by many twentieth-century Britons. The horns of this dilemma were on the one hand a de facto acceptance of a scientific, modern worldview and on the other a yearning for some metaphysical meaning beyond the truths offered by science. That is why Robinson's mode of argument in *Honest to God* now seems sometimes contradictory—the book was the product of a tension between the fundamentally modern desire to accommodate Christian belief to modern scientific and historical knowledge and a countervailing inclination to advocate myth's indispensable role in delivering truths beyond science. Robinson's attempt to reconcile these conflicting motivations animated the book.

The same tension, present in even clearer form, animated the next theological cause célèbre of the century, the publication of the symposium volume *The Myth of God Incarnate* in 1977. One lesson that many observers took from the *Honest to God* affair was that the media played a key role in creating theological controversies. As one historian of the *Honest to God* debate has noted, "[I]n the climate of the early 1960s, when the trade in new ideas was burgeoning media interest, a bishop expressing novel and possibly heretical ideas suited exactly the heavier Sunday papers and the middle-brow television discussion programmes."[3] This lesson was not lost on the group of theologians responsible for *The Myth of God Incarnate*, who deliberately courted controversy by holding a press conference to introduce their iconoclastic new book. Like *Honest to God*, *The Myth of God Incarnate* also became a bestseller, selling 30,000 copies in eight months. And its content was, if anything, more controversial than that of *Honest to God*. Whereas Robinson's volume had questioned the traditional Christian conception of God, *The Myth of God Incarnate* focused specifically on Christology by subjecting what the authors called "the traditional doctrine of the incarnation" to radical questioning. But like those in *Honest to God*, the essays in *The Myth of God Incarnate* were marked by the same tension between the modern and the mythical. The contributors to the volume believed that modern knowledge necessitated a reformulation of the traditional Christian conception of Jesus, but they also believed that Christian faith, precisely because it was expressed in the flexible language of myth, could successfully accommodate modern knowledge.

The *Honest to God* affair and the controversy surrounding *The Myth of God Incarnate* can be seen as the bookends marking a moment in the history of British theology. Adrian Hastings has described the period between the early 1960s and the late 1970s as a distinct cycle of liberal theology, which was the dominant strain in that period. Academic theologians in the seventies developed the earlier trends of the sixties, shaping them into a liberal orthodoxy. This resembled a process that had taken place earlier in the century when theologians of the 1920s forged a liberal synthesis out of the new theological ideas of the Edwardian period.[4] *Honest to God* signaled the resurgence of liberal theology in Britain, a resurgence that culminated with *The Myth of God Incarnate*. Significantly, both were works of *popular*, rather than academic theology, and they were intended to persuade the public that a proper understanding of the relationship between myth and Christianity could make the faith seem very attractive to modern men and women. What these two works and the debates surrounding them show is how deeply an understanding of myth as an inescapable aspect of religious belief was rooted in British liberal theology, and to some degree public opinion, during the post-Second World War period.

This movement of myth to the center of theological debate was part of an anthropological turn in British theology. It was anthropological in two senses: (1) the knowledge produced by the discipline of anthropology profoundly shaped theological discourse in Britain and 2) the understanding of myth that theologians borrowed from anthropology turned theology from divinity toward humanity by shifting its focus toward human religious experience and human expressions about that experience. This more human-centered orientation reflects the fact that theology of the post-Second World War period was an increasingly modest discipline, reluctant to make broad claims about the nature of God, and more content to concentrate on human religious experience and expressions of that experience. Robinson explained that this perspective controlled *Honest to God*, "[L]et's not start from a heavenly Being, whose very existence many would doubt. Let's start from what actually is most real to people in everyday life—and find God there."[5]

Theological interest in myth during this period was thus both an aspect and a cause of an intellectual shift that reoriented the agenda of theology around questions of human religious experience. Ironically, British theology's increasing interest in myth actually pushed the discipline into an uncomfortable intellectual gap between the humanities and the social sciences. This uncertain intellectual position is one reason its place in the university has been eclipsed by the field of religious studies. Because theologians were increasingly hesitant to make bold claims about their subject matter, they retreated to intellectual ground that was already occupied by other disciplines, in particular philosophy, anthropology, and religious studies. An attempt to make Christian meaning for modernity by drawing on the spiritual resources of myth resulted in a theology that was more modern than ever. In this sense the concept of myth was for twentieth-century theology an ambivalent ally: theologians turned to myth because it served their need to rethink Christianity for modernity, but in doing so they aligned their discipline and its methods even more closely with modernity. Twentieth-century British theology's turn to myth was thus a crucial step in a gradual marginalization of the discipline.

In an attempt to understand this process, this chapter examines how liberal theologians sought to balance the competing claims of modernity and myth in their work. It was this effort that produced the tension in *Honest to God*, *The Myth of God Incarnate*, and other myth-oriented theology of the period. Situating the work of myth-oriented theologians in the broader history of liberal theology, I show how these theologians came to see the category of myth as essential both to their response to modern unbelief and their response to intellectual challenges from modern science, critical history, and analytic philosophy. On the one hand these theologians took for granted what they termed the "modern scientific worldview," while on the other they argued that myth, as the natural idiom of religion, was not vulnerable to scientific, historical, or philosophical critiques because it was a form of discourse that transcended the empirical realm.

In the long run, however, the myth-oriented theologians were unable to maintain this dual loyalty to modernity and myth. This was because though in principle they claimed that myth transcended the empirical, in practice they did not treat it as something that referred to or had its roots in the transcendent. Rather they treated myth as human expressions about the meaning of existence. But this position was essentially that of anthropology; there was little distinctly theological about it at all. Their failure to define clearly a compelling theological view of myth explains why they largely failed to persuade the public to embrace a modern, myth-centered Christianity. By the late 1970s, after more than two decades of work on the topic, British theologians were acknowledging that their attempt to rebuild a modern Christianity around the concept of myth had been unsuccessful. As a member of the Church of England's Doctrine Commission concluded in 1981, "the term 'myth' raises more problems than it solves."[6] However, equally significant were the consequences that they did not acknowledge. Chief among these was that British theologians' efforts to resolve "the myth question" had actually helped marginalize the discipline of theology by erasing much of what made it distinct.

The theological background: Modernism and liberalism in British theology

British theologians' engagement with myth can be seen as part of what historians of religion have described as the modernist project in theology. The driving concern of modernist theology was to revise and adapt Christian doctrine into a belief system that was acceptable to moderns who had an essentially secularized, evolutionary worldview. The Irish priest George Tyrell, a leading Roman Catholic modernist, defined a modernist as a churchman who believed that a synthesis between the essential truth of Christianity and the essential truth of modernity was possible. As Adrian Hastings has described it, Anglican modernism was in the same spirit, but "a good deal more remote from traditional Christian belief than the mystical and sacramentalist Catholic 'modernism' of George Tyrell."[7] Modernist theology was essentially, then, an attempt to respond to the perceived challenge of modernity through a mixture of concession and resistance. The concessions centered on the acknowledgment that historical criticism of the Bible, combined with an evolutionary understanding of human origins, had shown that much biblical material reflected a primitive mythological cosmology. The resistance consisted in an insistence that scientific language was incapable of expressing the existential truths about humanity's relationship with God. Thus theology, with its ability to interpret the unique language of religion, was still a necessary discipline. The modernists of the 1910s and 1920s tended to take an experientialist view of the Bible, that is, they viewed it as a collection of texts that were interpretations of religious experience rather than a divine revelation. Versions of this idea would be central to the myth-oriented theology that developed in the 1960s.

"Modernist" theology was simply the cutting edge of "liberal" theology in the first quarter of the twentieth century. After that time the label "modernist" fell into disuse, in part because it had become negatively associated with an uncritical acceptance of science, with a vapid brand of philosophical idealism, and with advocacy of certain policies that eventually fell out of favor. However, the similar but broader term "liberal" remained a common self-designation for many theologians throughout the century. Theological liberalism was defined by three characteristics in particular: (1) an interest in accommodating Christian doctrine to modern knowledge, especially the knowledge produced by historical criticism of the Bible and modern science; (2) an emphasis on the humanity of Jesus, with a focus on the ethical values and human potential he represented; and (3) an anthropological turn in theological method in which human religious experience and symbolic expressions of that experience—rather than divine revelation—became the focus of inquiry. As J.F. Bethune-Baker, one of the leading liberal theologians in interwar Britain, put it in 1921: "To clear the ground I would start with two or three premisses, and the first of them is that 'orthodoxy', in beginning with God, began at the wrong end."[8] His point was that theologians would do better to ground their work in human expressions about the experience of God. Almost identical words would be written by John Robinson four decades later in the midst of the *Honest to God* controversy.

Bethune-Baker made his comments at the 1921 Girton Conference of the Churchman's Union, soon to be known as the Modern Churchman's Union (MCU). The conference occasioned one of the most significant theological controversies of the century in Britain.[9] The furor concerned controversial statements on Christology made by two of the conference's speakers, Hastings Rashdall and Bethune-Baker. The impression given by (in some cases erroneous) press reports of their speeches was that Rashdall had denied the divinity of Jesus while Bethune-Baker's skepticism about Jesus' divinity virtually amounted to a denial. The controversy that resulted forced the Archbishop of Canterbury, Randall Davidson, to convene an Archbishops' Commission on Doctrine in the Church of England, the purpose of which was to determine exactly what degree of doctrinal leeway was permitted in the church. The Commission did not issue its final report until 1938, but its statements and activities leading up to the report made it clear that the kind of inquiry pursued by liberals like Rashdall and Bethune-Baker was allowable and even commendable. In particular, a statement passed at the 1922 Canterbury Convocation stopped well short of disciplining the modernists, handing them what one historian has described as "an ecclesiastical victory."[10]

Thanks to the Girton Conference and its aftermath, the year 1922 had every appearance of marking the start of liberal theology's ascendancy on the British theological scene. Instead, the liberals were put on the defensive and would not emerge as a strong theological force until the 1960s. The upshot of the controversy in the short term was that liberal theologians enjoyed a kind of protected status in the Church. The presence of the liberal party within the Church of England was solidified, a development which also encouraged non-Anglican liberal theologians in an increasingly ecumenical age. This solidified presence did not mean, however, that theological liberalism was ascendant, for the theological tide of the next few decades would be against it. The failure of theological liberalism to make much headway in these decades was in part due to the fact that the Modern Churchmen were not cut out to be a bold vanguard for theological change. Ironically, most members of the MCU were deeply conservative in both temperament and politics, a characteristic epitomized most prominently in the 1920s and 1930s by Dean of St. Paul's Cathedral, longtime *Evening Standard* columnist, and sometime president of the MCU William Ralph Inge. But, more significantly, liberalism was outflanked by theological developments on the Continent. One of the main reasons for this was the appearance in Britain of the work of Karl Barth, for the very point of Barth's "neo-orthodoxy" was to attack the liberal theological program, in particular its focus on human religious experience. Only after the impact of Barth's work was superseded by that of Rudolf Bultmann would British theologians again focus their attention on human religious experience, a shift that provided the ideal context for discussions of myth's place in theology.[11] One historian of modernist and liberal theology in Britain has observed that the legacy of the modernism that culminated in the Girton Conference was "to have done some of the heavy spade work in turning over the soil and exposing to the air the issues that theology would have to tackle in the modern age."[12] However, most of these issues would not be tackled in earnest until the 1960s. But it was appropriate that when this renaissance of liberal British theology arrived, it was initiated by a theologian, Alec Vidler, who had been influenced and inspired by what he termed the "post-neo-orthodoxy" of Bultmann.[13]

Alec Vidler, the "Cambridge theologians," and the resurgence of liberal theology

When Robinson's *Honest to God* appeared it was widely described as the harbinger of a resurgence of liberal—soon to be called radical—theology in the 1960s.[14] That resurgence had first taken shape among a circle of Cambridge theologians that coalesced around Vidler at the beginning of the decade. Indeed it would be fair to say that their work marked a revival of liberal theology in Britain after several decades of relative quiescence. Vidler is a significant figure not only because of the shadow he cast as a scholar and theologian, but also because the trajectory of his career, which resembled many of his contemporaries', throws an instructive light on the theological context of the time. The "Cambridge theology" that he helped popularize in the early 1960s helped prepare the way for *Honest to God* by creating the impression, in Vidler's words, "that there was going to be a new deal in the presentation of the faith and a salutary upheaval in the Church."[15] Indeed Robinson's book caused such a stir in part because it followed hard on the heels of a collection of theological essays, edited by Vidler, entitled *Soundings*. Thus the media was able to portray *Honest to God* as the latest work of radical theology by a theologian with links to Cambridge.

By the early 1960s Vidler was a theologian and church historian of considerable stature with a long history of involvement in various schemes that sought to mobilize theological resources to shape society. Along with luminaries such as T.S. Eliot, John Middleton Murray, Michael Polanyi, and Karl Mannheim he had been one of the members of the group known as "the Moot." Organized by the ecumenical activist J.H. Oldham in the 1940s, this influential group met four times a year to present and discuss papers on the pressing issues of the day. Around the same time Vidler had also started his own discussion network known as St. Deiniol's Koinonia, named for the St. Deiniol's Library in Wales where Vidler was Warden. In the late 1940s he took over for Oldham as director of the Christian Frontier Council. This was an organization that Oldham had devised to help those in positions of societal importance—scientists, civil servants, teachers, and the like—develop ethical standards to guide their work.

Thus, when Vidler moved to Cambridge in 1956 to become dean of King's College, he brought with him several decades of experience working on the frontier where theology intersected with social life. During these decades his theology had moved from an early Anglo-Catholicism to, during the war years, a more eclectic theology influenced by Continental neo-Orthodoxy and Reinhold Niebuhr's theology of political and social realism. By the time he arrived at Cambridge he had distanced himself somewhat from neo-orthodoxy. He was convinced, in part by his involvement with the laypeople of the Christian Frontier Council, that the pressing theological need in Britain was for an interpretation of Christian belief and doctrine that answered to the concerns of the contemporary believer. Neo-orthodoxy no longer met this requirement, for it had become an overly-specialized theological enclave, keeping out the average believer with walls of jargon. Vidler was also dissatisfied with the trivialities of 1950s theological discourse, which in his view was all too taken up with pointless, incessant discussions of secondary matters. It was a time, he later said, "when theology was doughy rather than yeasty," a situation he sought to change.[16] It was these motivations that, with the example of the Moot in mind, motivated Vidler to convene a like-minded group of theologians who would be committed to critical inquiry into basic matters of belief.[17]

The group that Vidler invited to meet in his rooms was comprised of mostly younger theologians who shared his conviction that it was time for a new era of critical inquiry in the church, and this inquiry should be for the benefit of laypeople who could not relate to traditional statements of the Christian message. Ironically, John Robinson, whose name would become synonymous with radical theology, was not invited to join, as at the time he was considered to be too conservative.[18] The group's views appeared in public form in 1962 in a volume entitled *Soundings*. The essays were of course diverse, but a theme that linked them together was to take contemporary experience of laypeople as the starting point for theological reasoning. In other words, the controlling premise of the volume was that issues of Christian belief should be approached from the perspective of human experience, rather than from a desire to defend orthodoxy.

However controversial were some of the opinions expressed in *Soundings*, television media was mainly responsible for catapulting the volume through several printings. Just before the book appeared in print, Vidler appeared on the BBC religious affairs program *Meeting Point*. He took the opportunity to criticize harshly the current state of the Church of England, charging it with being complacent, intellectually stifling, and removed from the concerns of ordinary people. His remarks immediately sparked a media controversy that served as a publicity platform for the release of *Soundings*. Thanks to such publicity, "Cambridge theology"—critical, questioning and concerned with articulating a faith that would answer the needs of contemporary believers—came to be seen as the first stirrings of an emerging "radical" theology. This impression was reinforced when in 1963 Vidler and other Cambridge theologians put on a lecture series that was later published under the provocative title *Objections to Christian Belief*.[19] Vidler's significance in connection with myth-oriented theology, then, was as the instigator of a strand of radical theology that was centrally concerned with finding a new language for expressing the faith. Robinson's work both responded to and further developed this vein,[20] which would be at the center of British theology into the 1970s, culminating in books such as *The Myth of God Incarnate*. In other words, the myth-oriented theology of the 1960s and 1970s was one dimension of an emerging radical theology that had been given its original impetus by Vidler and associated "Cambridge theologians." Moreover, it was this Cambridge group's influence that helped give subsequent myth-oriented theology its orientation toward lay concerns.

Bultmann and demythologizing in Britain

Though the turn to myth in British theology was part of the ongoing development of the liberal wing of theology in Britain, it was also the result of developments within the narrower field of New Testament scholarship. Debates about myth in British theology were part of an extended interaction with modernity that had its roots in the Enlightenment. One of the major developments that shaped this interaction was historical and textual criticism of the Bible, which had its origins in the work of the French scholars like Richard Simon in the late seventeenth century and Jean Astruc in the early to mid-eighteenth century, before developing into the German "higher criticism" in the mid- to late eighteenth century. Post-Second World War examinations of the role of myth in the New Testament were in one sense an outgrowth of much older debates about the historical reliability of biblical texts.

In the twentieth century, around the time of the First World War, historical criticism and interpretation of the Bible became linked with the attempt by various theologians to respond to modernity. That is, historical study of the Bible was increasingly framed as a necessary response to perceived secularization, which was seen as partly due to the "modern" person's difficulties in believing traditional Christian doctrine. As Keith Clements explains, "By the years just prior to the First World War we find churchmen anxiously talking about the 'modern age' as something not only quite distinct from the realm of organized religion but threatening it—and seeing it implicitly as *the norm* for the population."[21] On this view, the task of theology was to reconceptualize traditional, now unintelligible, forms of belief so that they could be accepted by the modern believer. Historical criticism could aid this project by helping to identify the essential, indispensable elements in the biblical texts so that these could be shorn of the ancient cultural thought forms in which they were clothed.

Such a desire to extract the true meaning of biblical texts was at the heart of the work of the German New Testament scholar Rudolph Bultmann. Bultmann's work, especially his call to "demythologize" the New Testament, bears examination here because of its immense influence on British theology in the post-Second World War period. Thanks to English translations of his work that began to appear in the late 1940s, by mid-century questions that Bultmann raised "about the mythical character and meaning of the Christian faith dominated the agenda of modern theology."[22] Several of Bultmann's central ideas would become important in Britain when theologians there took up the question of myth's place in theology, in particular his notion of "demythologizing" and his understanding of myth as a symbolic expression of human experience of the world. As Rowan Williams has observed, Bultmann's work contributed to a theological shift in Britain whereby, from the late 1940s on, issues of New Testament interpretation, rather than doctrinal or systematic issues, came to occupy the center of theological debate.[23] This renewed focus on the New Testament was a precondition for the debates about Christianity and myth that would dominate theology in the 1960s.

When Bultmann began to develop his ideas on mythology in the Bible he was already a respected New Testament scholar and one of the pioneers of the method known as form criticism. He saw the purpose of his scholarly work as enabling a more effective proclamation of the Christian message. This was the motivation behind the 1941 lecture in which he first proposed the project of demythologizing the New Testament. The lecture was intended to offer practical guidance to former students who were serving as chaplains in the German army.[24] Bultmann wanted to suggest how unnecessary obstacles to hearing the Christian message, which he called the *kerygma*, could be cleared away. He argued that the mythological worldview of the New Testament was simply incredible to modern people, and prevented them from appreciating the core of the Christian message. He singled out two aspects of New Testament mythology that were especially problematic, its anthropomorphism and its premodern, prescientific cosmology. Bultmann contended: "Myth speaks of gods in the same way as of men, of their actions as human actions, with the difference that it imagines the gods to be endowed with superhuman power and their actions to be incalculable."[25] Such anthropomorphizing of God, which emphasized his action in the ordinary order of events, was unbelievable to modern Europeans who held a scientific view of the world. Similarly, the prescientific cosmology of the New Testament, with its three-story universe and world of spirits and miracles, could only be seen by moderns as hopelessly primitive.

At the same time, Bultmann contended that, since none of these aspects of the New Testament mythology were specifically Christian, they were obstacles that could be cleared away. They could be discarded at the same time that the *kerygma*, the core Christian message, was preserved. Bultmann was criticized for viewing myth too harshly, but he insisted that this was a misunderstanding. He maintained that myth is a vehicle for religious truth, in the sense that myth expresses humanity's understanding of its existential position in the world: "The real point in myth is not to give an objective world picture; what is expressed in it, rather, is how we human beings understand ourselves in our world."[26] Thus, Bultmann was not proposing a rejection of biblical myth on scientific grounds, but rather a translation of that myth so that the truths it embodied about the human situation would be apparent to moderns. In language that betrayed the influence of Heideggerian existentialism he insisted that "Myth does not want to be interpreted in cosmological terms but in anthropological terms—or better, in existentialist terms."[27] He insisted that he had no desire to make the *kerygma* "more acceptable to modern man by trimming traditional biblical texts, but to make clearer to modern man what the Christian faith is."[28] In other words, biblical myths were a vehicle for the Christian message, but not a necessary one: "In Bultmann's famous, if excruciatingly confusing, phrase, one must 'demythologize' myth, which means not eliminating, or 'demythicizing,' the mythology but instead extricating the true, existential meaning of that mythology."[29] Thus, the point of demythologizing was to "disclose the deepest religious truths that inhere within Christian myth."[30]

These arguments were grist to Robinson's mill in *Honest to God*. Robinson's book both revealed an intellectual debt to Bultmann's demythologizing thesis while at the same time emphasizing the theological necessity of mythical and symbolic language. Robinson made it clear that he had no objection to myth as such, for myth was inherent to all religious belief. Rather, his concern was to suggest that Christianity be purged of certain unnecessary mythical aspects that no longer resonated with moderns:

> To demythologize—as Bultmann would readily concede—is not to suppose that we can dispense with all myth or symbol. It is to cut our dependence upon one particular mythology—of what Tillich calls the 'superworld of divine objects'—which is in peril of becoming a source of incredulity rather than an aid to faith. Any alternative language ... is bound to be equally symbolic. But it may speak more 'profoundly' to the soul of modern man.[31]

The necessity of preserving only those mythical elements that were relevant to modern believers meant a new direction for theology,

Robinson argued. Instead of preservation, its task was a sort of continual renovation: "Without the constant discipline of theological thought, asking what we mean by symbols, purging out the dead myths...the Church can quickly become obscurantist."[32] Robinson essentially advocated, to the extent that it was possible, replacing Christian myths and symbols that no longer seemed meaningful with myths and symbols that did. His preferred option was to follow Paul Tillich in abandoning conceptions of a God "out there" in favor of language about God as the "ground of being." He acknowledged that the latter was no less mythical that the former, but he claimed that it was more relevant to modern concerns.

With each attempt to defend his book in the debates that followed its publication, Robinson clarified his views on myth further. In doing so he acknowledged how Bultmann had shaped his thinking and he framed his arguments as an effort to spell out his own understanding of the implications of Bultmann's thought. Robinson wanted to find a way to sever the mythology of the New Testament from a form of supernaturalism which he thought many modern people could not accept. He had no desire to discard mythology and in fact argued that it was indispensable not just to theology but also to human understanding of the world:

> Myth is of profound and permanent significance in human thought: most of us will always think and theologize in pictures. The crisis of our age is simply bound up with the necessity of being forced to distinguish myth for what it is, so that we may be able to evaluate it aright and use it without dishonesty and inhibition.[33]

Thus, the challenge for modern Christians, in Robinson's view, was to separate myth from history while realizing that mythological statements in the Bible were there to convey the theological significance of historical events. "God sent his only-begotten Son" was such a mythological statement, "*not* in the sense that it is not true, but in the sense that it represents the theological significance of the history.... The important thing is that what is history is no more true because it is history nor what is myth less true because it is myth."[34] He summarized the essence of his position by stating, "My concern...is not to throw out the myths, but precisely to enable us to use them."[35]

As Robinson's references to it suggest, Bultmann's work was in effect the door through which "the myth question" entered post-Second World War British theology. His proposal to demythologize the New

Testament was initially appealing to liberal theologians in Britain because it coincided with their efforts to craft an intellectually acceptable version of Christianity for the modern believer.[36] In the early 1950s Bultmann's main works began to appear in Britain in English and thereafter an attendant body of critical literature on him rapidly emerged. This literature soon began to reflect a theological consensus that Bultmann took his case too far, even though he drew attention to some important ways in which the New Testament was riddled with myth. British theologians criticized Bultmann's view of myth on two fronts. One was that his understanding of myth was based on discredited anthropology that viewed myth as the product of a primitive mentality. The other, related criticism was that Bultmann was too willing to jettison meaningful ancient myths out of deference to what the "modern mind" was able to accept. Whereas Bultmann seemed to assume that the modern mind had no taste for myth, many British theologians argued that myth was the natural idiom of religious language and theologians must therefore learn to use it in a way that was relevant to modern people.

This position was summed up by G.V. Jones, one of the first British theologians to engage at length with Bultmann's ideas. In his book-length critique of Bultmann, Jones contended that "myth is the language of religion and should be taken seriously as such."[37] Jones pointed out that Bultmann's peculiar definition of myth prevented him from realizing this and from recognizing that mythological thinking was part of the fabric of modern societies. A more recent critic of Bultmann has argued that "Bultmann is operating with a defective concept of myth. He is confusing presuppositions about worldview with myth as a genre."[38] This was essentially Jones's objection. He admitted that

> the Western mind has run into difficulty with religious and mythological language because it mistakes 'symbolical expressions of the inexpressible' for statements of objective truth. The modern mind, of which the philosophy of logical positivism is but one symptomatic expression, asks for "objective" facts and for literal intelligibility.[39]

Nevertheless, he contended, mythological thinking was deeply ingrained in modern societies, even though many did not realize this. He explained that

> Primitive peoples think mythologically, but not all who so think are primitive; indeed, mythological thinking may be evident in the most

fully developed religion and in advanced civilizations and may...be an indispensable mode of religious perception.[40]

This was because "myth is the 'symbolization of the infinite' and the only language adequate to this symbolization. For this reason the mythical is not merely a primitive type of mentality to be outgrown."[41] Jones's view that myth is the natural idiom of religion and that theologians should be unapologetic about this became a common view among British theologians.

Theologians like Jones who argued that myth was not merely a primitive thought form took support from the pathbreaking work of the Oxford anthropologist E.E. Evans-Pritchard. Evans-Pritchard's work minimized the gap between the primitive and the modern by emphasizing the continuing significance of mythic and religious thought. Since the late nineteenth century British theologians had been aware of research on myth by anthropologists and scholars of comparative religion. From this work they concluded that myth-making was an activity that took place in all ancient human cultures, including the cultures that had produced the Hebrew Bible and the New Testament. But, for the most part, British theologians saw this work as corrosive of Christian belief, for it was often presented as a debunking of foundational Christian texts and beliefs. Evans-Pritchard's work began to shift this widespread view. As Adrian Hastings has pointed out, in the post-Second World War period theologians were for the first time able to gain some support from a discipline that had since the late nineteenth century been inimical to religious belief. Evans-Pritchard's works on the Azande and Nuer tribes had shown that such "primitives" had more in common with "moderns" than the latter were willing to recognize. As Hastings puts it, in his work "Dichotomy is replaced by a continuity that finds room for rationality among 'primitives' and religion among 'moderns.' "[42]

Beginning in the 1950s Evans-Pritchard increasingly turned to theoretical work that developed themes often implicit in his earlier, field-study-based works. This eventually culminated in his influential 1965 work *Theories of Primitive Religion*. The book developed at length a criticism he had been voicing for at least a decade: prevailing anthropological theories of religion were wrongheaded, irrational, and biased. The work showed how most anthropologists proceeded on the unwarranted *a priori* assumption that religion was illusory. This assumption was reinforced by the tendency of anthropologists to attribute motivations to their subjects that are actually closer to those of the researchers themselves. What this amounted to, Evans-Pritchard argued, was a failure to understand primitive religion on its own terms. Anthropologists needed to recognize that religion was a unique phenomenon: it could not be understood in straightforward functional terms and religious beliefs, as well as the mythic language in which they were expressed, could not simply be taken as evidence of the "pre-logical" nature of a people. Such views shaped the thinking of British theologians as they responded to Bultmann's provocative thesis about the relation between myth and Christianity, giving them a basis for their criticism that his equation of "mythical" with "primitive" was unwarranted.

By early 1960s, the main tendency of theologians in Britain was to credit Bultmann for showing how the mythological language of the Bible could be an obstacle to belief, while disputing his suggestion that such language should be thrown overboard as unacceptable to the modern mind or translated into the vocabulary of Heiddegerian existentialism. As one theologian summed up this consensus, "Translation is desirable and necessary, but it is dangerous and cannot be allowed to go too far."[43] If religious believers were going to continue to speak about what was fundamentally inexpressible, British theologians reasoned, then they must speak using the language of myth or not at all. Characteristic of this position was a review of some of Bultmann's writings in the British journal *Theology*. The reviewer, James Mark, argued that myth, conceived of as "an account which is incapable of verification," would always be a necessary and important form of discourse for Christians:

> There are limits to human knowledge which, it seems, we cannot surpass. There are events of which we can form no conception.... If we wish to speak of these things, we must do so in the language of myth.... The question is whether we want to or not. Bultmann's assumption is that modern man either does not or finds it impossible.[44]

But Mark disagreed, arguing instead that the correct course was not to give up on myth, but to "learn afresh how to use the language of myth."[45]

A crisis of theological discourse and a new way forward

Mark's definition of myth as "an account which is incapable of verification" is a clue to why British theologians increasingly turned to myth in the 1960s. If myth was by definition incapable of verification, then it could not fall victim to the critiques of scientists or—of greater concern at the time—the critiques of analytic and linguistic philosophers.[46] This attempt to place the subject matter of theology beyond the reach of science and philosophy was a common move by British theologians of the period. It was a response to what they perceived to be a crisis of theological discourse.[47] Mark's review of Bultmann, the *Soundings* volume, and *Honest to God* can all be seen as efforts to resolve this crisis. And it was liberal theologians who felt this crisis most acutely, as they had historically emphasized the need to present Christian belief in language relevant and intelligible to the modern believer. What is more, for liberals the depth of the crisis was underscored by secularization itself, which they saw precisely as the result of the Church's failure to adapt its way of speaking to modern minds. To theologians confronting such a crisis the concept of myth offered a way forward, as evident in Mark's review of Bultmann's work. But the way forward involved a new strategy in liberal theology. Grounding theology in the explication of Christian myths was in harmony with traditional liberal concerns about articulating the faith in a way that was relevant and credible. At the same time it was a departure from traditional liberal tactics in that the focus was no longer on reconciling Christian belief with modern knowledge by minimizing incredible doctrines. Instead, the issue of Christianity's conflict with modern knowledge was virtually sidestepped. By defending myth as the natural idiom of religion, as a way of speaking about the meaning of human existence that by definition could not conflict with scientific or historical knowledge, liberal theologians sought to circumvent what they saw as some of the key obstacles to Christian faith in the modern world. This was a strategy born of crisis and anxiety about the status of theological discourse.

The anxieties of theologians during this period were primarily about finding a mode of expression for theology that would answer the intellectual charges then being leveled at the discipline. Editorials, articles, and book reviews in theological journals of the period were, as much as any other single topic, concerned with how theologians could and should say what they wanted to say. The intellectual challenges that were setting the agenda of British theology all seemed to boil down to the issue of theological discourse. More specifically, the repercussions of Bultmann's work and the implications of analytic philosophy forced theologians to confront the way they articulated the faith to a modern audience. The former suggested that the entire vocabulary of Christianity would need to be reformulated, while the latter suggested that what theologians said was actually meaningless.

In the mid-1960s the *New Yorker* essayist Ved Mehta went to Britain in an attempt to come to terms with the new, radical theology taking shape there. He found there as much anxiety about the state of the theological discipline as he did enthusiasm for the new theology then taking shape. And the anxiety was in part about how theologians could make an intellectually credible case for their faith. Mehta reported,

> Most of the theologians I met in England acknowledged at one time or another that the Achilles' heel of their calling might be a lack of extended training in philosophy, admitting that their reasoning powers were not always up to defending their faith, and this at a time when most theologians wished to have a reasoned faith and to be able to conduct a dialogue with agnostics and rationalists.[48]

Ninian Smart, one of the most prominent "Cambridge theologians," struck a similar note in a 1965 article diagnosing "The Intellectual Crisis of British Christianity."[49] Smart laid blame for the crisis on analytic and linguistic philosophy: "Christianity is in an intellectual crisis in Britain. This has to do, broadly, with philosophy." But theologians' scrambling attempts to respond to philosophical critiques had only made a muddle of theology. He explained that

> After the last war, linguistic philosophy boomed, and religious intellectuals became sensitive. You didn't want so much to show that religion is true as that it is meaningful.... But the intellectuals were sensitive too about empiricism. So we had analyses (or supposed analyses) of religious language which made its meaning look strange. These unrealistic accounts of religious language have proved quite incapable of providing a secret defence of Christianity.[50]

Such wrongheaded attempts to accommodate Christianity to modern philosophy had helped further a lamentable "modern trend towards formulating a non-theistic Christianity."[51] Smart's main point was that theologians were philosophically incompetent, and their incompetence resulted in theological ventures that were counterproductive, serving only to induce skepticism about the possibility of a transcendent God. Hence Smart's contention that "The way forward in discussion is by reconstructing the concept of a transcendent...being," something only possible if philosophy were to become "an integral part" of theological education.[52]

Smart envisioned a theological discipline that, without conceding everything to modern philosophy, could at least engage with it. His reference to an emerging "non-theistic Christianity" was a gibe at philosophers like R.B. Braithwaite. In the 1950s Braithwaite developed his own expressivist theory of religious belief,[53] which led him to join the Church of England. Seeking to respond to the extreme empiricist position which held that religious statements were meaningless, he contended that the Christian myth had value regardless of how historically true it might be: "A man is not, I think, a professing Christian unless he both purposes to live according to Christian moral principles and associates his intention with thinking of Christian stories; but he need not believe that the empirical propositions presented by the stories correspond to empirical fact."[54] Most observers found this position indistinguishable from atheism.

Far closer to the constructive engagement with philosophy that Smart had in mind was the work of the philosopher B.M.G. Reardon, who in the early 1960s offered a philosophically-informed defense of myth's fundamental importance for theology. Reardon was a leading example of a philosophically trained theologian who concluded that, far from dismissing myth as irrelevant to modernity, modern theories of myth emphasized the ongoing importance of mythic thinking as that type of discourse which articulated humanity's sense of its own existence. In his view, science had shown itself "incapable" of offering this sort of meaning. But science's inability pointed toward the necessity of theology, for "religion, as a projection of the mythical consciousness, can claim to be necessary for the authentification of man's being."[55] Reardon elaborated in terms that many of his peers in theology would have found it easy to agree with: "Theology, which is only a more overtly pictorial form of metaphysics, perpetuates myth not merely by its use of image-language but by its capacity to articulate those permanent impulses of our humanity of which myth is the archetypal expression."[56] This view was attractive to theologians who wanted to accord myth a central place in theological discourse. Writing a year later in 1963, John Robinson was already echoing them in an article on modern theology in *Twentieth Century*: "we are now getting used to the idea of myth in relation to, say, the Genesis stories. Today these are no longer understood as history. Their function, rather, is to give pictorial representation to certain theological truths about the human situation and the interpretation of the universe. It is an interpretation that cannot be expressed in anything other than poetic language."[57]

Thus, by the 1960s liberal theologians in Britain were divided into two camps. One camp, represented by figures like R.B. Braithwaite and Ian Ramsey, sought to continue the traditional liberal project of pushing theology in an empirical direction. This meant reformulating the faith so that it did not conflict with modern science, historical criticism, and philosophy. And of these, during the post-Second World War period the challenges of analytic and linguistic philosophy were of greatest concern to theologians. But the other camp of liberal theologians aimed to take theology in a new direction that would circumvent the scientific, philosophical and historical challenges that had traditionally concerned liberals. They would achieve this by explicating the mythical nature of Christian belief. Whereas liberal theologians of the pre-Second World War period had an essentially pejorative view of myth, these postwar liberals affirmed the value of myth as essentially the language of religion. Like many of their contemporaries in the field of English studies, these myth-inclined theologians assumed that myth was significantly related to the subject matter of their discipline. In their attempt to understand this relationship and argue for myth's central place in theological discourse, they drew on the insights about myth offered by the disciplines of anthropology, psychology, and comparative religion. As one observer of the theological scene put it:

[M]any earlier liberals were convinced theology had outgrown mythical thinking in favor of more scientific modes of thought grounded in philosophy, history, psychology, and sociology.... Modern myth studies have located the function of myth at the deepest levels of person and culture, and thus have provided a whole new basis for the positive evaluation of myth.[58]

The task of theology then became to interpret Christian myth and determine what normative theological role should be ascribed to the mythical content of the Bible. This is what Robinson had in mind in *Honest to God* when he advocated "the constant discipline of theological thought, asking what we mean by symbols, purging out the dead myths."[59]

These efforts of liberal British theologians to reorient their discipline around myth were premised on a shared understanding of modernity. According to this definition, modernity was characterized by the intellectual hegemony of science and a general acceptance of a scientific view of the world. At the same time, these theologians pointed out that most average people did not hold a consistent or informed scientific worldview, even though they liked to believe that they did. In other words, at the popular level modernity was defined by a reverence for science combined with an unacknowledged tendency to think in anything but scientific terms. This was pointed out by the theologian John Macquarrie, one of the most incisive British commentators on Bultmann. Following Karl Jaspers's critique of Bultmann, Macquarrie noted:

> The implied contrast in Bultmann's thought between the mythical and the scientific is quite misleading. The modern man certainly has a high regard for science and constantly appeals to it, but then... everyone appeals to science and very few are really acquainted with it.... [M]odern man has his quasi-myths...corresponding in many ways to the myths of former generations.[60]

On this view, moderns professed loyalty to a secular, scientific view of the world, yet continued to make sense of their existence through myths. British theologians saw this as an opportunity because if the average modern person was not immune to mythic thinking, then he or she could be persuaded that the Christian myth was more meaningful than modern quasi-myths. But this also posed a challenge to the myth-oriented theologians, for it meant that their efforts to tout the value of Christian myth would depend on the success of their attempts to convince the public that "myth" was not a category opposed to science.[61] As they began to realize in the 1970s, however, this was a more difficult task than they had anticipated.

A high water mark: *The Myth of God Incarnate*

The symposium *The Myth of God Incarnate* was the high water mark of theological engagement with myth in postwar Britain. The contributors to the volume were several of the leading liberal theologians of the period. These included Maurice Wiles, the chair of the Church of England's Doctrine Commission; John Hick, a leading authority on world religions; and Don Cupitt, who would go on to become the most famous of Britain's radical theologians. The symposium was prompted by the "growing knowledge...that the later conception of [Jesus] as God incarnate...is a mythological or poetic way of expressing his significance for us."[62] The strategy throughout the volume was to define myth as a unique form of thought that conveyed its own type of non-scientific, non-historical truth. The contributors conceded the validity of historical criticism and modern scientific knowledge, and they acknowledged that these made it impossible to believe some doctrines in the same way that first-century Christians had. But Christian belief was not therefore compromised, because the mythological language in which it was expressed was not subject to scientific or historical critiques. Because myth did not aspire to "literal" truth in the first place and because mythological language allowed for a considerable flexibility of interpretation, it could be continually adapted in light of new knowledge that changed how core doctrines were conceived. Thus the volume's preface noted that "the pressure upon Christianity is as strong as ever to go on adapting itself into something which can be believed."[63] Conceived of in this way, myth became a highly meaningful way of expressing the unknown or the inexpressible—such as the idea that God became a man—in terms of the known.

This view was clearly articulated by the New Testament scholar Frances Young in her contribution to the volume. She made a point of distinguishing how science and mythology gave very different, but non-conflicting, descriptions of reality:

> As Christian believers, then, we work with (i) the scientific model which finds explanations of phenomena, behavior and events in terms of natural causes, and (ii) what we can only describe as 'mythological' or symbolic models, models which however inadequately represent the religious and spiritual dimension of our experience. To call them 'mythological' is not to denigrate their status, but to indicate that they refer to realities which are not only inaccessible to the normal methods of scientific investigation, but are also indefinable in terms of human language, and in their totality, inconceivable within the limited powers and experience of the finite human mind.[64]

In other words, Young had accepted the view of myth that British theologians had begun articulating in the late 1950s and early 1960s.

Maurice Wiles went more deeply into the issue in his essay on "Myth in Theology." Wiles agreed with other contributors to the symposium that "The tendency in most theological discussions of myth is to think of myths as expressive of timeless truths about God and his relation to the world."[65] The incarnation was just such a myth, though it was also a myth in the sense of a narrative about a past event that defines a community. But what was most attractive to Wiles about myth was its elasticity, its capacity to expand to accommodate a range of belief. He explained: "If what held Christians together were seen as the use of the same myths rather than the holding of the same beliefs, it might be easier for Christians to accept the measure of variety that there both should and will be between them."[66] Viewed in this way, Christians were not necessarily people who believed the same things but rather people who expressed their religious commitments using similar language. Wiles conceded that many would rightly wonder what basis the incarnation myth had in history, asking "what sort of link is there between the myth and the history?"[67] His response was that the myth could still "function as a potent myth" even though "it is acknowledged that it is not literally true."[68] What was far more important than literal truth was that there be "some ontological truth corresponding to the central characteristic of the structure of the myth."[69] Myths that lacked such an ontological correlate should be abandoned as "inappropriate." The editor of the symposium, John Hick, took a similar position in his contribution. He echoed Wiles's language in arguing that myths ought not to be judged in terms of literal truth. Rather, "the truth of a myth is a kind of practical truth consisting in the appropriateness of the attitude to its object."[70]

Wiles conceded that his "ontological correlate" criterion was not easy to apply. And that was not the only note of pessimism in his essay. He doubted whether the mythical understanding of Christianity he recommended could ever serve an apologetic function, given that the popular understanding of myth was so far from the theological understanding. Most people understood myth as something delusive, in the sense that it was both untrue and led people astray. "This must be acknowledged," he admitted, "and the term may remain unusable in the general life of the church."[71] Such a note of pessimism among myth-oriented theologians was new, but it would soon become common. The fissures of doubt in Wiles's piece signaled the beginning of the end of British theologians' quest to reorient their discipline around a positive understanding of myth. Wiles concluded that myth "may still be a valuable tool for theological analysis," and he would be proven correct. But this fell far short of the hopes that British liberal theologians had had for myth in the early 1960s, when they had envisioned nothing less than the dawn of a new era of myth-driven apologetics.

If *The Myth of God Incarnate* and the publicity it generated were any indication, it seemed in the late 1970s that the liberal theology behind the myth and theology discussions of the previous decades was firmly in place. The symposium was but one of several noteworthy works of the 1970s by leading theologians written in a critical liberal spirit, including Geoffrey Lampe's *God as Spirit* (1976), a critique of traditional Trinitarian theology, and Dennis Nineham's *The Use and Abuse of the Bible* (1976). But, as Williams has noted in his evaluation of twentieth-century British theology, the end of the decade was not a moment of triumph for the long tradition of British theological liberalism: "The year 1977 was a high water mark, after which the assumptions and conclusions of the authors of the *Myth* symposium began to shift or fade in the overall intellectual map."[72] That tradition had from the start defined itself in response to "modernity" and, in particular, the intellectual challenges of modernity. The main focus of the liberal tradition had always been reformulating doctrine to make it more intellectually acceptable and relevant for the modern believer. However, by the 1970s theologians were increasingly turning their attention to other concerns as modernity's social and cultural dimensions began to supplant its intellectual dimensions in the theological imagination.

If *The Myth of God Incarnate* effectively marked the end of British theologians' engagement with the myth question, this was a chapter in the history of theology that ended more with a whimper than a bang. When liberal British theologians first began to turn their attention to myth two decades earlier, they had been hopeful that taking theology in this direction would both provide a more secure footing for the discourse of their discipline and allow for a dynamic flexibility in articulating the Christian faith. That is, Christianity was inescapably mythic, because all human attempts to make sense of human existence in religious terms were. But the precise way in which the myth was expressed could be adapted and translated into terms that were more comprehensible to the modern believer than the alien terminology of the New Testament. However, two decades of exploring the relationship between Christianity and myth did not result in the gains that theologians had intended. Despite the protestations of the *Myth* contributors that their hope was only "to release talk about God and about Jesus from confusions," as Adrian Hastings has pointed out, their conclusions seemed to imply "the necessity of winding up historic Christianity, with a minimum of pain to all concerned, as unacceptable to the modern mind."[73] Though liberal myth-oriented theologians advocated the value of myth, they, however unintentionally, reinforced a public perception that myth was unacceptable to the modern mind. In other words, the same tension between myth and modernity that hampered John Robinson's *Honest to God* also vitiated the *Myth* symposium. At the same time that the *Myth* contributors affirmed the unique religious power of myth, they framed their symposium as the latest in a series of "adjustments" that "have made it possible for many inhabitants of our modern science-oriented culture to be Christians today."[74] This was a position that was at once a dissent from and an acceptance of modernity. That such a tension was at the heart of their position perhaps helps explain, at least in part, why the public failed to embrace the proposed myth-centered Christianity.

Conclusion

The legacy of British theologians' attempts to deploy myth in an effort to articulate a modern faith had, at best, mixed results. In part this was because of damage they had done to their own cause. Episodes like the *Myth* symposium, portrayed in the media as an exercise in the debunking of Christian doctrine, reinforced a consensus among laypeople that when theologians talked of "myth" they meant a false narrative that could not stand up to the test of critical history.[75] This was not what most of the contributors to *The Myth* had intended to convey, but that is what many observers concluded.

With such unintended consequences in mind, the Church of England Doctrine Commission's 1981 report *Believing in the Church* warned against use of the term "myth" in theological discourse. No matter how carefully theologians tried to refine their use of the term, myth was still generally understood to mean falsehood. As John Barton and John Halliburton put it in their contribution to the volume, "'The Christian myth' is certainly understood by many people as a polite, theologians' way of saying that Christianity is not true, while trying to save appearances."[76] In particular, argued Anthony Thiselton in his contribution to the report, myth tended to be associated with a primitive worldview, it suggested a form of communication in which thought was wrapped in opaque language, and it was too often linked with subjectivist notions of truth.[77] "[T]he history of modern research into the nature of myth reveals pitfalls and difficulties which far outweigh any advantages" it might offer as a means of meeting critical challenges to Christian faith, Thiselton contended.[78] He acknowledged that myth was not wholly irrelevant to theological concerns, but concluded "that the category 'myth' does not in the end take us very far along the path of trying to clarify the nature of the relation between corporate knowledge and individual criticism. At very least it leaves too many loose ends which lend themselves easily to misunderstanding."[79]

The Doctrine Commission's report indicates how by the end of the 1970s the category of myth had at best an uneasy place in theological discourse, and theologians had lost confidence in using it to present the faith to the public. Barton and Halliburton observed that " 'myth', though potentially a useful word for describing some aspects of the Christian message, is also fraught with dangers and difficulties."[80] Chief among these dangers and difficulties was an endemic "vagueness" which, they concluded, "has been the death of 'myth.' "[81] Their judgment could be read as an epitaph: more than two decades of theological focus on myth had resulted in failure. But indications of potential failure had been there from the beginning. In 1963 John Robinson had observed "that the word 'myth' is still a source of misunderstanding to great numbers of people, and means simply that which is untrue."[82] But in the late 1970s British theologians were still saying the same thing; they knew that their repeated attempts to correct this misunderstanding had failed and they began to draw back from myth as a result. Myth would remain in use as a common category of analysis for many British theologians, though its apologetic efficacy and appropriateness were increasingly doubted. In the end, the "myth question" in contemporary theology was, as one observer noted, an "irreconcilable issue."[83] This was because the split between the liberal theologians who favored a normative role for philosophy in theology and those who ascribed a normative role to myth was unlikely to be resolved.

The turn to myth in British theology was part of an attempt to respond to and negotiate the challenges of modernity. By defending the religious significance of myth British theologians believed they were defending Christianity itself against the intellectual challenges of modernity. But instead of dealing effectively with these challenges, this strategy only succeeded in pushing British theology further in the direction of cultural irrelevance. By its own standards the attempt to make Christianity relevant by attending to its mythic dimensions was a failed project. This was in part because the understanding of myth embraced by theologians committed their discipline to an anthropological turn in which human expressions about God, rather than the relationship between humanity and God, became the discipline's primary subject matter. Such a project, driven as it was by conclusions and methods borrowed from anthropology, comparative religion, history, and philosophy, could only succeed in making theology into a hybrid that was a pale imitation of those disciplines. In *The Myth of God Incarnate* Maurice Wiles observed that theology was increasingly reliant on other disciplines,[84] but this reliance could be more of a crutch than a creative resource. Wiles's observation illustrates the ironic position of many twentieth-century advocates of myth: by turning to myth in order to limit modernity's impact on the faith, they in fact implicated themselves even more deeply in that very modernity. Without a distinct subject matter, methodology, or perspective of its own, theology's ability to offer a compelling interpretation of the human experience was eroded. Theology's current position as an academic discipline in Britain reflects this: it has been largely absorbed into the discipline of religious studies. This marginal position explains why so much theology is driven by a desire for "relevance" in attempt to recapture a lost position of cultural authority.

In response to broader social and cultural changes, British theologians in the 1970s were seeking new ways to be relevant. As Gary Dorrien has noted, modernist and liberal theologians often made global pronouncements about what "modern man" was capable of believing. But by the 1970s it was becoming increasingly difficult to frame theology in terms of confident pronouncements about the "modern" theological situation.[85] Instead of privileging the concerns of the "modern man," theologians began to listen to voices they had previously ignored. This meant that questions of social justice were brought to the forefront of theology as its agenda was increasingly defined by the concerns and experiences of marginalized religious communities instead of by the perceived needs of "modern man." Thus, during the 1970s theology on the left side of the theological spectrum was shifting from a liberal to a liberationist mode. In other words, myth-oriented theology was eclipsed from the theological left as liberal theologians shifted their attention from the intellectual challenges of modernity to its social and cultural challenges. Some fruits of this shift were the creative and highly productive fields of liberation theology, feminist theology, and—prompted in part by an increasingly multiethnic Britain—theology exploring the relationship of Christianity to other religions. Thus, in a fascinating and ironic turn of events, theologians who had once made it their business to explain the unique value of the Christian myth now began to come to grips with the myths at heart of other world religions.

Epilogue

During the heyday of twentieth-century mythic thinking, the novelist and philosopher Iris Murdoch observed, "The mythical is not something 'extra'; we live in myth and symbol all the time."[1] To live in modern Britain was to be surrounded by myth. The British path to modernity was winding, uncertain, and took travelers into unmarked territory. The modern problem was perforce to tread this path into the unknown, as well-worn structures of meaning were left behind. Along this path the British people constructed fencerows, planted hedges, established way stations, and erected signposts in the form of myth. These eased the journey and gave it meaning. This study has sought to illuminate some of those attempts to make meaning through myth.

My survey of mythic thinking as a characteristic of British modernity has been admittedly suggestive rather than exhaustive. It therefore leaves much scope for future research into the phenomenon. First, some of the best scholarship on the unique nature of British modernity has examined specific cases or individuals that embody its productive tensions. Noteworthy examples include Michael Saler's *The Avant-Garde in Interwar England* and Scott Anthony's *Public Relations and the Making of Modern Britain*.[2] One thing these studies highlight is the *imaginative* aspect of the making of British modernity, which was produced not simply by political, economic, and technological forces, but also by people who self-consciously embraced their imaginations without compromising their rationality.[3] Are historians willing to embrace "imagination" as a category of historical analysis? If so, future examinations of mythic thinking or related phenomena might do well to probe its links with different conceptions and uses of the imagination.

Second, there is a need for more in-depth studies of how mythic thinking manifested in popular and political culture, as opposed to literary and high culture. How did those who were not intellectuals use myth to construct and understand the experience of modernity? Myth was not alien to popular and political culture prior to the end of the period considered here. We know, for example, that the Suffragettes employed mythic iconography and dressed themselves as figures from classical mythology for parades and other public events.[4] It is also the case that images drawn from mythology appeared frequently in twentieth-century advertising, such as posters for the London Underground.[5] We know too that Tolkien's work was welcomed by and promoted among extreme right-wing British nationalists, as much as this dismayed Tolkien himself. The steps in the history of mythic thinking that I have examined here could well be retraced with an eye to elucidating the popular uses of myth throughout the century.

Finally, there is a related need for examinations of how myth has been used as a tool for refashioning the self and constructing characteristically modern forms of belief. One aspect of twentieth-century mythic thinking was its privatization or subjectivization. Charles Taylor has suggested that one aspect of the postmodern suspicion toward metanarratives is a "slide to subjectivism," evident in a shift toward "self-centered modes of the ideal of self-fulfilment [sic] in the popular culture of our time."[6] The recent history of mythic thinking seems to bear out his thesis. Perhaps the most salient example is the importance of myth to new age spirituality in Britain, a cultural phenomenon in which both Celtic and Arthurian mythology figure prominently and which has connections to the mythic fantasy literature that became a twentieth-century cultural phenomenon.[7] Mythic thinkers turned to myth because they saw it as timeless, but throughout the century the meaning of "myth" was continually changing in relation to the times. These shifting meanings, and the ways in which they illuminate the unique nature of British modernity, have by no means yet been fully explored.

Notes

1 Myth and the Modern Problem

1. W.H. Auden, "Yeats as an Example," *Kenyon Review* 10, no. 2 (1948): 191–92.
2. On attempts to create a common culture during the interwar period, see Dan LeMahieu, *A Cuture for Democracy: Mass Culture and the Cultivated Mind in Britain Between the Wars* (New York: Oxford University Press, 1988).
3. W.H. Auden, "A Contemporary Epic," *Encounter* 2, no. 2 (February 1954): 69; T.S. Eliot, "The Romantic Englishman, the Comic Spirit, and the Function of Criticism," in idem, *The Annotated* Waste Land *with Eliot's Contemporary Prose*, ed. Lawrence Rainey (New Haven, CT: Yale University Press, 2005), 141.
4. W.K.C. Guthrie, "Myth and Reason: Oration Delivered at the London School of Economics and Political Science on Friday, 12 December, 1952," (London: London School of Economics and Political Science, 1953), 7.
5. Ibid., 18–9. Italics in original.
6. Reprinted in Ted Hughes, *Winter Pollen: Occasional Prose*, ed. William Scammell (London: Faber and Faber, 1994), 151–52. This is a somewhat revised version of the address Hughes originally delivered in 1970.
7. See Philip Rahv, "The Myth and the Powerhouse," *Partisan Review* 20 (November–December 1953): 635–48.
8. Frank Kermode, "The Myth-Kitty," *Spectator*, 11 September 1959, 339.
9. For an excellent discussion of the difficulties involved in defining myth see Chapter 2 of William Doty, *Myth: A Handbook* (Westport, CT: Greenwood Press, 2004). Other key works in this body of literature include Bruce Lincoln, *Theorizing Myth: Narrative, Ideology, and Scholarship* (Chicago, IL: University of Chicago Press, 1999), Robert A. Segal, *Theorizing about Myth* (Amherst, MA: University of Massachusetts Press, 1999); idem, ed., *Psychology and Myth*, vol. 1 of idem, ed., *Theories of Myth: From Ancient Israel and Greece to Freud, Jung, Campbell and Lévi-Strauss* (New York: Garland Publishing, Inc., 1996); idem, ed., *Literary Criticism and Myth*, vol. 4 of idem, ed., *Theories of Myth: From Ancient Israel and Greece to Freud, Jung, Campbell and Lévi-Strauss* (New York: Garland Publishing, Inc., 1996); Laurence Coupe, *Myth* (London: Routledge, 1997); and Eric Csapo, *Theories of Mythology* (Malden, MA: Blackwell, 2005).
10. Elizabeth M. Baeten, *The Magic Mirror: Myth's Abiding Power* (Albany, NY: State University of New York Press, 1996).
11. Segal, *Theorizing about Myth*, 23.
12. C.S. Lewis, *Collected Letters: Volume I, Family Letters 1905–1931*, ed. Walter Hooper (London: HarperCollins, 2000), 976.
13. Lincoln, ix.
14. See H. Stuart Hughes, *Consciousness and Society: The Reorientation of European Social Thought, 1890–1930* (New York: Vintage Books, 1958).
15. J.R.R. Tolkien, "On Fairy-Stories," in *Essays Presented to Charles Williams* (Oxford: Oxford University Press, 1947), 72.

16. For some recent examples see Michael Bell, *Literature, Modernism and Myth: Belief and Responsibility in the Twentieth Century* (Cambridge: Cambridge University Press, 1997), Roslyn Reso Foy, *Ritual, Myth, and Mysticism in the Work of Mary Butts: Between Feminism and Modernism* (Fayetteville, AR: University of Arkansas Press, 2000), Randall Stevenson, *Modernist Fiction: An Introduction* (Lexington, KY: The University Press of Kentucky, 1992), Jewel Spears Brooker, *Mastery and Escape: T.S. Eliot and the Dialectic of Modernism* (Amherst, MA: University of Massachusetts Press, 1994); Milton Scarborough, *Myth and Modernity: Postcritical Reflections* (Albany, NY: State University of New York Press, 1994), Laurence Coupe, *Myth* (London: Routledge, 1997).

17. Examples included John B. Vickery, *The Literary Impact of* The Golden Bough (Princeton, NJ: Princeton University Press, 1973); Robert Fraser, ed., *Sir James Frazer and the Literary Imagination* (New York: St. Martin's Press, 1990); and Brian R. Clack, *Wittgenstein, Frazer, and Religion* (New York: St. Martin's Press, 1999). See also Martha Celeste Carpentier, *Ritual, Myth, and the Modernist Text: the Influence of Jane Ellen Harrison on Joyce, Eliot, and Woolf* (Amsterdam: Gordon and Breach, 1998) is a work in the same vein, though it traces Jane Harrison's influence rather than Frazer's.

18. Margaret Hiley's recent *The Loss and the Silence: Aspects of Modernism in the Works of C.S. Lewis, J.R.R. Tolkien and Charles Williams* (Zollikofen, Switzerland: Waking Tree Publishers, 2011) is perhaps an indication that scholars are beginning to take an interest in how seemingly disparate instances of mythic thinking might, in fact, be part of the same broader pattern.

19. Francis Mulhern, *The Moment of "Scrutiny,"* (London: New Left Books, 1979). See also Ian MacKillop, *F.R. Leavis: A Life in Criticism* (New York: St. Martin's Press, 1995); and Stefan Collini, "Cambridge and the Study of English," in *Cambridge Contributions*, ed. Sarah J. Omrod (Cambridge: Cambridge University Press, 1998), 42–64.

20. Michael Saler, "Modernity and Enchantment: A Historiographic Review," *American Historical Review* 111, no. 3 (June 2006): 694.

21. Max Weber, "Science as a Vocation," in H.H. Gerth and C. Wright Mills, eds., *From Max Weber: Essays in Sociology* (New York: Oxford University Press, 1958): 129–156.

22. Saler, 700.

23. Jane Bennett, *The Enchantment of Modern Life: Attachments, Crossings, and Ethics* (Princeton, NJ: Princeton University Press, 2001).

24. Alison Winter, *Mesmerized: Powers of Mind in Victorian Britain* (Chicago, IL: University of Chicago Press, 1998); Daniel Pick, *Svengali's Web: The Alien Enchanter in Modern Culture* (New Haven, CT: Yale University Press, 2000); Alex Owen, *The Place of Enchantment: British Occultism and the Culture of the Modern* (Chicago, IL: University of Chicago Press, 2004); and Michael Saler, *As If: Modern Enchantment and the Literary Prehistory of Virtual Reality* (Oxford: Oxford University Press, 2012). Though not limited to the British context, see also Joshua Landy and Michael Saler, eds., *The Re-Enchantment of the World: Secular Magic in a Rational Age* (Stanford, CA: Stanford University Press, 2009).

25. The meanings and implications of this phrase are dealt with perceptively and exhaustively in Charles Taylor, *A Secular Age* (Cambridge, MA: Harvard University Press, 2007).
26. See above, n. 16.
27. George S. Williamson, *The Longing for Myth in Germany: Religion and Aesthetic Culture from Romanticism to Nietzsche* (Chicago, IL: University of Chicago Press, 2004). For other examples of the emerging interest in the relationship between myth and modernity see Andrew Von Hendy's sweeping, impressive study *The Modern Construction of Myth* (Bloomington, IN: Indiana University Press, 2002); Dan Edelstein and Bettina R. Lerner, eds., *Myth and Modernity* (New Haven, CT: Yale University Press, 2007), which focuses on uses of myth in modern France; and Angus Nicholls, "Anglo-German Mythologics: The Australian Aborigines and Modern Theories of Myth in the Work of Baldwin Spencer and Carl Strehlow," *History of the Human Sciences* 20, no. 1 (February 2007): 83–114.

2   Golden Boughs, Fairy Books, and Holy Grails: The Making of a Myth-Saturated Culture

1. T.S. Eliot, "Ulysses, Order and Myth," *The Dial* 75 (November 1923), 483.
2. J.R.R. Tolkien, *Letters of J.R.R. Tolkien*, ed. Humphrey Carpenter (London: George Allen & Unwin, 1981), 144–45, 147.
3. Hans G. Kippenberg, *Discovering Religious History in the Modern Age*, trans. Barbara Harshaw (Princeton, NJ: Princeton University Press, 2002), 41–42.
4. See Robert Ackerman, *The Myth and Ritual School: J.G. Frazer and the Cambridge Ritualists* (New York: Routledge, 2002), 31–32.
5. The first to assess the impact of Tylor's career was fellow anthropologist R.R. Marrett, *Tylor* (New York: J. Wiley and Sons, Inc., 1936). More recently Tylor's thought has been examined by Joan Leopold, *Culture in Comparative and Evolutionary Perspective: E.B. Tylor and the Making of Primitive Culture* (Berlin: Reimer, 1980), who provides an excellent analysis of the sources and development of Tylor's thought.
6. Ackerman, *Myth and Ritual*, 37.
7. See Henrika Kuklick, "Tribal Exemplars: Images of Political Authority in British Authority in British Anthropology, 1885–1945," in George W. Stocking, Jr., ed., *Functionalism Historicized* (Madison, WI: University of Wisconsin Press, 1984), 63.
8. Edward B. Tylor, *Anthropology: An Introduction to the Study of Man and Civilization*, rev. ed. (London: Macmillan, 1924), 387.
9. Kippenberg, 63.
10. The main events of Smith's life are sketched in T.O. Beidelman, *W. Robertson Smith and the Sociological Study of Religion* (Chicago, IL: University of Chicago Press, 1974). See also Marjorie Wheeler-Barclay, *The Science of Religion in Britain, 1860–1915* (Ph.D. diss.: Northwestern University, 1987); and idem, "Victorian Evangelicalism and the Sociology of Religion: The Career of William Robertson Smith," *Journal of the History of Ideas* 54, no. 1 (January 1993): 59–78.
11. Beidelman, 64.

12. William Robertson Smith, *Religion of the Semites* (1889; reprint, London: Transaction Publishers, 2002), 17–18.
13. Robert Alun Jones, "Smith and Frazer on Religion," in Stocking, Jr., ed., *Functionalism Historicized*, 38.
14. Roger Lancelyn Greene, *Andrew Lang: A Critical Biography* (Leicester: Edmund Ward, 1946), 86.
15. Ibid., vii.
16. See Kippenberg, 107.
17. There are four different editions of *The Golden Bough*. The first two-volume edition appeared in 1890. The second edition of 1900 had three volumes. The third edition ballooned to 12 volumes, which appeared between 1911 and 1915. This was followed in 1922 by a one-volume abridged edition. Perhaps the first piece of imaginative literature to draw on *The Golden Bough* was Grant Allen's novel *The Great Taboo* (1890), which explicitly takes its inspiration from Frazer's book. *The Great Taboo* is discussed in Gillian Beer, "Speaking for the Others: Relativism and Authority in Victorian Anthropological Literature," in Robert Fraser, ed., *Sir James Frazer and the Literary Imagination* (New York: St. Martin's Press, 1990), 38–60.
18. Stanley Edgar Hyman, *The Tangled Bank: Darwin, Marx, Frazer and Freud as Imaginative Writers* (New York: Atheneum, 1962).
19. Hyman, 439.
20. The best recent biographical studies of Frazer are Robert Ackerman, *J.G. Frazer: His Life and Work* (Cambridge: Cambridge University Press, 1987); and Robert Fraser, *The Making of* The Golden Bough*: The Origins and Growth of an Argument* (London: Palgrave, 2001).
21. These figures can be found in Ackerman, *J.G. Frazer*, 256–57.
22. Ackerman, *J.G. Frazer*, 256.
23. See Mary Beard, "Frazer, Leach, and Virgil: The Popularity (and Unpopularity) of *The Golden Bough*," *Comparative Studies in Society and History* 24, no. 2 (April, 1992): 212–16. Despite the undeniable popularity of *The Golden Bough* in terms of commercial success, Beard remains skeptical of the book's contemporary cultural influence. She argues that "It would be naïve to imagine that Frazer's theories and arguments had much to do with [*The Golden Bough*'s contemporary] popularity," and she notes George Steiner's verdict that the book must rank with *Capital* and *The Origin of Species* as one of the great unread classics of non-fiction. See ibid., 223; and ibid. n. 55.
24. The most vociferous of Frazer's critics was the Cambridge anthropologist Edmund Leach, who was insistent that *The Golden Bough* was a product of sustained plagiarism by Frazer. See his articles "Golden Bough or Gilded Twig?," *Deadalus* 90 (1961): 371–99; and "On the 'Founding Fathers': Frazer and Malinowski," *Encounter* 25, no. 5 (November 1965): 24–36.
25. The critics were not just the next generation of anthropologists like Malinowski and R.R. Marett. Frazer's fellow comparativist Andrew Lang was highly critical of *The Golden Bough*, and exposed many of its flaws and inconsistencies in his *Magic and Religion* (1901). Even though its ultimate conclusion is questionable, one of the most sustained, careful, and interesting evaluations of the argument of *The Golden Bough* is Jonathan Z. Smith "When the Bough Breaks" Chapter 10 in idem, *Map is not Territory: Studies in the History of Religions* (Leiden: E.J. Brill, 1978), 208–39. Smith suggests that

Frazer knew the central argument of the book was untenable and he concludes that *The Golden Bough* was an elaborate joke. Smith's piece is only one of the better known examples of a body of scholarship examining how *The Golden Bough* functions as text. In addition to the work of Beard (see above, n. 23) and many of the essays in *Sir James Frazer and the Literary Imagination*, Marty Roth, "Sir James Frazer's *The Golden Bough*: A Reading Lesson," in Marc Manganaro, ed., *Modernist Anthropology: From Fieldwork to Text* (Princeton, NJ: Princeton University Press, 1990), 69–79 offers a postmodernist reading of *The Golden Bough* as an "imaginative construction."

26. For an excellent detailed synopsis of *The Golden Bough* see Ackerman, *Myth and Ritual*, 50–53.
27. Qtd. in Smith, 239.
28. Beard, 219.
29. Frazer, *Golden Bough*, 2nd ed., vol. I, xx.
30. Frazer, *Golden Bough*, 3rd ed., vol. I, xxv.
31. Ackerman, *Myth and Ritual*, 53.
32. The emergence of social anthropology in Britain has been examined by numerous scholars, an unusual number of whom are themselves anthropologists. Key studies include George W. Stocking, Jr., *After Tylor: British Social Anthropology, 1888–1951* (Madison, WI: University of Wisconsin Press, 1995); idem, ed., *Functionalism Historicized: Essays on British Social Anthropology* (Madison, WI: University of Wisconsin Press, 1984), Jack Goody, *The Expansive Moment: The Rise of Social Anthropology in Britain and Africa 1918–1970* (Cambridge: Cambridge University Press, 1995); Henrika Kuklick, *The Savage Within: The Social History of British Anthropology, 1885–1945* (Cambridge: Cambridge University Press, 1991); Adam Kuper, *Anthropology and Anthropologists: The Modern British School*, rev. ed. (London: Routledge and Kegan Paul, 1983), Michael W. Young, *Malinowski: Odyssey of an Anthropologist, 1884–1920* (New Haven, CT: Yale University Press, 2004), and Roy Ellen, ed., *Malinowski Between Two Worlds: the Polish Roots of an Anthropological Tradition* (Cambridge: Cambridge University Press, 1988).
33. John B. Vickery, *The Literary Impact of* The Golden Bough (Princeton, NJ: Princeton University Press, 1973), 28.
34. Frazer, *Golden Bough*, 2nd ed., vol. I, xx.
35. Frazer, *Golden Bough*, 3rd ed., vol. I, xxvi.
36. Vickery, 36.
37. Ackerman, *Myth and Ritual*, 50.
38. Frazer, *Golden Bough*, 3rd ed., vol. xi, 308.
39. J.G. Frazer, "The Scope of Social Anthropology," in *Psyche's Task: A Discourse Concerning the Influence of Superstition on the Growth of Institutions*, 2nd ed., (London: Macmillan & Co., 1913), 170. See also Ackerman, *J.G. Frazer*, 212–23 for Frazer's concerns about the fragility of civilization.
40. On the Victorians' relationship to the classical past see Frank M. Turner, *The Greek Heritage in Victorian Britain* (New Haven, CT: Yale University Press, 1981).
41. Jane Ellen Harrison, *Prolegomena to the Study of Greek Religion*, 3rd ed. (Cambridge: Cambridge University Press, 1922), 657.
42. A number of biographers have tried to take the measure of Harrison's charismatic persona and her eventful life. The most thorough is Annabel

Robinson, *The Life and Work of Jane Ellen Harrison* (Oxford: Oxford University Press, 2002); the most interesting is Mary Beard, *The Invention of Jane Harrison* (Cambridge, MA: Harvard University Press, 2000). Sandra J. Peacock, *Jane Ellen Harrison: The Mask and the Self* (New Haven, CT: Yale University Press, 1988) offers a psychobiographical approach. A shorter study that focuses on Harrison's significance for classical studies is R. Schleiser, "Jane Ellen Harrison," in Ward W. Briggs and William M. Calder III, eds., *Classical Scholarship. A Biographical Encyclopedia* (New York: Taylor & Francis, 1990), 127–41. For an examination of Harrison's intellectual achievement in context see Harry C. Payne, "Modernizing the Ancients: The Reconstruction of Ritual Drama 1870–1920," *Proceedings of the American Philosophical Society* 122, no. 3 (Jun. 9, 1978), 182–92.

43. Jane Ellen Harrison, *Mythology and Monuments of Ancient Athens* (London, 1890), iii. Italics in original.

44. Harrison was a lifelong campaigner for the removal of prohibitions against women, whether academic, social, or legal. She was a passionate and articulate polemicist for women's suffrage and in 1909 wrote *Homo Sum*, a highly-regarded pamphlet for the National Union of Women's Suffrage Societies.

45. Jane Ellen Harrison, "Unanimism and Conversion," in *Alpha and Omega* (London: Sidgwick and Jackson, 1915), 51.

46. Robert Ackerman, Introduction to Jane Ellen Harrison, *Prolegomena to the Study of Greek Religion* (Princeton, NJ: Princeton University Press, 1991), xxii.

47. Kippenberg, 109.

48. Jane Ellen Harrison, *Themis; A Study of the Social Origins of Greek Religion, with an Excursus on the Ritual Forms Preserved in Greek Tragedy by Professor Gilbert Murray and a Chapter on the Origin of the Olympic Games by Mr F.M. Cornford* (Cambridge: Cambridge University Press, 1912), 122.

49. Ibid., xi.

50. Ibid., xii.

51. Ibid., 16. Italics in original.

52. Robinson, 9.

53. Harrison, *Themis*, xix.

54. Jane Ellen Harrison, *Epilegomena to the Study of Greek Religion* (Cambridge: Cambridge University Press, 1921), 38.

55. Ibid., 36.

56. Ibid.

57. There is a relative paucity of scholarship on life and work of Jessie Weston. Janet Grayson, "In Quest of Jessie Weston," in *Arthurian Literature* XI, ed. Richard Barber (Cambridge: Boydell and Brewer, 1992), 1–80, is perhaps the most thorough study of her life. A helpful biographical sketch is provided in Stanley Edgar Hyman, "Jessie Weston and the Forest of Broceliande," *Centennial Review* 9 (1965): 509–21. Robert Ackerman's description of the connections between Weston and the myth and ritual school is illuminating though brief. See idem, *The Myth and Ritual School*, 181–84.

58. Ackerman, *Myth and Ritual*, 219–20, n. 34.

59. See Jessie Weston, *From Ritual to Romance* (London: Cambridge University Press, 1920), vii–viii; 35, n. 2.

60. Weston, 67.
61. Weston, 7.
62. See *Times* (London), 10 February 1927, 15.
63. Richard Barber, *The Grail: Imagination and Belief* (Cambridge, MA: Harvard University Press, 2004), 249.
64. See Marc Girouard, *Return to Camelot: Chivalry and the English Gentleman* (New Haven, CT and London: Yale University Press, 1981).
65. Ibid., 297.
66. John B. Vickery, "Frazer and the Elegiac: The Modernist Connection," in Manganaro, ed., 51.
67. Martha Celeste Carpentier has undertaken a project that does for Harrison's literary influence what Vickery did for *The Golden Bough's*. See her *Ritual, Myth, and the Modernist Text: The Influence of Jane Ellen Harrison on Joyce, Eliot, and Woolf* (Amsterdam: Gordon and Breach, 1998). There is a well-established but still growing body of scholarship that explores the influence of myth and ritual anthropology on the modernists. See following chapter, n. 2
68. Wallace W. Douglas, article "The Meanings of 'Myth' in Modern Criticism," *Modern Philology* 50, no. 4 (May 1953), 241.

3   "The Grail Is Stirring": Modernist Mysticism, the Matter of Britain, and the Quest for Spiritual Renewal

1. T.S. Eliot, "Ulysses, Order and Myth," *The Dial* 75 (November 1923): 483.
2. For typical examples of this tendency to focus on a select few canonical modernists see David Spurr, "Myths of Anthropology: Eliot, Joyce, Lévy-Bruhl," *PMLA* 109, no. 2 (March 1994): 266–80; K.J. Phillips, "Jane Harrison and Modernism," *Journal of Modern Literature* 17, no. 4 (spring 1991): 465–76; Lee Oser, *The Ethics of Modernism: Moral Ideas in Yeats, Eliot, Joyce, Woolf and Beckett* (Cambridge: Cambridge University Press, 2006). See also notes 3 and 4 below. Notable exceptions to this tendency have tended to come from scholars pursuing or incorporating gender-based analysis. See, for example, Ruth Hoberman, *Gendering Classicism: The Ancient World in Twentieth-Century Women's Historical Fiction* (Albany, NY: State University of New York Press, 1997); Jane Garrity, *Step-daughters of England: British Women Modernists and the National Imaginary* (Manchester: Manchester University Press, 2003); and Jane Goldman, *Modernism, 1910–1945: Image to Apocalypse* (New York: Palgrave Macmillan, 2004). Tim Armstrong, *Modernism: A Cultural History* (Cambridge: Polity Press, 2005) is also exemplary in considering canonical writers alongside lesser known figures.
3. See Michael Bell, *Literature, Modernism and Myth: Belief and Responsibility in the Twentieth Century* (Cambridge: Cambridge University Press, 1997).
4. Andrew Von Hendy, *The Modern Construction of Myth* (Bloomington and Indianapolis, IN: Indiana University Press, 2002), 137–38.
5. Ibid., 146.
6. I am indebted to Hunter Heyck for helping me to see the importance of this distinction and for his invaluable comments on this chapter.

7. Richard Barber, *The Holy Grail: Imagination and Belief* (Cambridge, MA: Harvard University Press, 2004), 297.

8. This attitude was expressed most forcefully by David Jones, who contended that ancient Celtic versions of the Grail myth were "far more solemn and significant" than late medieval versions, which utterly mangled the power and beauty of the Celtic originals. He then quotes C.S. Lewis to the effect that the medieval romance makers "destroyed more magic than they ever invented." See David Jones, *In Parenthesis* (London: Faber & Faber Ltd., 1937), 200–01.

9. Confusingly, in some versions of the tale the castle is occupied by two kings, the "Wounded King," who is identified as Pellam or Pellehan, and his son or grandson Pelles, who is called the "Fisher King."

10. The relevant passage is quoted at the beginning of Chapter 2 above.

11. Jewel Spears Brooker, *Mastery and Escape: T.S. Eliot and the Dialectic of Modernism* (Amherst, MA: University of Massachusetts Press, 1994), 11.

12. T.S. Eliot, *The Use of Poetry and the Use of Criticism* (London: Faber and Faber, 1933), 130.

13. *The Waste Land* had first been published a few days earlier in the first issue of the *Criterion*. Both the version in the *Criterion* and the one in the *Dial* appeared without notes. At the beginning of December the poem first appeared as a book and included Eliot's annotations.

14. T.S. Eliot, *The Annotated* Waste Land *with Eliot's Contemporary Prose*, ed. Lawrence Rainey (New Haven, CT: Yale University Press, 2005), 71.

15. See T.S. Eliot, *On Poetry and Poets* (London: Faber and Faber, 1957), 122.

16. Brooker, 13. Brooker's volume, especially the four essays collected under the heading "The Mind of Europe: Anxiety, Crisis, and Therapy," offers what is probably the single best elucidation and analysis of Eliot's mythical method, in large part because of her skill in contextualizing Eliot's thought in relation early twentieth-century social science. My discussion of Eliot here relies heavily on Brooker's insights.

17. It is important to note that Eliot's views on myth and the function of art underwent significant change after his conversion to Anglicanism in the late 1920s. The shift in Eliot's thought, however, did not diminish the influence of his earlier views on the function of myth within a modernist aesthetic project, views that continued to reverberate across the cultural landscape for decades. For an excellent analysis of the gradual change in Eliot's thought from the time of *The Waste Land*'s appearance to the publication of *The Idea of a Christian Society* see John Margolis, *T.S. Eliot's Intellectual Development: 1922–1939* (Chicago, IL: The University of Chicago Press, 1972).

18. Qtd. in Morine Krissdottir, *John Cowper Powys and the Magical Quest* (London: Macdonald and Jane's Publishing Group Ltd., 1980), x.

19. Glen Cavaliero, *John Cowper Powys: Novelist* (Oxford: Clarendon Press, 1973), 183.

20. See, for example, John Cowper Powys, *Petrushka and the Dancer: The Diaries of John Cowper Powys, 1929–1939*, ed. Morine Krissdottir (Manchester: Carcanet Press Limited, 1995), 15.

21. John Cowper Powys, *The Complex Vision* (New York: Dodd, Mead and Company, 1920), 111.

22. Ibid., 105–06.

23. Ibid., 249.
24. Ibid., 5.
25. Powys, *Complex Vision*, 17.
26. Ibid., 243.
27. Ibid., 243.
28. Ibid., 241.
29. Ibid., 318.
30. Ibid.
31. Qtd. in Krissdottir, 84.
32. Krissdottir, 17.
33. John Cowper Powys, *A Glastonbury Romance* (London: Macdonald and Co. Publishers Ltd., 1955), xv. The novel originally appeared in 1932, but the 1955 edition included a new preface in which Powys explained some of the motivations and ideas behind the work.
34. Ibid., xiii; xv.
35. Ibid., xi.
36. Ibid., xii.
37. Ibid., 230.
38. Ibid., 233.
39. Ibid., 232.
40. John Cowper Powys, *Autobiography* (London: John Lane, The Bodley Head, 1934), 104.
41. See especially the entries for 1931 in Powys, *Diaries*.
42. Cavaliero, 181.
43. Powys, *Diaries*, 15.
44. Powys, *A Glastonbury Romance*, 923.
45. Bradley W. Buchanan, "Armed with Questions: Mary Butts's Sacred Interrogative," *Twentieth Century Literature* 49, no. 3 (Autumn 2003): 360. One consequence of this renewed interest is a recent biography of Butts: Nathalie Blondel, *Mary Butts: Scenes from the Life* (Kingston, NY: McPherson, 1998). In addition to the works cited below, see also the entry on Mary Butts by Robin Blaser in Jennifer Gariepy, et al, eds., *Twentieth-Century Literary Criticism, vol. 77* (Detroit: Gale Research, 1998): 69–109; Christopher Wagstaff, ed., *A Sacred Quest: The Life and Writings of Mary Butts* (New York: McPherson & Company, 1995); Andrew D. Radford, "Defending Nature's Holy Shrine: Mary Butts, Englishness, and the Persephone Myth," *Journal of Modern Literature* 29, no. 3 (Winter 2006): 126–49; Laura Marcus, "Mysterious Mary Butts," *Times Literary Supplement*, 24 August 2001, 3–4.
46. Mary Butts, *The Journals of Mary Butts*, ed. Nathalie Blondel (New Haven, CT: Yale University Press, 2002), 263–64. Butts's use of the Grail myth is contrasted with Eliot's by Jennifer Kroll, "Mary Butts's 'Unrest Cure' for The Waste Land," *Twentieth Century Literature* 45, no. 2 (summer 1999): 159–173.
47. See Blondel, introduction to Butts, *Journals*, 8. A fascinating discussion of the ways in which modernist women writers made use of the work of the myth and ritual school is offered in Hoberman, *Gendering Classicism*. Hoberman argues that female modernists used myth "to explore and challenge their culture's assumptions about gender" (22). This was unquestionably the case. Hoberman, however, contends that modernist women writers did not experience the supposedly typical modernist anxiety about cultural

fragmentation, because they could not mourn the dissolution of a culture premised on their exclusion. This seems less clear, especially in light of the work of a writer like Butts, who certainly did express anxiety about cultural fragmentation. Jane Garrity's assessment (quoted herein, see n. 50) is much closer to the mark than Hoberman's.

48. Butts, *Journals*, 216.
49. Ibid., 325–36.
50. Garrity, 189.
51. See, for example, Butts, *Journal*, 342; 367.
52. Ibid., 342.
53. Ibid., 461.
54. Ibid., 218.
55. Ibid., 461.
56. Ibid., 249.
57. See Blondel, introduction, 8.
58. Butts, *Journal*, 410.
59. Ibid., 426.
60. Mary Butts, *The Crystal Cabinet: My Childhood at Salterns* (Manchester: Carcanet Press Limited, 1988), 33.
61. Butts, *Journals*, 407; 430; 410; 421.
62. See Roslyn Reso Foy, *Ritual, Myth, and Mysticism in the Work of Mary Butts: Between Feminism and Modernism* (Fayetteville, AR: The University of Arkansas Press, 2000), 60.
63. Foy, 58.
64. In classical mythology, Picus is both a wise and foolish trickster, a role the Picus of Butts's novel plays by initiating and manipulating the game that becomes a Grail quest. There are two Scyllas in classical mythology, one a monster and one a royal scion whose love for the King of Minos destroys her father's kingdom.
65. Mary Butts, *Armed with Madness* (London: Penguin, 2001 [1928]), 140. The novel's reliance on ideas drawn from the Ritualists is exhaustively documented by Foy; see especially Chapter Three, " 'Dis-ease,' " 51–71.
66. Jed Esty, *A Shrinking Island: Modernism and National Culture in England* (Princeton, NJ: Princeton University Press, 2004), 118.
67. Esty, 75.
68. Alan Jacobs, *The Narnian: The Life and Imagination of C.S. Lewis* (New York: Harper Collins, 2005), 196.
69. Qtd. in Charles Williams, *The Image of the City and Other Essays*, ed. Anne Ridler (London: Oxford University Press, 1958), xxviii.
70. Barber, 293.
71. Roma A. King, "The Occult as Rhetoric in the Poetry of Charles Williams," in Charles A. Huttar and Peter J. Schakel, eds., *The Rhetoric of Vision: Essays on Charles Williams* (Lewisburg, PA: Bucknell University Press, 1996), 165.
72. See Scott McLaren, "Hermeticism and the Metaphysics of Goodness in the Novels of Charles Williams," *Mythlore* 24, no. 3–4 (winter–spring 2006): 5–6.
73. Arthur Edward Waite, *The Hidden Church of the Holy Graal* (London: Rebman, 1909); revised as *The Holy Grail, its Legends and Symbolism: An Explanatory Survey of Their Embodiment in Romance Literature and a Critical Study of the Interpretations Placed Thereon* (London: Rider and Co., 1933), 534.

74. Charles Williams, *War in Heaven* (London: Victor Gollancz, 1930), 37.
75. Charles Williams, "The Figure of Arthur," in idem and C.S. Lewis, *Arthurian Torso* (London: Oxford University Press, 1948), 83.
76. Ibid. 84, 83.
77. See Angelika Schneider, "Coinherent Rhetoric in *Taliessin through Logres*," in Huttar and Schakel, eds., 186–87.
78. Williams, "Figure of Arthur," 13.
79. Ibid., 23.
80. Jones, *In Parenthesis*, ix.
81. Ibid.
82. Ibid., 201.
83. See for example, ibid., 203–04, n. 12; 204, n. 15; 206, n. 24; 210, n. 37; 219, n. 15; 223, n. 29.
84. Ibid., 200.
85. David Jones, "The Myth of Arthur," in idem, *Epoch and Artist* (London: Faber and Faber, 1959), 243.
86. Ibid., 242.
87. David Jones, "The Arthurian Legend," in idem, *Epoch and Artist*, 203. The meaning of the Latin is "cup of my blood." Jones is quoting from the words of consecration of the wine in the Roman Catholic mass. See also ibid., 206.
88. Ibid., 205; see also ibid., 210.
89. Ibid., 206.
90. Ibid., 203.
91. Brooker, 141.
92. See Alex Owen, *The Place of Enchantment: British Occultism and the Culture of the Modern* (Chicago, IL: University of Chicago Press, 2004).

4   "The Mythical Mode of Imagination": J.R.R. Tolkien, C.S. Lewis, and the Epistemology of Myth

1. C.S. Lewis, "First and Second Things," in idem, *Essay Collection and Other Short Pieces*, ed. Lesley Walmsley (London: HarperCollins Publishers, 2000), 653.
2. Ibid.
3. Ibid.
4. J.R.R. Tolkien, *Letters of J.R.R. Tolkien*, ed. Humphrey Carpenter (London: George Allen and Unwin, 1981), 55–6.
5. There is a substantial body of scholarship on the Inklings as a group. Humphrey Carpenter's *The Inklings: C.S. Lewis, J.R.R. Tolkien, Charles Williams, and Their Friends* (London: Allen and Unwin, 1978) was for a long while the standard reference, though it has recently been superseded in both thoroughness and theoretical sophistication by Diana Pavlac Glyer's *The Company They Keep: C.S. Lewis and J.R.R. Tolkien as Writers in Community* (Kent, OH: Kent State University Press, 2007). Pavlac Glyer places much greater emphasis than Carpenter on the degree to which the Inklings influenced each other. See also Gareth Knight, *The Magical World of the Inklings* (Longmead: Element Books, 1990); Colin Duriez, *Tolkien and C.S. Lewis: The Gift of Friendship* (Mahwah, NJ: HiddenSpring, 2003).

6. Tolkien, *Letters*, 144; C.S. Lewis, "The Mythopoeic Gift of Rider Haggard," [1960] in *On Stories and Other Essays on Literature*, ed. Walter Hooper (New York: Harcourt Brace Jovanovich, 1966), 100.

7. C.S. Lewis, *The Collected Letters of C.S. Lewis, Volume III: Narnia, Cambridge, and Joy 1950–1963*, ed. Walter Hooper (San Francisco, CA: HarperSanFrancisco, 2007), 462.

8. Jed Esty, *A Shrinking Island: Modernism and National Culture in England* (Princeton, NJ: Princeton University Press, 2004), 122. Esty's book exemplifies a welcome development in scholarship on the Inklings: the attempt to situate their work in relation to broader literary, cultural, and intellectual trends. A pioneering work in this regard is Valentine Cunningham, *British Writers of the Thirties* (Oxford: Oxford University Press, 1988). See also Margaret Hiley, *The Loss and the Silence: Aspects of Modernism in the Works of C.S. Lewis, J.R.R. Tolkien and Charles Williams* (Zollikofen, Switzerland: Waking Tree Publishers, 2011).

9. See Tolkien, *Letters*, 54.

10. Humphrey Carpeter, *Tolkien: A Biography* (Boston, MA: Houghton Mifflin Company, 1977), 131.

11. Meredith Veldman, *Fantasy, the Bomb, and the Greening of Britain: Romantic Protest, 1945–1980* (Cambridge: Cambridge University Press, 1994), 58. Michael Saler has emphasized the influence of fin-de-siècle aestheticism, including the Arts and Crafts movement, on Tolkien. See idem, *As If: Modern Enchantment and the Literary Prehistory of Virtual Reality* (Oxford: Oxford University Press, 2012), Chapter 5. Dimitra Fimi, *Tolkien, Race, and Cultural History: From Fairies to Hobbits* (London: Palgrave Macmillan, 2008) also discusses the evolution of Tolkien's legendarium in relation to his cultural and intellectual context.

12. Carpenter, 31.

13. The story of the T.C.B.S. and its profound influence on Tolkien's life and work is told in John Garth, *Tolkien and the Great War: The Threshold of Middle-earth* (New York: Houghton Mifflin, 2003). T.C.B.S. *stood for 'Tea Club and Barrovian Society'*.

14. See Carpenter, 73; Garth 57–9.

15. Carpenter, 59.

16. J.R.R. Tolkien, "On Fairy-Stories," in *Essays Presented to Charles Williams* (Oxford: Oxford University Press, 1947), 64.

17. See Garth 114; and Carpenter, 78.

18. See Verlyn Flieger, *Interrupted Music: The Making of Tolkien's Mythology* (Kent, OH: Kent State University Press, 2005), 14.

19. Tolkien, *Letters*, 144. On Tolkien's desire to create "a mythology for England" see Paul H. Kocher, "A Mythology for England," in *J.R.R. Tolkien*, ed. Harold Bloom (Philadelphia, PA: Chelsea House Publishers, 2000), 103–11; Jane Chance, *Tolkien's Art: A Mythology for England*, rev. ed. (Lexington, KY: University of Kentucky Press, 2000). There are also numerous studies of the making and development of Tolkien's mythology, the best of which have tended to come from medievalists. See for example the essays collected in Jane Chance, ed., *Tolkien the Medievalist* (London: Routledge, 2003). T.A. Shippey, *The Road to Middle Earth* (London: George Allen and Unwin, 1982) focuses on the philological material from which

Tolkien constructed his mythology; it is a rigorous, groundbreaking study by one of the best Tolkien scholars. Also excellent is the aforementioned Verlyn Flieger, *Interrupted Music: The Making of Tolkien's Mythology*. The significance of speech and soil (as opposed to blood and soil) in Tolkien's concept of race is helpfully discussed by Michael Drout in his introduction to *J.R.R. Tolkien, Beowulf and the Critics*, ed. Michael D. Drout (Tempe, AZ: Arizona Center for Medieval and Renaissance Studies, 2002).

20. C.S. Lewis, *Surprised by Joy: The Shape of My Early Life* (New York: Harcourt Brace and Company, 1955), 17.
21. Lewis, *Joy*, 139.
22. Lewis, *Joy*, 170.
23. Ibid., 174.
24. Ibid., 60; ibid., 59.
25. See C.S. Lewis, *Collected Letters: Volume I, Family Letters 1905–1931*, ed. Walter Hooper (London: HarperCollins, 2000), 601.
26. Carpenter, 143; C.S. Lewis, *All My Road Before Me: The Diary of C.S. Lewis 1922–1927*, ed. Walter Hooper (San Diego: Harcourt Brace Jovanovich, 1991), 393.
27. Lewis, *Joy*, 216.
28. For an excellent account of these conversations, their concern with myth, and their role in Lewis's conversions see Alan Jacobs, *The Narnian: The Life and Imagination of C.S. Lewis* (New York: HarperCollins, 2005), pages 139–151.
29. See Carpenter, 147; Tolkien, "Fairy-Stories," 71.
30. Lewis, *Letters*, i, 976–77. Emphasis in the original.
31. Ibid., 977. Emphasis in the original.
32. Carpenter, 147.
33. The poem can be found in J.R.R. Tolkien, *Tree and Leaf: Including the Poem Mythopoeia* (New York: Houghton Mifflin Harcourt, 1989).
34. See above, Chapter 3.
35. For an extended investigation of this premise see Pavlac Glyer, *The Company They Keep*. See also Andrew Lazo, "A Kind of Mid-Wife: J.R.R. Tolkien and C.S. Lewis—Sharing Influence," in Chance, ed., *Tolkien the Medievalist*, 36–49.
36. Carpenter, 170.
37. Tolkien ultimately attempted, but never completed, two related time travel stories, "The Lost Road" and "The Notion Club Papers." These have since been published in collections edited by Tolkien's son Christopher. The first can be found in J.R.R. Tolkien, *The Lost Road and Other Writings: The History of Middle Earth, Vol. 5*, ed. Christopher Tolkien (London: HarperCollins, 2002); the second in J.R.R. Tolkien, *Sauron Defeated: The History of the Lord of the Rings, Part Four: The History of Middle Earth, Vol. 9*, ed. Christopher Tolkien (London: HarperCollins, 2002).
38. See Tolkien, *Letters*, 34; 36; 38; 41; 68; and 366.
39. Tolkien, "On Fairy-Stories," 83.
40. J.R.R. Tolkien, *Beowulf: The Monsters and the Critics* [Sir Israel Gollancz Memorial Lecture British Academy 1936] (Oxford: Oxford University Press, 1936), 14–15. In his introduction to a critical edition of the lecture, Tolkien scholar Michael Drout argues convincingly that the basis of the lecture

was composed between August 1933 and October 1935. See *J.R.R. Tolkien, Beowulf and the Critics*, ed. Michael D. Drout (Tempe, AZ: Arizona Center for Medieval and Renaissance Studies, 2002).

41. T.A. Shippey has identified the relationship between Collingwood and Tolkien as one of the next frontiers in Tolkien studies. See Tom Shippey, "Guest Editorial: An Encyclopedia of Ignorance," *Mallorn* 45 (spring 2008): 3–5.

42. Verlyn Flieger offers a helpful discussion of Tolkien's engagement with alternative theorists of myth in "'There Would Always Be a Fairy-Tale': J.R.R. Tolkien and the Folklore Controversy," in Chance, ed., *Tolkien the Medievalist*, 26–35.

43. Tolkien, "On Fairy-Stories," 47.

44. Ibid., 49. The power of myth was an issue that fascinated Tolkien, and he did not think that power could be explained in scientific terms. As a character in "The Notion Club Papers" puts it: "I don't think any of us realize, the force, the daimonic force that the great myths and legends have. From the profundity of the emotions and perceptions that begot them, and from the multiplication of them in many minds....They are like an explosive." See Tolkien, *Sauron Defeated*, 228.

45. Ibid., 50.

46. Ibid., 57.

47. Ibid., 62.

48. Ibid., 58.

49. Ibid., 66.

50. Ibid.

51. Tolkien quotes the relevant passage in "On Fairy-Stories," 71–72. See also Carpenter, 147–8.

52. Ibid., 72.

53. Saler, 159.

54. "On Fairy-Stories," 74.

55. Ibid., 74.

56. Ibid., 81.

57. Ibid., 82.

58. Ibid., 83.

59. Andrew Von Hendy, *The Modern Construction of Myth* (Bloomington & Indianapolis, IN: Indiana University Press, 2002), 136. This has been helpfully described as Yeats's "redemptive Revivalism" in Gregory Castle, *Modernism and the Celtic Revival* (Cambridge: Cambridge University Press, 2001). See especially Chapter 2.

60. Von Hendy, 136.

61. Hiley, *The Loss and the Silence*, 113.

62. C.S. Lewis, "Sometimes Fairy Stories May Say Best What's to Be Said," in *On Stories*, 48.

63. Lewis, "Myth Became Fact," 65.

64. See Lewis, *Surprised by Joy*, 217–19.

65. Lewis, "Myth Became Fact," 66.

66. Ibid.

67. Barfield was a member of the Inklings and his views on meaning and myth also influenced Tolkien. This influence has been traced by Verlyn Flieger,

Splintered Light: Logos and Language in Tolkien's World (Kent, OH: Kent State University Press, 2002); Margaret Hiley, "Stolen Language, Cosmic Models: Myths and Mythology in Tolkien," *Modern Fiction Studies* 50, no. 4 (winter 2004): 838–60; Judith Klinger, "'More Poetical, Less Prosaic': The Convergence of Myth and History in Tolkien's Work," *Hither Shore* 3: 180–95; and Jonathan Padley and Kenneth Padley, "'From Mirrored Truth the Likeness of the True': J. R. R. Tolkien and Reflections of Jesus Christ in Middle-Earth," *English* 59, no. 224 (spring 2010): 70–92. Barfield's influence on Lewis's understanding of myth has been examined in Hiley, *The Loss and the Silence* (see pages 182–84) as well as by Colin Duriez (see following note).

68. The aspects of Barfield's influence on Lewis, among others, are discussed in Colin Duriez, "Myth, Fact and Incarnation," in Eduardo Segura and Thomas Honegger, eds., *Myth and Magic: Art According to the Inklings* (Zollikofen, Switzerland: Walking Tree Publishers, 2007), 71–98. See especially pages 85–89. Additional helpful discussions of Lewis's view of myth include Mark Edwards Freshwater, *C.S. Lewis and the Truth of Myth* (Lanham, MD: University Press of America, 1988); Peter J. Schakel, *Reason and Imagination in C.S. Lewis: A Study of Till We Have Faces* (Grand Rapids: Eerdmans, 1984); and a number of essays in Bruce L. Edwards, ed., *C.S. Lewis: Life, Work, and Legacy*, 4 vols. (Santa Barbara, CA: Praeger Publishers, 2007).

69. C.S. Lewis, *Miracles: A Preliminary Study* (New York: Macmillan, 1968), 134.
70. Lewis, "First and Second Things," 4.
71. Tolkien, *Letters*, 77.
72. Carpenter, 244.
73. Lewis, "*De Descriptione Temporum*," in idem, *Selected Literary Essays*, ed. Walter Hooper (Cambridge: Cambridge University Press, 1969), 12.
74. Lewis, *Joy*, 207.
75. On the reasons for Lewis's failure to obtain a chair at Oxford see A.N. Wilson, *C.S. Lewis: A Biography* (New York: Norton, 1990), 158.
76. Lewis, "*De Descriptione Temporum*," 7.
77. Ibid., 11.
78. One of Lewis's most highly regarded novels, the allegorical *Till We Have Faces*, is an extended meditation on precisely this issue.
79. Tolkien, *On Fairy-Stories*, 72; idem, *Letters*, 147.
80. Lewis, *The Abolition of Man* [1943] (New York: Macmillan Publishing Company, 1955), 86.
81. Lewis, *Letters*, ii, 1010.
82. Ibid. Emphasis in original.
83. Lewis, *Letters*, ii, 594. Emphasis in original.
84. See, for example, Alastair Fowler, "C.S. Lewis: Supervisor," *Yale Review* 91, 4 (October 2003): 64–80. See especially pp. 70–71.
85. See Tolkien, *Letters*, 377.
86. Lewis, *Abolition*, 86.
87. Ibid., 87; ibid., 88.
88. See C.S. Lewis, *That Hideous Strength* [1945] (New York: Macmillan, 1965). There is some reason to think that the book influenced George Orwell's *Nineteen Eighty-Four*. Orwell reviewed Lewis's novel, which shares many elements with *Nineteen Eighty-Four*, positively in the *Manchester Evening News* in 1945. See George Orwell, "The Scientist Takes Over," in idem,

The Complete Works of George Orwell, vol. xvii, ed. Peter Davidson (London: Secker and Warburg, 1998), 250–51.

89. Lewis, *Abolition*, 89.
90. See Lewis, *Letters*, iii, 1324.
91. See C.S. Lewis, "Psycho-Analysis and Literary Criticism," in *Selected Literary Essays*, 286–300. For a useful comment on Lewis's thoughts about Jung's theory of myth see Michael Ward, *Planet Narnia: The Seven Heavens in the Imagination of C.S. Lewis* (Oxford: Oxford University Press, 2007), 230.
92. C.S. Lewis, "The Anthropological Approach," in *Selected Literary Essays*, 309.
93. Lewis, *Letters*, iii, 1084. For further comments by Lewis on Jung see idem, "On Science Fiction," in *On Stories*, 66–7.
94. Jacobs notes how Lewis's thought was marked by a deep suspicion toward explanations that seemed reductive. See *The Narnian*, p. 142.
95. As one of Lewis's biographers has put it, "Lewis was never interested in literature as a substitute for Christian faith." See Jacobs, *The Narnian*, 294. Lewis attacked the idea in print as early as 1940. See C.S. Lewis, "Christianity and Culture," *Theology* 40 (March 1940), 166–79.
96. In 1954 Lewis moved from Oxford to Cambridge, where Leavis's influence was palpable and inescapable. For a succinct statement of Lewis's objections to Leavisite evaluative criticism see idem, *Letters*, iii, 1371. For a more extended response see the following note.
97. C.S. Lewis, *An Experiment in Criticism* [1961] (Cambridge: Cambridge University Press, 1979), 139.
98. Lewis, "The Mythopoeic Gift of Rider Haggard," 100.
99. See C.S. Lewis, "Equality," in idem, *Present Concerns* (New York: Harcourt, 1987), 16–20.
100. Lewis, *Experiment*, 60.
101. Ibid., 57; 59.
102. Ibid., 60.
103. See Lewis, *Experiment*, 70.
104. *Fifty Years of Publishing Books That Matter* [author unknown] (London: George Allen and Unwin, 1964), 5. See also the exhaustive investigation of *The Lord of the Rings*'s publishing history compiled by the online reference *An Illustrated Tolkien Bibliography*: http://www.tolkienbooks.net/php/lotr-print-runs.php. Accessed 14 March 2013.
105. The poll results are reported in Shippey, *Author*, xx–xxi. Tolkien's place at the top of the poll left many critics in Britain aghast, a reaction analyzed in idem xxi–xxiv and 305–328. See also Joseph Pearce, *Tolkien: Man and Myth* (London: HarperCollins, 1998), 1–12.
106. Given the multiplicity of editions and publishers, exact sales figures for Lewis's novels are probably impossible to determine. Two of his biographers comment in passing on the strong sales of Lewis's fiction, though without providing citations. See Jacobs, x; and Michael White, *C.S. Lewis: Creator of Narnia* (New York: Carroll and Graf, 2005), 122.
107. For a fascinating study of Tolkien's influence on Campaign for Nuclear Disarmament and the environmental movement in Britain see Veldman, *Fantasy, the Bomb, and the Greening of Britain*.
108. See Chapter 5 below.

109. For a criticism of some implications of this latter pole of Tolkien and Lewis's thought by a contemporary see Donald Davie, *These Companions: Recollections* (Cambridge: Cambridge University Press, 1982), 170.

5 Coping with the Catastrophe: J.G. Ballard, the New Wave, and Mythic Science Fiction

1. See Graeme Revell, "Essay on J.G. Ballard," *RE/Search* no. 8/9 (1984): 144. See also Ballard's own account in "J.G. Ballard," interview by Alan Burns, in Alan Burns and Charles Sugnet, eds., *The Imagination on Trial: British and American Writers Discuss Their Working Methods* (London: Allison and Busby, 1981), 22–23. John Baxter in *The Inner Man: The Life of J.G. Ballard* (London: Weidenfeld & Nicholson, 2011) has suggested that Ballard may have embellished his account of this incident over the years (see page 230).
2. John Baxter, who had connections to the New Wave group, has described it as "a house with many mansions." See Baxter, 161.
3. Michael Moorcock, "A New Literature for the Space Age," *New Worlds* 142 (May–June 1964): 2. Italics in original.
4. Though not everyone got the joke. When Lord Goodman, then chairman of the Arts Council, was considering withdrawing the Council's support of *New Worlds*, he was reassured when he saw Paolozzi's name on the masthead. See Michael Moorcock, "Introduction," in idem, ed., *New Worlds: An Anthology* (London: Fontana, 1983), 23.
5. This was a tension the New Wave writers themselves were aware of. See for example J.G. Ballard's editorial "Which Way to Inner Space?," *New Worlds* 118 (May 1962): 2–3, 116–18, in which he acknowledges that if the New Wave project is to succeed, "most of the hard work will fall . . . on the readers. The onus is on them to accept a more oblique narrative style, understated themes, private symbols and vocabularies." The editorial is reprinted in J.G. Ballard, *A User's Guide to the Millennium: Essays and Reviews* (New York: Picador, 1996); see p. 198.
6. The grant helped bridge the period until a new distributor was found. See Michael Moorcock, "Introduction," *New Worlds: An Anthology*, 19. The story of *New Worlds*'s eventful history is also told in Colin Greenland, *The Entropy Exhibition: Michael Moorcock and the British "New Wave" in Science Fiction* (London: Routledge & Kegan Paul, 1983), Chapter 2, "The 'Field' and the 'Wave': The History of *New Worlds*."
7. Moorcock, "Introduction," *New Worlds: An Anthology*, 22.
8. Ibid., 16.
9. Moorcock, "Introduction," *New Worlds: An Anthology*, 13. For Ballard's caustic assessment of the Angry Young Men see idem, "Memories of Greeneland," in *User's Guide to the Millennium*, 138; and Charles Platt, *Who Writes Science Fiction?* (Manchester: Savoy Books, 1980), 250. For Aldiss's view see Brian Aldiss, "Magic and Bare Boards," in idem and Harry Harrison, eds., *Hell's Cartographers: Some Personal Histories of Science Fiction Writers* (London: Weidenfeld and Nicolson, 1975), 189.
10. Ballard, "Which Way to Inner Space?," *A User's Guide to the Millennium*, 198.

11. Ibid.
12. Brian Aldiss, *The Shape of Further Things* (New York: Doubleday & Company, Inc., 1971), 91. First published in the U.K. by Faber & Faber in 1970.
13. J.G. Ballard, interview by Thomas Frick, in *Paris Review* 94 (Winter 1984): 158.
14. Though in the late 1950s Moorcock did work as an editor for *Current Topics*, the policy discussion magazine of the Liberal party, and later canvassed for the Labour party. The problems of finding an appropriate political label for Moorcock are manifest, as he himself has acknowledged: "My own politics is a mix. I'm a person of the left who writes mostly, at the moment, for right-wing journals and newspapers like *The Spectator* and *The Telegraph*. I'm an anarcho-syndicalist who believes in keeping the British House of Lords (unelected upper house) unreformed. What label exists for that mix?" See interview with Moorcock at http://juandahlmann.wordpress.com/tag/michael-moorcock/. Accessed 5 November 2012.
15. Ballard, interview by Frick, 158.
16. Aldiss, "Magic and Bare Boards," 190.
17. Norman Spinrad, *The Star Spangled Future* (New York: Ace, 1979), 6.
18. An experience Aldiss novelized in *A Soldier Erect* and *A Rude Awakening*. Other fiction by Aldiss that reflects on imperialism, both British and otherwise, includes his novel *The Dark Light Years* (London: Faber and Faber, 1964) and the story "So Far From Prague," in Langdon Jones, ed., *The New S.F.: An Original Anthology of Modern Speculative Fiction* (London: Hutchison & Co Ltd, 1969), 55–70.
19. J.G. Ballard, "Theatre of War," in *Myths of the Near Future* (London: Jonathan Cape, 1982), 118. See also Ballard's 1969 short story "The Killing Ground," in *J.G. Ballard: The Complete Short Stories* (London: Flamingo, 2001), 781–87. For further examples of New Wave writings that deal with imperialism see Moorcock's novels *A Cure for Cancer* (London: Allison and Busby, 1971) and *Breakfast in the Ruins* (London: New English Library, 1972); and Aldiss's *The Dark Light Years*.
20. Aldiss, "Magic and Bare Boards," 189.
21. Patrick Parrinder, *Shadows of the Future: H.G. Wells, Science Fiction, and Prophecy* (Liverpool: Liverpool University Press, 1995), 145.
22. J.G. Ballard, "The Terminal Beach," in idem, *Chronopolis and Other Stories* (New York: G.P. Putnam's Sons, 1971), 51. First published in *New Worlds* in 1964.
23. Aldiss, "Magic and Bare Boards," 208.
24. The question appeared on the cover of *New Worlds* 182 (July 1961) and it was particularly common in Moorcock's fiction of the 1960s and 1970s.
25. J.G. Ballard, interview by Graeme Revell, in *RE/Search* no. 8/9 (1984): 44.
26. See for example Brian Aldiss, *Shape of Further Things*, 38; 51–52.
27. J.G. Ballard, interview by James Goddard and David Pringle, in Goddard and Pringle, eds., *J.G. Ballard: The First Twenty Years* (Hayes: Bran's Head, 1976), 26.
28. See for example J.G. Ballard, "Introduction to Crash," *RE/Search* 8/9 (1984): 96. This oft-reprinted piece was originally written for the French edition of *Crash* in 1974 and first appeared in English as "Some Words about *Crash!*," *Foundation* 9 (November 1975): 45–54.

29. See for example Moorcock, "Aspects of Fantasy," in Darrell Schweitzer, ed., *Exploring Fantasy Worlds: Essays on Fantastic Literature* (San Bernardino, CA: Borgo Press, 1985), 12–13.
30. Thomas M. Disch, et al., "The Lessons of the Future," *New Worlds* 173 (July 1967): 2–3. Italics in original. A similar dismissal of the modernist literary tradition is offered by Ballard in an essay on Salvador Dali that originally appeared in *New Worlds* in 1969. See "The Innocent as Paranoid," *A User's Guide to the Millennium*, 92–93. The influence of surrealism on Ballard is examined in Jeannette Baxter, *J.G. Ballard's Surrealist Imagination: Spectacular Authorship* (Farnham: Ashgate Publishing Limited, 2009).
31. Thomas M. Disch, "Introduction: Mythology and Science Fiction," in idem and Charles Naylor, eds., *New Constellations: An Anthology of Tomorrow's Mythologies* (New York: Harper & Row, 1976), x. Though Disch is American, he lived in London during the 1960s and was very much a part of the New Wave intellectually. He made his name by publishing in *New Worlds* when it was under Moorcock's editorship. Disch's novel *Camp Concentration*, serialized in *New Worlds* in 1967, was one of the most noteworthy pieces to appear in the magazine during Moorcock's tenure.
32. See Olaf Stapledon, "Preface to English Edition," *Last and First Men* (New York: Dover, 1968; London: Methuen, 1930), 9–11; C.S. Lewis, "On Science Fiction," in idem, *Of Other Worlds: Essays and Stories* (London: Geoffrey Bles, 1966), 59–73; J.B. Priestley, "They Came From Inner Space," in idem, *Thoughts in the Wilderness* (London: William Heinemann Ltd., 1957), 20–26; Raymond Williams, "Science Fiction," *The Highway* 48 (December 1956): 41–45.
33. Brian Aldiss, "British Science Fiction Now: Studies of Three Writers," *SF Horizons* no. 2 (winter 1965), 26. Aldiss started *SF Horizons* in 1964 on the grounds that, as serious literature, contemporary science fiction was worthy of serious literary criticism. The magazine was short-lived, but others soon appeared to fill the void. Descriptions of science fiction as a form of contemporary myth began to proliferate in the 1970s as critics began to ask whether science fiction was indeed the literary genre that most authentically expressed contemporary concerns. For examples see John Radford, "Science Fiction as Myth," *Foundation* 10 (June 1976): 28–34; K.V. Bailey, "A Prized Harmony: Myth, Symbol and Dialectic in the Novels of Olaf Stapledon," *Foundation* 15 (January 1979): 53–66; Peter Nicholls, "Mythology," in idem, ed., *The Encyclopaedia of Science Fiction* (St Albans: Granada, 1979), 416–18; Russell Blackford, "Myth and the Art of Science Fiction Commentary," *Science Fiction: A Review of Speculative Literature* 3, no. 2 (May 1981): 52–6; Alexei Panshin and Cory Panshin, "Science Fiction and the Dimension of Myth," *Extrapolation* 22, no. 2 (summer 1981): 127–39; Gary K. Wolfe, "Mythic Structures in Cordwainer Smith's 'The Game of Rat and Dragon,'" *Science Fiction Studies* 4, no. 2 (July 1977): 144–50; Elizabeth Cummins Cogell, "The Middle-Landscape Myth in Science Fiction," *Science Fiction Studies* 5, no. 2 (July 1978): 134–42.
34. Brian Aldiss, *Shape of Further Things*, 39.
35. The phrases are from Moorcock, "Aspects of Fantasy," 10; and Ballard, interview by Burns, 26. The Moorcock essay was originally serialized in the magazine *Science Fantasy* in 1963–64. For further examples of Moorcock speaking

in similar terms see his essays, "The Secret Life of Elric of Melniboné: The Creation of an Archetype," and "New Worlds—Jerry Cornelius: The History of a Magazine, The Nature of a Character," in idem, *Sojan* (Manchester: Savoy Books Ltd., 1977), 127; 150–51. In fact, nearly all of Moorcock's fiction deals with a core "mythology" that he developed early in his career. For examples of New Wave fiction that explicitly acknowledges Jung's influence see Brian Aldiss, "The Source," *New Worlds* 153 (August 1965): 61–77; and William Barclay [Moorcock], "The Golden Barge," *New Worlds* 155 (October 1965): 36–51; and idem, *Behold The Man*, in which the central character is a devotee of Jung. Ballard has also acknowledged Jung's influence; see interview by Graeme Revell, 45.

36. Disch, "Introduction," xi.
37. New Wave writers Thomas M. Disch and Charles Naylor edited a collection entitled *New Constellations: An Anthology of Tomorrow's Mythologies* (see above n. 31), with an introduction by Disch on "Mythology and Science Fiction." Some notable examples of reworked myths include Moorcock's *Behold The Man*, a retelling of the story of Jesus; and Aldiss's *Frankenstein Unbound*, a retelling of the Frankenstein story.
38. See for example Ballard's homage to William Burroughs, "Mythmaker of the Twentieth Century," in *RE/Search* 8/9 (1984): 105–07. The piece originally appeared in *New Worlds* 142 (May–June 1964).
39. The title Ballard gave to one of his short story collections was *Myths of the Near Future*. See n. 19 above.
40. Ballard, interview by Alan Burns, 20; 21.
41. The entry reads: "**BALLARDIAN**: (adj) 1. of James Graham Ballard (J.G. Ballard; born 1930), the British novelist, or his works (2) resembling or suggestive of the conditions described in J.G. Ballard's novels and stories, esp. dystopian modernity, bleak man-made landscapes and the psychological effects of technological, social or environmental developments."
42. J.G. Ballard, *The Kindness of Women* (London: Harper Collins, 1991), 197.
43. J.G. Ballard, "Disasters," interview by Rodney Smith, in *The Listener*, 14 February 1980, 208.
44. J.G. Ballard, "Fictions of Every Kind," *RE/Search* 8/9 (1984): 99. The piece originally appeared in *Books and Bookmen* in 1971.
45. J.G. Ballard, "The New Science Fiction: A Conversation Between J.G. Ballard and George MacBeth," interview by George Macbeth, in Langdon Jones, ed., *The New S.F.: An Original Anthology of Modern Speculative Fiction* (London: Hutchinson, 1969), 53; 54.
46. Ballard, interview by Thomas Frick, 158.
47. J.G. Ballard, *Crash* (London: Cape, 1973), 53.
48. Andrzej Gasiorek, *J.G. Ballard* (Manchester: Manchester University Press, 2005), 112.
49. J.G. Ballard, "Quotations by Ballard," *RE/Search* 8/9 (1984): 154.
50. Ibid.
51. Ballard, "Introduction to Crash," 96.
52. Ibid., 97. Italics in original.
53. Ballard, "Fictions of Every Kind," 205.
54. Ballard, "The Car, The Future," *User's Guide to the Millennium*, 262. First published in *Drive* magazine in 1971.

55. Ballard, interview by Rodney Smith, 209; Ballard, "Introduction to Crash," 98.
56. Ballard, "Introduction to Crash," 98, 96.
57. Ibid., 98.
58. See Ballard, "The Consumer Consumed," *User's Guide to the Millennium*, 259–61. First published in 1971.
59. Qtd. in Jerome Tarshis, "Krafft-Ebing Visits Dealey Plaza: The Recent Fiction of J.G. Ballard," *Evergreen Review* no. 96 (Spring 1973): 145–46.
60. See J.G Ballard, "Ballard at Home," interview by Catherine Bresson, *Metaphores* 7 (March 1982): 16. Samuel Francis has noted the influence of Jungian ideas on Ballard's early fiction, especially of the 1960s. This influence is evident not only in use of stock Jungian concepts and symbols, but also explicit references to Jung and his theories. See *The Psychological Fictions of J.G. Ballard* (London: Continuum, 2011), 43–52.
61. Ballard, "The Pleasures of Reading," *A User's Guide to the Millennium*, 181. For examples of similar comments by Ballard see idem, interview by MacBeth, 50; and idem, interview by Brendan Hennessy, *The Transatlantic Review* no. 39 (Spring 1971): 62.
62. Ballard, "Hobbits in Space?" *User's Guide to the Millennium*, 14. First published in *Time Out* 1977.
63. Ballard, "Back to the Heady Future," *User's Guide to the Millennium*, 193–94.
64. Ballard, "Mythmaker of the Twentieth Century," 105, 107.
65. Ballard, interview by Rodney Smith, 209.
66. See Ballard, interview by Thomas Frick, 136; and idem, "Waiting for Silver Coconuts," interview by Charles Shaar Murray, *New Musical Express*, 22 October 1983: 28.
67. See for example Ballard, *Concrete Island* (London: Cape, 1973), 22; and idem, "The Terminal Beach," 62.
68. Ballard, interview by Pringle and Goddard, 40.
69. Ballard, interview by Frick, 158.
70. Ballard, interview by Revell, 42.
71. Ibid., 45.
72. J.G. Ballard, interview by Andrea Juno and V. Vale, *RE/Search* 8/9 (1984): 31.
73. Ballard, interview by Burns, 20; ibid.; ibid.
74. Ballard, "The Innocent as Paranoid," *User's Guide to the Millennium*, 93. First published in *New Worlds* in 1969.
75. Ballard, interview by MacBeth, 46.
76. Ballard, interview by Revell, 42.
77. Ballard, interview by MacBeth, 51–52.
78. Ballard, interview by Revell, 46.
79. Ballard, "Quotations by Ballard," 164.
80. Ballard, "Innocent as Paranoid," 93.
81. Ballard, interview by Revell, 42.
82. Gasiorek, 206.
83. See J.G. Ballard, "Grave New World," interview by David Gale. The interview originally aired on BBC Radio 3 in 1998 and can be found at http://www.jgballard.ca/media/1998_nov11_BBC3_radio.html. Accessed 5 November 2012.

84. See Ballard, interview by Graeme Revell, 42. The interviewer explains Barthes's understanding of myth to Ballard, who does not seem to be familiar with it.
85. See the partial bibliography of these interviews prepared by Ballard scholar David Pringle at http://www.solaris-books.co.uk/Ballard/Pages/Miscpages/interviewsbib.htm. Accessed 5 November 2012.
86. Baxter, 32.
87. Roger Luckhurst, "A Writer and His Quirk," *Science Fiction Studies* 26, no. 2 (July 1999): 333.
88. Ballard, interview by Revell, 45.
89. Greenland, 111.
90. Michael Moorcock, "Modern Metaphors," in Goddard and Pringle, eds., *J.G. Ballard: The First Twenty Years*, 61. Ballard had the same opinion of the modernists. See Ballard, "Fictions of Every Kind," 98.
91. The transcript of this conversation, at which Kingsley Amis was also present, was published as "C.S. Lewis Discusses Science Fiction with Kingsley Amis," in *SF Horizons* no. 1 (spring 1964): 5–12.
92. Moorcock, *Wizardry and Wild Romance: A Study of Epic Fantasy* (London: Victor Gollancz Ltd, 1987), 125. The chapter in which this assessment appears, "Epic Pooh," was originally published in pamphlet form in 1976.

6   Myth and the Quest for Psychological Wholeness: C.G. Jung as Spiritual Sage

1. "C.G. Jung," *Manchester Guardian*, 26 July 1955, 6.
2. Vincent Brome, "The Man Who Woke the World," *Guardian*, 19 July 1975, 9.
3. "Professor C.G. Jung," *Times* (London), 8 June 1961, 19.
4. "Professor Carl G. Jung," *Guardian*, 7 June 1961, 6.
5. "Garl Gustav Jung," *Guardian*, 8 June 1961, 8.
6. H. I'A. F., "Dr. Jung," review of *Modern Man in Search of a Soul*, by C.G. Jung, *Manchester Guardian*, 13 September 1933, 5.
7. Some of these reverberations are examined above in Chapters 4 and 5 and below in Chapters 6 and 7.
8. Andrew Von Hendy, *The Modern Construction of Myth* (Bloomington and Indianapolis, IN: Indiana University Press, 2002), xvi–xvii.
9. The literature on Jung is extensive and multidisciplinary. For a meticulous and historically informed study of the development of Jung's psychology see Sonu Shamdasani, *Jung and the Making of Modern Psychology: The Dream of a Science* (Cambridge: Cambridge University Press, 2003). The more recent biographies of Jung include Deirdre Bair, *Jung: A Biography.* (Boston, MA: Little, Brown and Company, 2003); Ronald Hayman, *A Life of Jung* (New York: W.W. Norton and Co., 2001); Richard Noll, *Aryan Christ: The Secret Life of Carl Jung* (New York: Random House, 1997); Frank McLynn, *Carl Gustav Jung* (London: Bantam Press, 1996). Noll's biography and his earlier *The Jung Cult: Origins of a Charismatic Movement* (Princeton, NJ: Princeton University Press, 1994) have been severely criticized by Shamdasani and Anthony Stevens [see below] among others. See Sonu Shamdasani, *Cult Fictions: C.G. Jung and the Founding of Analytical Psychology* (London: Routledge, 1998); and *Jung Stripped*

Bare: By his Biographers, Even (London: Karnac, 2005), which also contains criticisms of the McLynn and Bair biographies. It seems the definitive biography of Jung has yet to be written. For a concise, highly regarded exposition of Jung's thought see Anthony Stevens, *On Jung*, 2nd ed. (Princeton, NJ: Princeton University Press, 1999).

10. Bair, 621.
11. McLynn, 80. Shamdasani in *Jung Stripped Bare* has drawn attention to the shortcomings of this work and has highlighted how it should be read with caution. Although McLynn's claims are often tendentious, his biography delves into the connections between Jung and Britain in ways others do not.
12. Ibid., 252.
13. Bair, 304.
14. On the attempt to reconcile science and religion in theses years see Peter J. Bowler, *Reconciling Science and Religion: The Debate in Early-Twentieth-Century Britain* (Chicago, IL: University of Chicago Press, 2001). The Bampton Lectures for 1930 were published as L.W. Grensted, *Psychology and God: A Study of the Implications of Recent Psychology for Religious Belief and Practice* (London: Longmans, Green and Co., 1931).
15. R.G. Collingwood, *The Philosophy of Enchantment: Studies in Folktale, Cultural Criticism, and Anthropology*, ed. David Boucher, Wendy James, and Philip Smallwood (Oxford: Clarendon Press, 2007), 170.
16. Ibid., 173.
17. See Maud Bodkin, *Archetypal Patterns in Poetry: Psychological Studies of the Imagination* (London: Oxford University Press, 1934). For an example of Knight's approach see *The Wheel of Fire: Interpretations of Shakespearian Tragedy* (London: Oxford University Press, 1930).
18. Charles was almost certainly introduced to Jung's thought by Laurens van der Post. See Charles, Prince of Wales, "My Life, My Future," *Guardian*, 30 August 1982, 3. *The Guardian's* editorial board took the Prince's interest in Jung as a positive sign and devoted a leader to the subject. See "The Prince and Dr Jung," *Guardian*, 31 August 1982, 10.
19. Nicholas de Jongh, "In the Colonies of the Mind," *Guardian*, 27 January 1990, 23.
20. Though of course Jung's connections with what James Webb called the "occult revival" went back well before the War. See James Webb, *The Occult Establishment* (La Salle, IL: Open Court, 1976). See especially Chapter 6.
21. See Stanley Reynolds, "Jung's Xanadu," *The Guardian*, 31 May 1976, 8; and also Bill Harpe, "They Tried to Tell Us We're too Jung," *Guardian*, 6 June 1977, 10. The dream is described by Jung in C.G. Jung, *Memories, Dreams, Reflections*, rev. ed., ed. Aniela Jaffé, trans. Richard and Clara Winston (New York: Vintage Books, 1989), 197–99.
22. Anthony Storr, "Commonsense About Jung," *Times Literary Supplement*, 18 May 1962, 356.
23. Shamdasani, *Jung and the Making of Modern Psychology*, 156–57.
24. Ibid., 23. Based on his comparison of Jung's original manuscript with that eventually published by Jaffé, Shamdasani has argued that *Memories, Dreams, Reflections* cannot be considered an autobiography composed by Jung. He writes, "Jung never saw or approved the final manuscript, and

the manuscripts he did see went through considerable editing after his death," (ibid., 24). An extended version of this can be found in idem, "Memories, Dreams, Omissions," *Spring: Journal of Archetype and Culture* 54 (October 1993): 100–31. More recently, Carrie B. Dohe has offered a helpful and concise overview of questions surrounding the reliability of *Memories, Dreams, Reflections*. Dohe seems to endorse Paul Bishop's view that, although the book needs to be read critically, it portrays "what [Jung] wanted us to think about him." See Carrie B. Dohe, "Analytical Psychology as Modern Revelation: C.G. Jung between Master and Scientist," (paper presented at "Master-Disciple Relationships in Interdisciplinary Discourse" Workshop, The Free University in Berlin, Germany, April 23–25, 2010), 4, http://www.academia.edu/420626/_Analytical_Psychology_ as_Modern_Revelation_C._G._Jung_Between_Master_and_Scientist_. Accessed March 17, 2013.

25. Jung, *Memories, Dreams, Reflections*, 165.
26. See Jung, *Memories, Dreams, Reflections*, 280–82.
27. Ibid., 282.
28. Ibid., 228.
29. Ibid., 300.
30. See ibid., 300–01.
31. Ibid., 340.
32. As nearly every student of Jung's work has observed, he can be infuriatingly inconsistent in his definition and use of key concepts such as individuation, symbol, archetype and myth. This terminal inconsistency bedevils any attempt to summarize his thought. It is not my purpose here to provide a synoptic discussion of Jung's understanding of myth, and I do not want to give the impression that the view expressed in *Memories, Dreams, Reflections* represents the culmination of Jung's thinking on the subject. It does represent his most widely-read discussion of the subject, however. One of the best attempts to summarize and evaluate the entirety of Jung's view of myth is the chapter "Jung on Mythology" in Robert A. Segal, *Theorizing about Myth* (Amherst, MA: University of Massachusetts Press, 1999), pp. 67–98.
33. Brome, "The Man Who Woke the World," 9.
34. Roy Perrot, "The Relevance of Jung," *Observer*, 28 January 1973, 34.
35. Young's interview with Jung was published in the *Sunday Times* (London) on 17 July 1960.
36. Carl Gustav Jung interviewed by Gordon Young, "The Art of Living," in William McGuire and R.F.C. Hull eds., *C.G. Jung Speaking: Interviews and Encounters* (London: Thames and Hudson, 1978), 429–30.
37. Jung's desire to communicate his views to non-specialists is also discussed by John Freeman in his introduction to *Man and His Symbols*. See John Freeman, "Introduction," in C. G. Jung ed., *Man and His Symbols* (New York: Anchor Books, 1964), 9–15. See also Bair, 619–21.
38. Philip Toynbee, "Jung's Inner Life," *Observer*, 7 July 1963, 23.
39. Anthony Storr, "Commonsense About Jung," 356. See also idem, "Two Faces of Jung," *Times Literary Supplement*, 2 August 1963, 592.
40. Oliver Louis Zangwill, "Introductions to Jung," *Times Literary Supplement*, 30 July 1954, 489.

41. Kathleen Raine, "Job and the Unconscious," *Encounter* 4, no. 4 (April 1955): 86.
42. Kathleen Raine, "A Serious Call," *Times Literary Supplement*, 2 September 1955, 513.
43. See Raine, "Job and the Unconscious," 87.
44. Ibid., 86.
45. Philip Toynbee, "Jung's Inner Life," *Observer*, 7 July 1963, 23.
46. Philip Toynbee, "Symbols of Our Time," *Observer*, 25 October 1964, 26.
47. Philip Toynbee, "God and Dr Jung," *Observer*, 20 June 1976, 27.
48. Toynbee documented his spiritual questioning during this period in idem, *Part of a Journey: An Autobiographical Journal 1977–1979* (London: Collins, 1981); and idem, *End of a Journey: An Autobiographical Journal 1979–1981*, ed. John Bullimore (London: Bloomsbury, 1988).
49. Toynbee, "God and Dr Jung," 27.
50. Ibid.
51. Storr, "Commonsense About Jung," 356.
52. On this relationship see Ann Conrad Lammers, *In God's Shadow: The Collaboration of Victor White and C.G. Jung* (New York: Paulist Press, 1994). Most of the Jung–White correspondence has been collected in Ann Conrad Lammers and Adrian Cunningham eds., *The Jung-White Letters* (London: Routledge, 2007). This volume includes a helpful biographical essay on White by Cunningham.
53. See H.L. Philp, *Jung and the Problem of Evil* (London: Rockliff, 1958); and David Cox, *Jung and St Paul: A Study of the Doctrine of Justification by Faith and its Relation to the Concept of Individuation* (London: Longmans, Green and Co., Ltd., 1959).
54. Priestley's friendship with Jung is discussed in William Schoenl, *C.G. Jung: His Friendships with Mary Mellon and J.B. Priestley* (Wilmette, IL: Chiron Press, 1998). See also idem, "BBC Broadcasters' Unpublished Views on Jung: Priestley and Freeman," *International Journal of Jungian Studies* 1 no. 2 (2009): 158–162. In *Storyteller: The Many Lives of Laurens Van Der Post* (London: John Murray, 2001) J.D.F. Jones argues that van der Post characteristically exaggerated his friendship with Jung as he did so much else.
55. Laurens van der Post, *Jung and the Story of Our Time* (London: Hogarth Press, 1976), 232.
56. J.B. Priestley, "Jung and the Writer," *Times Literary Supplement*, 6 August 1954, 508. See also J.B. Priestley, "Books in General," *New Statesman and Nation*, 30 October 1954, 541–42. Priestley's 1951 play *Dragon's Mouth* (written with Jacquetta Hawkes) is essentially a dramatization of Jung's psychological theory.
57. Geoffrey Wansell, "Explorer of the Unconscious," *Times* (London), 20 November 1971, 12.
58. van der Post, *Jung and the Story of Our Time*, 237.
59. Robert Ellwood, *The Politics of Myth: A Study of C.G. Jung, Mircea Eliade, and Joseph Campbell* (Albany, NY: State University Press of New York, 1999), 3.
60. For a typical example of praise for Jung's warnings about the Nazis see the leader "The Prince and Dr Jung," *Guardian*, 31 August 1982, 10. For rare references to Jung's alleged Nazi sympathies see *The Guardian*'s obituary (n. 4 above) which mentions how Jung was "criticized for accepting editorship of

a nazified journal." See also Philip Toynbee's comments in "Letters to the Editor," *Observer*, 28 July 1963, 22. The issue of Jung's alleged anti-Semitism remains an unresolved issue in Jung studies.

61. As a typical example see Storr, "Two Faces of Jung."

62. See George Seddon, "Briefing," *Observer*, 14 March 1965, 23. McLynn notes that the program "was a great success and introduced Jung to a new audience" (McLynn, 526). For some reactions to the program shortly after its broadcast see Bernard Campbell, "Jung on TV," *Observer*, 15 November 1959, 12. *The Times* also felt it necessary to mention the impact of the broadcast in its obituary for Jung. See above, n. 3.

63. See, for example, Maurice Richardson, "Buridan's Ass's Night," *The Observer*, 25 October 1959, 24.

64. Part of this controversy was played out in the pages of *The Listener* in 1957.

65. Renford Bambrough, "Bread and Stones: Introduction to the Dunford Dialogues," film no. T120, Script Library, Talks Scripts DUM-DUN, BBC Written Archives Centre, p. 2. Talk broadcast 7 October 1961. For a discussion of analytic philosophers' anxieties about public perception of their work see Matthew Sterenberg, "Tradition and Revolution in the Rhetoric of Analytic Philosophy," *Philosophy and Literature* 34 no. 1 (April 2010): 161–72.

66. For a typical example of how commentators emphasized Jung's boundary-transgressing intellectual exuberance see John Cohen, "Jung on Myths," *Manchester Guardian*, 16 April 1957, 4.

67. C.P. Snow, *The Two Cultures and the Scientific Revolution* (Cambridge: Cambridge University Press, 1959), 4.

68. F.R. Leavis, "Two Cultures? The Significance of C.P. Snow," *Spectator*, 9 March 1962, 297–303.

69. For an excellent recent interpretation of this episode see Guy Ortolano, *The Two Cultures Controversy: Science, Literature, and Cultural Politics in Postwar Britain* (Cambridge: Cambridge University Press, 2009).

70. Storr, "Two Faces of Jung," 592.

71. John A.T. Robinson, *Honest to God* (London: SCM Press, 1963). A more detailed discussion of this episode can be found in Chapter 8 below.

72. Grace Davie, *Religion in Britain since 1945: Believing without Belonging* (Oxford: Blackwell, 1994), 94.

73. Grace Davie, "From Obligation to Consumption: A Framework for Reflection in Northern Europe," *Political Theology* 6 no. 3 (2005): 281–301.

74. "The Art of Living," 435.

75. Anthony Storr, "Child and Man," *Times Literary Supplement*, 29 September 1961, 647.

76. G.C. Bunn, A.D. Lovie, and G.D. Richards eds., *Psychology in Britain: Historical Essays and Personal Reflections* (Leicester: BPS Books, 2001).

77. Von Hendy, 178.

7 Minding the Myth-Kitty: Myth, Cultural Authority, and the Evolution of English Studies

1. William Righter, *Myth and Literature* (London: Routledge & Kegan Paul, 1975), 10–11.

2. Christopher Norris, "Literary Theory, Science and Philosophy of Science," in Christa Knellwolf and Christopher Norris eds., *Twentieth-Century Historical, Philosophical and Psychological Perspectives*, vol. 9 of *The Cambridge History of Literary Criticism* (Cambridge: Cambridge University Press, 2001), 407.

3. See A.S. Byatt, "'The Omnipotence of Thought': Frazer, Freud and Post-Modernist Fiction" in idem, *Passions of the Mind: Selected Writings* (New York: Turtle Bay Books, 1992), 109. The piece originally appeared in Robert Fraser, ed., *Sir James Frazer and the Literary Imagination* (London: Macmillan, 1980).

4. On this shift as change in literary studies more generally, that is, beyond the British context, see Jonathan Culler, *Framing the Sign: Criticism and Its Institutions* (Norman: University of Oklahoma Press, 1988), esp. pp. 33–35.

5. See Chris Baldick, *Criticism and Literary Theory 1890 to the Present* (London: Longman, 1996), 134–36; also Randall Stevenson, *1960–2000: The Last of England?*, vol. 12 of *The Oxford English Literary History* (Oxford: Oxford University Press, 2004), 90, 94. The same view is implicit in Harry Blamires, *A History of Literary Criticism* (London: Macmillan, 1991); Blamires situates his discussion of Northrop Frye's importance within a broader discussion of post-Second World War criticism.

6. Baldick, 134.

7. Some of Fiedler's early essays are collected in the volumes *An End to Innocence* (1955) and *No! in Thunder* (1960). Francis Fergusson's best-known foray into myth criticism was *The Idea of a Theater*. For a typical example of American myth criticism during its golden age see the special issue of *Chimera* IV (spring 1946).

8. See S.E. Hyman, "Myth, Ritual, and Nonsense," *Kenyon Review* 11 (summer, 1949): 455–75; and Philip Rahv, "The Myth and the Powerhouse," *Partisan Review* 20 (November-December 1953): 635–48.

9. There is of course an immense literature on Frye's thought and its legacy. Two of the best book-length studies of Frye's criticism are A.C. Hamilton, *Northrop Frye: Anatomy of His Criticism* (Toronto: University of Toronto Press, 1990) and Jonathan Locke Hart, *Northrop Frye: The Theoretical Imagination* (London: Routledge, 1994). Frye's criticism is helpfully contextualized in relation to other critical movements in Frank Lentricchia, *After the New Criticism* (London: Athlone Press, 1980). Frye's cultural politics are discussed in David Cook, *Northrop Frye: A Vision of the New World* (New York: St. Martin's Press, 1985). Frye's theories were still shaping influential works of criticism decades after his *Anatomy* appeared. One particularly significant example was Paul Fussel's *The Great War and Modern Memory* (New York: Oxford University Press, 1975).

10. Baldick, 134.

11. William Righter, "Myth and Interpretation," *New Literary History* 3 (1972–3): 319–44.

12. David Daiches, *English Literature* (Englewood Cliffs, NJ: Prentice-Hall, Inc., 1964), 126.

13. Paul West, "On Myth and Modernity," in idem, *The Wine of Absurdity: Essays on Literature and Consolation* (University Park, PA: The Pennsylvania State University Press, 1966), 212.

14. David Daiches, *The Present Age: After 1920*; vol. 5 of Bonamy Dobreé, gen. ed., *Introductions to English Literature* (Folcroft Library Editions, 1972), 135.

15. See above, Chapter 2.

16. Wallace W. Douglas, article "The Meanings of 'Myth' in Modern Criticism," *Modern Philology* 50, no. 4 (May 1953): 241.

17. Brian Coates, "Anthropological Criticism," in Knellwolf and Norris, eds., *Twentieth-Century Historical, Philosophical and Psychological Perspectives*, 266.

18. Frank Kermode, "The Myth-Kitty," *Spectator*, 11 September 1959, 339.

19. M.J.C. Hodgart, "In the Shade of the Golden Bough," *The Twentieth Century* 157, no. 936 (February 1955): 111.

20. Ibid., 113.

21. Ibid.

22. Ibid., 118.

23. F.W. Bateson, "The Function of Criticism at the Present Time," *Essays in Criticism* 3, no. 1 (January 1953): 25.

24. Ibid.

25. F.W. Bateson, "Editorial Commentary: The Second Breath," *Essays in Criticism* 15, no. 1 (January 1965): 3.

26. Baldick, 161.

27. Raman Selden, Introduction to *From Formalism to Poststructuralism*, ed. idem, vol 8 of *The Cambridge History of Literary Criticism* (Cambridge: Cambridge University Press, 1995), 1. Randall Stevenson concurs with Selden. See Stevenson, *The Last of England?*, Chapter 3.

28. Norris, 407.

29. Frank Kermode, *Not Entitled: A Memoir* (New York: Farrar, Straus and Giroux, 1995), 214; qtd. in Bernard Bergonzi, *Exploding English: Criticism, Theory, Culture* (Oxford: Clarendon Press, 1990), 23.

30. Frank Kermode, *The Sense of an Ending: Studies in the Theory of Fiction* (New York: Oxford University Press, 1967), 31.

31. Paul West, "The Nature of Fiction," *Essays in Criticism* 13, no. 1 (January 1963): 100.

32. Daiches, *English Literature*, 128.

33. West, "On Myth and Modernity," 231, 236.

34. Ibid., 213.

35. Ibid., 236.

36. See for example Graham Hough, *Image and Experience* (London: Duckworth & Co. Ltd., 1960).

37. Graham Hough, "Criticism as a Humanist Discipline," in idem, *Selected Essays* (Cambridge: Cambridge University Press, 1978), 13.

38. David Daiches, "Myth, Metaphor, and Poetry," in idem, *More Literary Essays* (London: Oliver & Boyd, 1968), 1.

39. Ibid.

40. Ibid., 2.

41. Ibid., 3.

42. Ibid., 5.

43. Ibid., 6

44. Ibid., 9

45. Ibid., 11.

46. Ibid., 13–14.

47. Ibid., 14.
48. C.P. Snow, Introduction to John Holloway, *A London Childhood* (New York: Charles Scribner's Sons, 1968; first published 1966).
49. See, for instance, John Holloway, "Science & Literature: A Reply to Sir Peter Medawar," *Encounter* 33, no. 1 (July 1969): 81–85.
50. John Holloway, "Our Contracting Universities," in *The Colours of Clarity: Essays on Contemporary Literature and Education* (London: Routledge & Kegan Paul, 1964), 10.
51. C.S. Lewis was also scheduled to present a paper but was prevented by illness.
52. John Holloway, "The Concept of Myth in Literature," in L.C. Knights and Basil Cottle, eds., *Metaphor and Symbol: Proceedings of the Twelfth Symposium of the Colston Research Society held in the University of Bristol* (London: Butterworths Scientific Publications, 1960), 123.
53. Ibid., 125–26.
54. Holloway, "The Concept of Myth in Literature," 127.
55. Ibid., 131.
56. Ibid., 132.
57. Ibid.
58. John Holloway, *The Establishment of English* (Cambridge: Cambridge University Press, 1972), 25.
59. Ibid., 26; 27.
60. For a thoughtful discussion of Hough's approach to criticism see Peter Schwendener, "In Quest of Graham Hough," *American Scholar* 67 no. 1 (January 1998): 139–45.
61. Graham Hough, "Crisis in Literary Education," in J.H. Plumb, ed., *Crisis in the Humanities* (Baltimore: Penguin, 1964), 103.
62. Graham Hough, *The Dream and the Task: Literature and Morals in the Culture of Today* (London: Gerald Duckworth & Co. Ltd., 1963), 99. Hough broadcast numerous times on the BBC Third Programme, and the six pieces that make up *The Dream and the Task* were originally broadcast talks.
63. Ibid., 100.
64. Ibid.
65. Ibid., 101–02.
66. Graham Hough, "Criticism as a Humanist Discipline," in idem, *Selected Essays* (Cambridge: Cambridge University Press, 1978), 13.
67. Ibid., 20.
68. Ibid.
69. See Iris Murdoch, "Against Dryness," *Encounter* 16, no. 1 (January 1961): 16–20.
70. Graham Hough, *An Essay on Criticism* (London: Gerald Duckworth & Co. Ltd., 1966), 151–52.
71. Ibid., 152.
72. Ibid.
73. See Graham Hough, "The Muse as Mentor," in idem, *The Dream and the Task*, 11–27.
74. Graham Hough, "The Modernist Lyric," in idem, *Selected Essays*. For Auden's statement of the modern problem see above, Chapter 1.

75. Graham Hough, "The Moral Censor," in idem, *The Dream and the Task*, 28.
76. Hough, *Essay in Criticism*, 155.
77. Hough, "The Modernist Lyric," 241.
78. Frank Kermode, *The Sense of an Ending: Studies in the Theory of Fiction* (Oxford: Oxford University Press, 1967), 1.
79. Ibid., 132.
80. All citations in this paragraph from Frank Kermode, "The Myth-Kitty," 339.
81. Frank Kermode, "On David Jones," *Encounter* 13, no. 5 (November 1959): 76.
82. Ibid., 79.
83. Ibid., 78.
84. Ibid., 76; ibid., 79.
85. Ibid., 77.
86. Frank Kermode, "Hunter and Shaman," *Spectator*, 1 April 1960, 477.
87. Kermode, "On David Jones," 76. Emphasis in original.
88. Ibid., 478.
89. Frank Kermode, "The House of Fiction: Interviews with Seven English Novelists," *Partisan Review* 30, no. 1 (spring 1963), 74. The interviews were originally aired on the BBC Third Programme before appearing in article form *Partisan Review*. Versions of the piece also appeared in *The Listener* under the title "Myth, Reality, and Fiction" (see following note), in *Abstracts of English Studies* (February 1964), as well as in the influential Malcolm Bradbury edited volume *The Novel Today* (London: Fontana, 1977).
90. Frank Kermode, "Myth Reality, and Fiction," *The Listener* 68 (30 August 1962): 311.
91. Murdoch, "Against Dryness," 19.
92. Kermode, *Sense of an Ending*, 39.
93. Ibid.
94. Ibid., 43.
95. Ibid., 132.
96. John Bayley, "The Flexner Sonata," *Essays in Criticism* 18, no. 2 (April 1968): 212.
97. K.K. Ruthven, *Myth* (London: Methuen & Co Ltd, 1976), 82.
98. Righter, *Myth and Literature*, 13.
99. Raymond Williams, *Keywords: A Vocabulary of Culture and Society* (Oxford: Oxford University Press, 1976), 177.
100. Righter, *Myth and Literature*, 1.
101. Righter, *Myth and Literature*, 14.
102. Williams, 178.
103. Ruthven, 82.
104. Ibid., 1.
105. Righter, *Myth and Literature*, 122.
106. Ibid., 2.
107. Hough, "The Modernist Lyric," 237.
108. Josephine M. Guy, "Specialisation and Social Utility: Disciplining English Studies," in Martin Daunton, ed., *The Organisation of Knowledge in Victorian Britain* (Oxford: Oxford University Press, 2005), 199.
109. Ibid., 206.

110. Ibid., 216.
111. Bayley, "The Flexner Sonata," 211.
112. A.D. Moody, "Disillusionment," *Essays in Criticism* 17, no. 4 (October 1967): 499.

8 Making a Modern Faith: Myth in Twentieth-Century British Theology

1. This view was expressed most forcefully by Alasdair MacIntyre in *Encounter*. See idem, "God and the Theologians," *Encounter* 21 no. 3 (September 1963): 3–10.
2. Many of these reviews are helpfully collected in David L. Edwards, ed., *The Honest to God Debate: Some Reaction to the Book 'Honest to God,'* (London: SCM Press Ltd., 1963).
3. Keith W. Clements, *Lovers of Discord: Twentieth-Century Theological Controversies in England* (London: SPCK, 1988), 179.
4. Adrian Hastings, *A History of English Christianity 1920–1990* (London: SCM Press, 1991), 649.
5. John A.T. Robinson, "Why I Wrote It," in Edwards, ed., *The Honest to God Debate*, 277.
6. Anthony Thiselton, "Knowledge, Myth and Corporate Memory," in The Doctrine Commission of the Church of England, *Believing in The Church: The Corporate Nature of Faith* (London: SPCK, 1981): 68.
7. Hastings, 231.
8. Qtd. in S.W. Sykes, "Theology," in C.B. Cox and A.E. Dyson, eds., *The Twentieth Century Mind: History, Ideas, and Literature in Britain, vol. II: 1918–1945* (Oxford: Oxford University Press, 1972), 148.
9. The story of this controversy is well told in Clements, Chapter 4, "From Miracles to Christology: Hensley Henson and the 'Modern Churchmen.'"
10. Sykes, 149.
11. Though Bultmann was older than Barth by about two years, his work did not appear in English until the late 1940s, whereas Barth's groundbreaking commentary *Epistle to the Romans* had been available in English since the 1930s. Barth's influence thus preceded Bultmann's in Britain.
12. Clements, 104.
13. See Alec R. Vidler, *20th Century Defenders of the Faith: Some Theological Fashions Considered in the Robertson Lectures for 1964* (London: SCM Press Ltd., 1965), 103.
14. A historical account of radical theology by a first-hand observer can be found in David L. Edwards, *Tradition and Truth: The Challenge of England's Radical theologians 1962–1989* (London: Hodder and Stoughton, 1989).
15. Vidler, *20th Century Defenders of the Faith*, 107.
16. Alec R. Vidler, *The Church in an Age of Revolution: 1789 to the Present Day*, rev. ed., vol. 5 of *The Pelican History of the Church* (Harmondsworth, England: Penguin Books, 1971), 274.
17. Vidler gives a brief account of how the group was founded in Ved Mehta, *The New Theologian* (New York: Harper & Row, 1965), 73–74.

18. See Vidler, *Defenders*, 106.
19. Donald MacKenzie MacKinnon et al., *Objections to Christian Belief* (London: Constable, 1963).
20. In *Honest to God* Robinson acknowledges Vidler's influence on his thinking and quotes from the *Soundings* volume more than once.
21. Clements, 17.
22. Gary Dorrien, *The Word as True Myth: Interpreting Modern Theology* (Louisville: Westminster John Knox Press, 1997), 106. Some works that evidence this impact include Roger Lloyd, *The Ferment in the Church* (London: SCM Press, Ltd., 1964); David Cairns, *A Gospel Without Myth?: Bultmann's Challenge to the Preacher* (London: SCM Press Ltd., 1960); Ian Henderson, *Myth in the New Testament* (London: Robert Cunningham and Sons Ltd., 1952); Philip Edgcumbe Hughes, *Scripture and Myth: An Examination of Rudolf Bultmann's Plea for Demythologization* (London: The Tyndale Press, 1956); Geraint Vaughan Jones, *Christology and Myth in the New Testament: An Inquiry into the Character, Extent and Interpretation of the Mythological Element in New Testament Christology* (London: George Allen & Unwin Ltd., 1956); John Macquarrie, *The Scope of Demythologizing: Bultmann and his Critics* (London: SCM Press Ltd., 1960); L. Malevez, S.J., *The Christian Message and Myth: The Theology of Rudolf Bultmann*, trans. Olive Wyon (London: SCM Press Ltd., 1958); H.P. Owen, *Revelation and Existence: A Study in the Theology of Rudolf Bultmann* (Cardiff: University of Wales Press, 1957). There were also several American interpretations of Bultmann that were widely read in Britain including Schubert M. Ogden, *Christ Without Myth: A Study Based on the Theology of Rudolf Bultmann* (New York: Harper & Row, 1961); Burton Throckmorton, *The New Testament and Mythology* (Philadelphia, PA: Westminster Press, 1959); and John Knox, *Myth and Truth: An Essay on the Language of Faith* (Charlottesville, VA: University Press of Virginia, 1964).
23. Rowan Williams, "Theology in the Twentieth Century," in Ernest Nicholson, ed., *A Century of Theological and Religious Studies in Britain* (Oxford: Oxford University Press, 2003), 244.
24. This lecture, other key texts by Bultmann, and essays by his critics were translated into English and collected in Hans Werner Bartsch, ed., *Kerygma and Myth: A Theological Debate*, vol. 1, trans. Reginald H. Fuller (London: SPCK, 1953); and idem, ed., *Kerygma and Myth: A Theological Debate*, vol. 2, trans. Reginald H. Fuller (London: SPCK: 1962). Some of Bultmann's writings have been retranslated in the more recent collection *New Testament and Mythology and Other Basic Writings*, trans. and ed. Schubert M. Ogden, (Philadelphia, PA: Fortress Press, 1984).
25. Bultmann, in Bartsch, ed., vol. 1, 183.
26. Bultmann, "New Testament and Mythology," in Ogden, ed., 9.
27. Ibid.
28. Bultmann in Bartsch, ed., vol. 2, 183.
29. Robert Segal, "Does Myth Have a Future?," in Laurie L. Patton and Wendy Doniger, eds., *Myth and Method* (Charlottesville, VA: University Press of Virginia, 1996), 90.
30. Dorrien, 104.
31. John A.T. Robinson, *Honest to God* (London: SCM Press, Ltd., 1963), 132.

32. Ibid., 133.
33. Robinson, "The Debate Continues," in Edwards, ed. *The Honest to God Debate*, 264.
34. Ibid., 266–67.
35. Ibid., 267.
36. This despite the fact that Bultmann was an avowed critic of liberal theology, which he believed turned Christianity into a sentimental moralism. See Bultmann, "New Testament and Mythology," in Ogden, ed., 12.
37. Qtd. in Jones, 13.
38. Paul Avis, *God and the Creative Imagination: Metaphor, Symbol and Myth in Religion and Theology* (London: Routledge, 1999), 162.
39. Jones, 13.
40. Ibid., 241
41. Ibid., 270.
42. Hastings, 498.
43. H.E. Root, "What is the Gospel?," *Theology* 66, no. 516 (June, 1963), 222.
44. James Mark, "Myth and Miracle, or the Ambiguity of Bultmann," *Theology* 66, no. 514 (April 1963), 137.
45. Ibid., 140.
46. Analytic philosophy's challenge to theology is discussed in Stewart Sutherland, "Philosophy of Religion in the Twentieth Century" in Ernest Nicholson, ed., *A Century of Theological and Religious Studies in Britain*, 253–69.
47. For works of the period that reflect this anxiety see John Macquarrie, *Twentieth-Century Religious Thought: The Frontiers of Philosophy and Theology, 1900–1960* (London: SCM Press Ltd., 1963); R.W. Hepburn, *Christianity and Paradox* (London: Watt, 1958); Ian T. Ramsey, *Religious Language* (London: SCM Press Ltd., 1957); Donald MacKinnon, *The Borderlands of Theology* (Cambridge: Cambridge University Press, 1961).
48. Mehta, 117.
49. Ninian Smart, "The Intellectual Crisis of British Christianity," *Theology* 67, no. 535 (January 1965): 31–38.
50. Ibid., 32.
51. Ibid.
52. Ibid., 36; 37.
53. On Braithwaite's theory religious statements were really declarations of loyalty to a specific set of moral or religious principles.
54. R.B. Braithwaite, *An Empiricist's View of the Nature of Religious Belief* (Cambridge: Cambridge University Press, 1955), 22.
55. B.M.G. Reardon, "Philosophy and Myth," *Theology* 65, no. 502 (April 1962): 138.
56. Ibid., 137.
57. The Bishop of Woolwich [John Robinson], "Keeping in Touch with Theology," *Twentieth Century* 172, no. 1018 (summer 1963), 87.
58. Tyron Inbody, "Myth in Contemporary Theology: The Irreconcilable Issue," *Anglican Theological Review* 58, no. 2 (April 1976), 139–40.
59. Robinson, *Honest to God*, 133.
60. Macquarrie, *The Scope of Demythologizing*, 233–34. The "quasi-myth" that Macquarrie had in mind was the thoroughly secular belief that humans had

achieved self-sufficiency through science. See also Karl Jaspers and Rudolf Bultmann, *Myth and Christianity: An Inquiry into the Possibility of Religion Without Myth* (New York: The Noonday Press, 1958).

61. Perhaps the most philosophically sophisticated attempt to do so was Ian G. Barbour, *Myths, Models, and Paradigms: The Nature of Scientific and Religious Language* (London: SCM Press, 1974), which aimed to show that the categories of "science" and "myth" were not nearly as antithetical as Bultmann and his followers had supposed.
62. John Hick, ed., *The Myth of God Incarnate* (London, SCM Press, 1977), ix.
63. Ibid.
64. Frances Young, "Two Roots or a Tangled Mass?," in Hick, ed., 34.
65. Maurice Wiles, "Myth in Theology," in Hick, ed., 163.
66. Ibid., 164.
67. Ibid., 158.
68. Ibid., 165.
69. Ibid., 161.
70. John Hick in idem, ed., 178.
71. Wiles, 164.
72. Williams, 246.
73. Hick, x; Hastings, 650.
74. Hick, x.
75. See Avis, 173. Cf. Hastings, 650.
76. John Barton and John Halliburton, "Story and Liturgy," in *Believing in the Church*, 81.
77. See Thiselton, "Knowledge, Myth and Corporate Memory," 67–72.
78. Ibid., 70.
79. Ibid., 72.
80. John Barton and John Halliburton, "Story and Liturgy," in *Believing in the Church*, 79.
81. Ibid., 80.
82. Robinson, "The Debate Continues," 263.
83. Inbody, 139.
84. See Wiles, 164.
85. Gary Dorrien, "The Golden Years of Welfare Capitalism: The Twilight of the Giants," in Gregory Baum, ed., *The Twentieth Century: A Theological Overview* (Maryknoll, NY: Orbis Books 1999), 100.

Epilogue

1. Iris Murdoch, "Mass, Might and Myth," *Spectator*, 7 September 1962, 338.
2. Michael Saler, *The Avant-Garde in Interwar England: "Medieval Modernism" and the London Underground* (New York: Oxford University Press, 1999); and Scott Anthony, *Public Relations and the Making of Modern Britain: Stephen Tallents and the Birth of a Progressive Media Profession* (Manchester: Manchester University Press, 2012).
3. See, for instance, Saler's notion of the ironic imagination. Michael Saler, "Modernity, Disenchantment, and the Ironic Imagination," *Philosophy and Literature* 28, no. 1 (April 2004): 137–49.

4. Lisa Tickner, *The Spectacle of Women: Imagery of the Suffragette Campaign, 1870–1914* (London: Chatto and Windus, 1987), 125–26.

5. As documented in Oliver Green, *Underground Art: London Transport Poster 1908-Present* (London: Studio Vista, 1990).

6. Charles Taylor, *The Ethics of Authenticity* (Cambridge, MA: Harvard University Press, 1991), 60. See also idem, *A Secular Age* (Cambridge, MA: Harvard University Press, 2007).

7. Graham Harvey notes that many self-identified contemporary pagans came to the religion via a childhood interest in fantasy literature. See idem, *Contemporary Paganism* (New York: New York University Press, 1996), 182.

Selected Bibliography

Primary sources

Newspapers and periodicals

Encounter
Essays in Criticism
Guardian
Listener
Manchester Guardian
New Statesman
New Statesman and Nation
New Worlds
Observer
Partisan Review
Theology
Times (London)
Times Literary Supplement
Twentieth Century
SF Horizons
Spectator
Sunday Times

Other printed sources

Aldiss, Brian. *The Dark Light Years*. London: Faber and Faber, 1964.
——. *Frankenstein Unbound*. London: Jonathan Cape, 1973.
—— and Harry Harrison, eds. *Hell's Cartographers: Some Personal Histories of Science Fiction Writers*. London: Weidenfeld and Nicolson, 1975.
——. *The Shape of Further Things*. New York: Doubleday & Company, Inc., 1971.
Allen, Grant. *The Great Taboo*. London: Chatto & Windus, 1890.
Auden, W.H. "Yeats as an Example." *Kenyon Review* 10, no. 2 (1948): 187–95.
Bailey, K.V. "A Prized Harmony: Myth, Symbol and Dialectic in the Novels of Olaf Stapledon." *Foundation* 15 (January 1979): 53–66.
Ballard, J.G. "Ballard at Home," interview by Catherine Bresson. *Metaphores* 7 (March 1982): 3–30.
——. *Chronopolis and Other Stories*. New York: G.P. Putnam's Sons, 1971.
——. *Concrete Island*. London: Cape, 1973.
——. *Crash*. London: Cape, 1973.
——. "Disasters," interview by Rodney Smith. *The Listener*, 14 February 1980: 208–09.
——. "Interview by Brendan Hennessy." *The Transatlantic Review* no. 39 (spring 1971): 60–64.
——. "Interview by Thomas Frick." *Paris Review* 94 (winter 1984): 133–60.

——. *J.G. Ballard: Conversations.* ed. V. Vale and Marian Wallace. San Francisco, CA: RE/Search Publications, 2005.

——. *J.G. Ballard: The Complete Short Stories.* London: Flamingo, 2001.

——. *The Kindness of Women.* London: HarperCollins, 1991.

——. *Myths of the Near Future.* London: Jonathan Cape, 1982.

——. "Some Words about *Crash!*" *Foundation* 9 (November 1975): 45–54.

——. *A User's Guide to the Millennium: Essays and Reviews.* New York: Picador, 1996.

——. "Waiting for Silver Coconuts," interview by Charles Shaar Murray. *New Musical Express,* 22 October 1983: 28–29, 52.

Barbour, Ian G. *Myths, Models, and Paradigms: The Nature of Scientific and Religious Language.* London: SCM Press, 1974.

Bartsch, Hans Werner, ed. *Kerygma and Myth: A Theological Debate,* vol. 1. Trans. Reginald H. Fuller. London: SPCK, 1953.

——, ed. *Kerygma and Myth: A Theological Debate,* vol. 2. Trans. Reginald H. Fuller. London: SPCK, 1962.

Baudrillard, Jean. "Two Essays." *Science Fiction Studies* 55 no. 18 (November 1991): 309–19.

Bergonzi, Bernard. *Exploding English: Criticism, Theory, Culture.* Oxford: Clarendon Press, 1990.

Blackford, Russell. "Myth and the Art of Science Fiction Commentary." *Science Fiction: A Review of Speculative Literature* 3, no. 2 (May 1981): 52–56.

Bodkin, Maud. *Archetypal Patterns in Poetry: Psychological Studies of the Imagination.* London: Oxford University Press, 1934.

Braithwaite, R.B. *An Empiricist's View of the Nature of Religious Belief.* Cambridge: Cambridge University Press, 1955.

Bultmann, Rudolf. *New Testament and Mythology and Other Basic Writings.* Trans. and ed. Schubert M. Ogden. Philadelphia, PA: Fortress Press, 1984.

Butts, Mary. *Armed with Madness.* London: Wishart & Company, 1928; reprint, London: Penguin, 2001.

——. *The Crystal Cabinet: My Childhood at Salterns.* Manchester: Carcanet Press Limited, 1988.

——. *The Journals of Mary Butts.* ed. Nathalie Blondel. New Haven, CT: Yale University Press, 2002.

Byatt, A.S. *Passions of the Mind: Selected Writings.* New York: Turtle Bay Books, 1992.

Cairns, David. *A Gospel Without Myth?: Bultmann's Challenge to the Preacher.* London: SCM Press Ltd., 1960.

Chase, Richard. *The American Novel and Its Tradition.* Garden City, NY: Doubleday, 1957.

——. *Quest for Myth.* Baton Rouge, LA: Louisiana State University Press, 1949.

Cogell, Elizabeth Cummins. "The Middle-Landscape Myth in Science Fiction." *Science Fiction Studies* 5, no. 2 (July 1978): 134–42.

Collingwood, R.G. *The Philosophy of Enchantment: Studies in Folktale, Cultural Criticism, and Anthropology.* ed. David Boucher, Wendy James, and Philip Smallwood. Oxford: Clarendon Press, 2007.

Cox, C.B., and A.E. Dyson, eds. *The Twentieth Century Mind: History, Ideas, and Literature in Britain, vol. II: 1918–1945.* Oxford: Oxford University Press, 1972.

Cox, David. *Jung and St Paul: A Study of the Doctrine of Justification by Faith and its Relation to the Concept of Individuation*. London: Longmans, Green and Co., Ltd., 1959.

Daiches, David. *English Literature*. Englewood Cliffs, NJ: Prentice-Hall, Inc., 1964.

——. *Literary Essays*. London: Oliver & Boyd, 1956.

——. *More Literary Essays*. London: Oliver & Boyd, 1968.

——. *The Present Age: After 1920*. Vol. 5 of gen. ed. Bonamy Dobreé, *Introductions to English Literature*. Folcroft, PA: Folcroft Library Editions, 1972.

Disch, Thomas M., and Charles Naylor, eds. *New Constellations: An Anthology of Tomorrow's Mythologies*. New York: Harper & Row, 1976.

Douglas, Wallace W. "The Meanings of 'Myth' in Modern Criticism." *Modern Philology* 50, no. 4 (May 1953) 232–242.

Eliot, T.S. *The Annotated Waste Land with Eliot's Contemporary Prose*. ed. Lawrence Rainey. New Haven, CT: Yale University Press, 2005.

——. *On Poetry and Poets*. London: Faber and Faber, 1957.

——. "Ulysses, Order and Myth," *The Dial* 75 (November 1923): 480–83.

——. *The Use of Poetry and the Use of Criticism*. London: Faber and Faber, 1933.

Ferguson, Francis. *The Idea of a Theater*. Garden City, NY: Doubleday, 1949.

Fiedler, Leslie A. *An End to Innocence: Essays on Culture and Politics*. Boston, MA: Beacon Press, 1955.

——. *No! in Thunder: Essays on Myth and Literature*. Boston, MA: Beacon Press, 1960.

Frazer, James George. *The Golden Bough: A Study in Magic and Religion*. 3rd ed. 13 vols. London: Macmillan & Co., 1911–1915.

——. *Psyche's Task. A Discourse Concerning the Influence of Superstition on the Growth of Institutions*. 2nd ed. London: Macmillan & Co., 1913.

Fussel, Paul. *The Great War and Modern Memory*. New York: Oxford University Press, 1975.

Grensted, L.W. *Psychology and God: A Study of the Implications of Recent Psychology for Religious Belief and Practice*. London: Longmans, Green and Co., 1931.

Guthrie, W.K.C. "Myth and Reason: Oration Delivered at the London School of Economics and Political Science on Friday, 12 December, 1952." London: London School of Economics and Political Science, 1953.

Harrison, Jane Ellen. *Alpha and Omega*. London: Sidgwick and Jackson, 1915.

——. *Epilegomena to the Study of Greek Religion*. Cambridge: Cambridge University Press, 1921.

——. *Mythology and Monuments of Ancient Athens*. London: Macmillan & Co., 1890.

——. *Prolegomena to the Study of Greek Religion*. 3rd ed. Cambridge: Cambridge University Press, 1922.

——. *Themis; A Study of the Social Origins of Greek Religion, with an Excursus on the Ritual Forms Preserved in Greek Tragedy by Professor Gilbert Murray and a Chapter on the Origin of the Olympic Games by Mr F.M. Cornford*. Cambridge: Cambridge University Press, 1912.

Henderson, Ian. *Myth in the New Testament*. London: Robert Cunningham and Sons Ltd., 1952.

Hepburn, R.W. *Christianity and Paradox*. London: Watt, 1958.

Holloway, John. *The Colours of Clarity: Essays on Contemporary Literature and Education*. London: Routledge & Kegan Paul, 1964.

——. *The Establishment of English*. Cambridge: Cambridge University Press, 1972.

——. *A London Childhood*. New York: Charles Scribner's Sons, 1968.

Hough, Graham. *The Dream and the Task: Literature and Morals in the Culture of Today*. London: Gerald Duckworth & Co. Ltd., 1963.

——. *An Essay on Criticism*. London: Gerald Duckworth & Co. Ltd., 1966.

——. *Image and Experience*. London: Duckworth & Co. Ltd., 1960.

——. *Selected Essays*. Cambridge: Cambridge University Press, 1978.

Hughes, Philip Edgcumbe. *Scripture and Myth: An Examination of Rudolf Bultmann's Plea for Demythologization*. London: The Tyndale Press, 1956.

Hughes, Ted. *Winter Pollen: Occasional Prose*. ed. William Scammell. London: Faber and Faber, 1994.

Hyman, Stanley Edgar. "Myth, Ritual, and Nonsense." *Kenyon Review* XI (summer 1949): 455–75.

——. *The Tangled Bank: Darwin, Marx, Frazer and Freud as Imaginative Writers*. New York: Atheneum, 1962.

Jaspers, Karl, and Rudolf Bultmann. *Myth and Christianity: An Inquiry into the Possibility of Religion Without Myth*. New York: The Noonday Press, 1958.

Jones, David. *Epoch and Artist*. London: Faber and Faber, 1959.

——. *In Parenthesis*. London: Faber & Faber Ltd., 1937.

Jones, Geraint Vaughan. *Christology and Myth in the New Testament: An Inquiry into the Character, Extent and Interpretation of the Mythological Element in New Testament Christology*. London: George Allen & Unwin Ltd., 1956.

Jones, Langdon, ed. *The New S.F.: An Original Anthology of Modern Speculative Fiction*. London: Hutchison & Co Ltd., 1969.

Jung, C.G., ed. *Man and His Symbols*. New York: Anchor Books, 1964.

——. *Memories, Dreams, Reflections*. Rev. ed. Aniela Jaffé. Trans. Richard and Clara Winston. New York: Vintage Books, 1989.

——. *Modern Man in Search of a Soul*. Trans. W.S. Dell and Cary Baynes. London: Routledge & Kegan Paul, 1933.

Kermode, Frank. *Not Entitled: A Memoir*. New York: Farrar, Straus and Giroux, 1995.

——. *The Sense of an Ending: Studies in the Theory of Fiction*. Oxford: Oxford University Press, 1967.

Kirk, Geoffrey S. *Myth*. Cambridge: Cambridge University Press, 1970.

Knights, L.C., and Basil Cottle, eds. *Metaphor and Symbol: Proceedings of the Twelfth Symposium of the Colston Research Society Held in the University of Bristol*. London: Butterworths Scientific Publications, 1960.

Knox, John. *Myth and Truth: An Essay on the Language of Faith*. Charlottesville, VA.: University Press of Virginia, 1964.

Lang, Andrew. *Magic and Religion*. London: Longmans, Green & Co., 1901.

Leach, Edmund. *The Abolition of Man*. London: Oxford University Press, 1943; reprint, New York: Macmillan Publishing Company, 1955.

——. "Golden Bough or Gilded Twig?" *Deadalus* 90 (1961): 371–99.

——. *All My Road Before Me: The Diary of C.S. Lewis 1922–1927*. ed. Walter Hooper San Diego: Harcourt Brace Jovanovich, 1991.

——. *Collected Letters, Volume I: Family Letters 1905–1931*. ed. Walter Hooper. London: HarperCollins, 2000.

——. *The Collected Letters of C.S. Lewis, Volume II: Books, Broadcasts, and the War, 1931–1949.* ed. Walter Hooper. San Francisco, CA: HarperSanFrancisco, 2004.

——. *The Collected Letters of C.S. Lewis, Volume III: Narnia, Cambridge, and Joy 1950–1963.* ed. Walter Hooper. San Francisco, CA: HarperSanFrancisco, 2007.

——. *Essay Collection and Other Short Pieces.* ed. Lesley Walmsley. London: Harper CollinsPublishers, 2000.

——. *An Experiment in Criticism.* Cambridge: Cambridge University Press, 1961.

——. *Of Other Worlds: Essays and Stories.* London: Geoffrey Bles, 1966.

——. *On Stories and Other Essays on Literature.* ed. Walter Hooper. New York: Harcourt Brace Jovanovich, 1966.

——. *Selected Literary Essays.* ed. Walter Hooper. Cambridge: Cambridge University Press, 1969.

——. *Surprised by Joy: The Shape of My Early Life.* New York: Harcourt Brace and Company, 1955.

——. *That Hideous Strength.* New York: Macmillan, 1965.

——. *Till We Have Faces, A Myth Retold.* London: Geoffrey Bles, 1956.

Lloyd, Roger. *The Ferment in the Church.* London: SCM Press, Ltd., 1964.

MacKinnon, Donald MacKenzie. *The Borderlands of Theology.* Cambridge: Cambridge University Press, 1961.

MacKinnon, Donald MacKenzie., H.A. Williams, A.R. Vidler, and J.S. Bezzant. *Objections to Christian Belief.* London: Constable, 1963.

Macquarrie, John. *The Scope of Demythologizing: Bultmann and his Critics.* London: SCM Press Ltd., 1960.

——. *Twentieth-Century Religious Thought: The Frontiers of Philosophy and Theology, 1900–1960.* London: SCM Press Ltd., 1963.

Malevez, L., S.J. *The Christian Message and Myth: The Theology of Rudolf Bultmann.* Trans. Olive Wyon. London: SCM Press Ltd., 1958.

McGuire, William and R.F.C. Hull, eds. *C.G. Jung Speaking: Interviews and Encounters.* London: Thames and Hudson, 1978.

Mehta, Ved. *The New Theologian.* New York: Harper & Row, 1965.

Moorcock, Michael. *Breakfast in the Ruins.* London: New English Library, 1972.

——. *A Cure for Cancer.* London: Allison and Busby, 1971.

——, ed. *New Worlds: An Anthology.* London: Fontana, 1983.

——. *Sojan.* Manchester: Savoy Books Ltd., 1977.

——. *Wizardry and Wild Romance: A Study of Epic Fantasy.* London: Victor Gollancz Ltd., 1987.

Nicholls, Peter, ed. *The Encyclopaedia of Science Fiction.* St. Albans: Granada, 1979.

Ogden, Schubert M. *Christ Without Myth: A Study Based on the Theology of Rudolf Bultmann.* New York: Harper & Row, 1961.

Orwell, George. *The Complete Works of George Orwell.* Vol. 17. ed. Peter Davidson. London: Secker and Warburg, 1998.

Owen, H.P. *Revelation and Existence: A Study in the Theology of Rudolf Bultmann.* Cardiff: University of Wales Press, 1957.

Panshin, Alexei, and Cory Panshin. "Science Fiction and the Dimension of Myth." *Extrapolation* 22, no. 2 (summer 1981): 127–39.

Philp, H.L. *Jung and the Problem of Evil.* London: Rockliff, 1958.

Platt, Charles. *Who Writes Science Fiction?.* Manchester: Savoy Books, 1980.

Plumb, J.H., ed. *Crisis in the Humanities.* Baltimore: Penguin, 1964.

Powys, John Cowper. *Autobiography.* London: John Lane, The Bodley Head, 1934.

——. *The Complex Vision.* New York: Dodd, Mead and Company, 1920.

——. *A Glastonbury Romance.* London: Macdonald and Co. Publishers Ltd., 1955.

——. *Petrushka and the Dancer: The Diaries of John Cowper Powys, 1929–1939.* ed. Morine Krissdottir. Manchester: Carcanet Press Limited, 1995.

Priestley, J.B. *Thoughts in the Wilderness.* London: William Heinemann Ltd., 1957.

Radford, John. "Science Fiction as Myth." *Foundation* 10 (June 1976): 28–34.

Rahv, Philip. "The Myth and the Powerhouse." *Partisan Review* 20 (November–December, 1953): 635–48.

Ramsey, Ian T. *Religious Language.* London: SCM Press Ltd., 1957.

RE/Search no. 8/9: J.G. Ballard. ed. V. Vale and Andrea Juno. San Francisco, CA: RE/Search Publications, 1984.

Righter, William. "Myth and Interpretation." *New Literary History* 3 (1972–3): 319–44.

——. *Myth and Literature.* London: Routledge & Kegan Paul, 1975.

Robinson, John A.T. *Honest to God.* London: SCM Press, Ltd., 1963.

Ruthven, K.K. *Myth.* London: Methuen & Co Ltd., 1976.

Self, Will. *Junk Mail.* London: Penguin, 1996.

Snow, C.P. *The Two Cultures and the Scientific Revolution.* Cambridge: Cambridge University Press, 1959.

Spinrad, Norman. *The Star Spangled Future.* New York: Ace, 1979.

Stapledon, Olaf. *Last and First Men.* New York: Dover, 1968; London: Methuen, 1930.

Tarshis, Jerome. "Krafft-Ebing Visits Dealey Plaza: The Recent Fiction of J.G. Ballard." *Evergreen Review* no. 96 (spring 1973): 137–48.

Throckmorton, Burton. *The New Testament and Mythology.* Philadelphia, PA: Westminster Press, 1959.

Tolkien, J.R.R. *Letters of J.R.R. Tolkien.* ed. Humphrey Carpenter. London: George Allen and Unwin, 1981.

——. "On Fairy-Stories." In *Essays Presented to Charles Williams.* Oxford: Oxford University Press, 1947: 38–89.

Trilling, Lionel. *Beyond Culture.* New York: Viking Press, 1965.

Tylor, Edward B. *Anthropology: An Introduction to the Study of Man and Civilization.* Rev. ed. London: Macmillan, 1924.

Van der Post, Laurens. *Jung and the Story of Our Time.* London: Hogarth Press, 1976.

Vidler, Alec R. *20th Century Defenders of the Faith: Some Theological Fashions Considered in the Robertson Lectures for 1964.* London: SCM Press Ltd., 1965.

——. *The Church in an Age of Revolution: 1789 to the Present Day.* Rev. ed. Vol. 5 of *The Pelican History of the Church.* Harmondsworth: Penguin Books, 1971.

Waite, Arthur Edward. *The Hidden Church of the Holy Graal.* London: Rebman Limited, 1909. Revised as *The Holy Grail: The Galahad Quest in the Arthurian Literature.* London: Rider, 1933.

West, Paul. *The Wine of Absurdity: Essays on Literature and Consolation.* University Park, PA: The Pennsylvania State University Press, 1966.

Weston, Jessie. *From Ritual to Romance.* London: Cambridge University Press, 1920.

Wiles, Maurice F. "'Myth' in Theology." *Bulletin of the John Rylands University Library* 59, no. 1 (autumn 1976): 227–46.

Williams, Charles, and C.S. Lewis. *Arthurian Torso.* London: Oxford University Press, 1948.

——. *The Image of the City and Other Essays.* ed. Anne Ridler. London: Oxford University Press, 1958.

——. *War in Heaven.* London: Victor Gollancz, 1930.

Williams, Raymond. *Keywords: A Vocabulary of Culture and Society.* Oxford: Oxford University Press, 1976.

——. "Science Fiction." *The Highway* 48 (December 1956): 41–45.

Wolfe, Gary K. "Mythic Structures in Cordwainer Smith's 'The Game of Rat and Dragon.' " *Science Fiction Studies* 4, no. 2 (July 1977): 144–50.

Secondary Sources

Ackerman, Robert. Introduction. In Jane Ellen Harrison, *Prolegomena to the Study of Greek Religion.* Princeton, NJ: Princeton University Press, 1991. pp. xiii–xxx.

——. *J.G. Frazer: His Life and Work.* Cambridge: Cambridge University Press, 1987.

——. *The Myth and Ritual School: J.G. Frazer and the Cambridge Ritualists.* New York: Routledge, 2002.

Anthony, Scott. *Public Relations and the Making of Modern Britain: Stephen Tallents and the Birth of a Progressive Media Profession.* Manchester: Manchester University Press, 2012.

Armstrong, Tim. *Modernism: A Cultural History.* Cambridge: Polity Press, 2005.

Avis, Paul. *God and the Creative Imagination: Metaphor, Symbol and Myth in Religion and Theology.* London: Routledge, 1999.

Baeten, Elizabeth M. *The Magic Mirror: Myth's Abiding Power.* Albany, NY: State University of New York Press, 1996.

Bair, Deirdre. *Jung: A Biography.* Boston, MA: Little, Brown and Company, 2003.

Baldick, Chris. *Criticism and Literary Theory 1890 to the Present.* London: Longman, 1996.

Barber, Richard. *The Grail: Imagination and Belief.* Cambridge, MA: Harvard University Press, 2004.

Baum, Gregory, ed. *The Twentieth Century: A Theological Overview.* Maryknoll, NY: Orbis Books, 1999.

Baxter, Jeannette and Wymer, Roland, eds. *J.G. Ballard: Visions and Revisions.* London: Palgrave Macmillan, 2012.

Baxter, John. *The Inner Man: The Life of J.G. Ballard.* London: Weidenfeld & Nicholson, 2011.

Beard, Mary. "Frazer, Leach, and Virgil: The Popularity (and Unpopularity) of *The Golden Bough.*" *Comparative Studies in Society and History* 24, 2 (April, 1992): 203–24.

——. *The Invention of Jane Harrison.* Cambridge, MA: Harvard University Press, 2000.

Beidelman, T.O. *W. Robertson Smith and the Sociological Study of Religion.* Chicago, IL: University of Chicago Press, 1974.

Bell, Michael. *Literature, Modernism and Myth: Belief and Responsibility in the Twentieth Century.* Cambridge: Cambridge University Press, 1997.

——, and Peter Poellner, eds. *Myth and the Making of Modernity: The Problem of Grounding in Early Twentieth-Century Literature.* Amsterdam: Rodopi, 1998.

Bennett, Jane. *The Enchantment of Modern Life: Attachments, Crossings, and Ethics.* Princeton, NJ: Princeton University Press, 2001.

Blamires, Harry. *A History of Literary Criticism.* London: Macmillan, 1991.

Blondel, Nathalie. *Mary Butts: Scenes from the Life.* Kingston, NY: McPherson, 1998.

Bloom, Harold, ed. *J.R.R. Tolkien.* Philadelphia, PA: Chelsea House Publishers, 2000.

Bowler, Peter J. *Reconciling Science and Religion: The Debate in Early-Twentieth-Century Britain.* Chicago, IL: University of Chicago Press, 2001.

Brooker, Jewel Spears. *Mastery and Escape: T.S. Eliot and the Dialectic of Modernism.* Amherst, MA: University of Massachusetts Press, 1994.

Buchanan, Bradley W. "Armed with Questions: Mary Butts's Sacred Interrogative," *Twentieth Century Literature* 49, no. 3 (Autumn 2003): 360–87.

Bunn, G.C., A.D. Lovie, and G.D. Richards, eds. *Psychology in Britain: Historical Essays and Personal Reflections* Leicester: BPS Books, 2001.

Burns, Alan, and Charles Sugnet, eds. *The Imagination on Trial: British and American Writers Discuss Their Working Methods.* London: Allison and Busby, 1981.

Carpenter, Humphrey. *The Inklings: C.S. Lewis, J.R.R. Tolkien, Charles Williams, and Their Friends.* London: Allen and Unwin, 1978.

——. *Tolkien: A Biography.* Boston, MA: Houghton Mifflin Company, 1977.

Carpentier, Martha Celeste. *Ritual, Myth, and the Modernist Text: The Influence of Jane Ellen Harrison on Joyce, Eliot, and Woolf.* Amsterdam: Gordon and Breach, 1998.

Cavaliero, Glen. *John Cowper Powys: Novelist.* Oxford: Clarendon Press, 1973.

Chance, Jane. *Tolkien's Art: A Mythology for England.* Rev. ed. Lexington, KY: University of Kentucky Press, 2000.

——, ed. *Tolkien the Medievalist.* London: Routledge, 2003.

Clack, Brian R. *Wittgenstein, Frazer, and Religion.* New York: St. Martin's Press, 1999.

Clements, Keith W. *Lovers of Discord: Twentieth-Century Theological Controversies in England.* London: SPCK, 1988.

Cook, David. *Northrop Frye: A Vision of the New World.* New York: St. Martin's Press, 1985.

Coupe, Laurence. *Myth.* London: Routledge, 1997.

Csapo, Eric. *Theories of Mythology.* Malden, MA: Blackwell, 2005.

Culler, Jonathan. *Framing the Sign: Criticism and Its Institutions.* Norman: University of Oklahoma Press, 1988.

Cunningham, Valentine. *British Writers of the Thirties.* Oxford: Oxford University Press, 1988.

Curry, Patrick. *Defending Middle-earth: Tolkien, Myth, and Modernity.* Edinburgh: Floris Books, 1997.

Davie, Donald. *These Companions: Recollections.* Cambridge: Cambridge University Press, 1982.

Davie, Grace. "From Obligation to Consumption: A Framework for Reflection in Northern Europe," *Political Theology* 6, no. 3 (2005): 281–301.

——. *Religion in Britain since 1945: Believing Without Belonging*. Oxford: Blackwell, 1994.

Delville, Michel. *J.G. Ballard*. Plymouth: Northcote House, 1998.

Dorrien, Gary. *The Word as True Myth: Interpreting Modern Theology*. Louisville: Westminster John Knox Press, 1997.

Doty, William. *Myth: A Handbook*. Westport, CT: Greenwood Press, 2004.

Duriez, Colin. *Tolkien and C.S. Lewis: The Gift of Friendship*. Mahwah, NJ: HiddenSpring, 2003.

Edelstein, Dan, and Bettina R. Lerner, eds. *Myth and Modernity*. New Haven, CT: Yale University Press, 2007.

Edwards, Bruce L., ed. *C.S. Lewis: Life, Work, and Legacy*. 4 vols. Santa Barbara, CA: Praeger Publishers, 2007.

Edwards, David L., ed. *The Honest to God Debate: Some Reaction to the Book* 'Honest to God.' London: SCM Press Ltd, 1963.

——. *Tradition and Truth: The Challenge of England's Radical Theologians 1962–1989*. London: Hodder and Stoughton, 1989.

Ellen, Roy, ed. *Malinowski Between Two Worlds: The Polish Roots of an Anthropological Tradition*. Cambridge: Cambridge University Press, 1988.

Ellwood, Robert. *The Politics of Myth: A Study of C.G. Jung, Mircea Eliade, and Joseph Campbell*. Albany, NY: State University Press of New York, 1999.

Esty, Jed. *A Shrinking Island: Modernism and National Culture in England*. Princeton, NJ: Princeton University Press, 2004.

Fifty Years of Publishing Books That Matter [author unknown]. London: George Allen and Unwin, 1964.

Fimi, Dimitra. *Tolkien, Race, and Cultural History: From Fairies to Hobbits*. London: Palgrave Macmillan, 2008.

Flieger, Verlyn. *Interrupted Music: The Making of Tolkien's Mythology*. Kent, OH: Kent State University Press, 2005.

Fowler, Alastair. "C.S. Lewis: Supervisor." *Yale Review* 91, 4 (October 2003): 64–80.

Foy, Roslyn Reso. *Ritual, Myth, and Mysticism in the Work of Mary Butts: Between Feminism and Modernism*. Fayetteville, AR: University of Arkansas Press, 2000.

Francis, Samuel. *The Psychological Fictions of J.G. Ballard*. London: Continuum, 2011.

Fraser, Robert. *The Making of* The Golden Bough*: The Origins and Growth of an Argument*. London: Palgrave, 2001.

——, ed. *Sir James Frazer and the Literary Imagination*. New York: St. Martin's Press, 1990.

Freshwater, Mark Edwards. *C.S. Lewis and the Truth of Myth*. Lanham, MD: University Press of America, 1988.

Gariepy, Jennifer, et al., ed. *Twentieth-Century Literary Criticism*, vol. 77. Detroit: Gale Research, 1998.

Garrity, Jane. *Step-daughters of England: British Women Modernists and the National Imaginary*. Manchester: Manchester University Press, 2003.

Garth, John. *Tolkien and the Great War: The Threshold of Middle-earth*. New York: Houghton Mifflin, 2003.

Gasiorek, Andrzej. *J.G. Ballard*. Manchester: Manchester University Press, 2005.

Girouard, Marc. *Return to Camelot: Chivalry and the English Gentleman*. New Haven, CT: Yale University Press, 1981.

Glyer, Diana Pavlac. *The Company They Keep: C.S. Lewis and J.R.R. Tolkien as Writers in Community*. Kent, OH: Kent State University Press, 2007.

Goddard, James, and David Pringle, eds. *J.G. Ballard: The First Twenty Years*. Hayes: Bran's Head, 1976.

Goldman, Jane. *Modernism, 1910–1945: Image to Apocalypse*. New York: Palgrave Macmillan: 2004.

Goody, Jack. *The Expansive Moment: The Rise of Social Anthropology in Britain and Africa 1918–1970*. Cambridge: Cambridge University Press, 1995.

Grayson, Janet. "In Quest of Jessie Weston." In Barber, Richard, ed. *Arthurian Literature XI*. Cambridge: Boydell and Brewer, 1992: 1–80.

Green, Oliver. *Underground Art: London Transport Posters 1908-Present*. London: Studio Vista, 1990.

Greene, Roger Lancelyn. *Andrew Lang: A Critical Biography*. Leicester: Edmund Ward, 1946.

Greenland, Colin. *The Entropy Exhibition: Michael Moorcock and the British "New Wave" in Science Fiction*. London: Routledge & Kegan Paul, 1983.

Hamilton, A.C. *Northrop Frye: Anatomy of His Criticism*. Toronto: University of Toronto Press, 1990.

Hart, Jonathan Locke. *Northrop Frye: The Theoretical Imagination*. London: Routledge, 1994.

Harvey, Graham. *Contemporary Paganism*. New York: New York University Press, 1996.

Hastings, Adrian. *A History of English Christianity 1920–1990*. London: SCM Press, 1991.

Hayman, Ronald. *A Life of Jung*. New York: W.W. Norton and Co., 2001.

Hick, John, ed. *The Myth of God Incarnate*. London: SCM Press, 1977.

Hiley, Margaret. *The Loss and the Silence: Aspects of Modernism in the Works of C.S. Lewis, J.R.R. Tolkien and Charles Williams*. Zollikofen: Waking Tree Publishers, 2011.

Hoberman, Ruth. *Gendering Classicism: The Ancient World in Twentieth-Century Women's Historical Fiction*. Albany, NY: State University of New York Press, 1997.

Howard, Thomas. *The Novels of Charles Williams*. Oxford: Oxford University Press, 1983.

Hughes, H. Stuart. *Consciousness and Society: The Reorientation of European Social Thought, 1890–1930*. New York: Vintage Books, 1958.

Huttar, Charles A., and Peter J. Schakel, eds. *The Rhetoric of Vision: Essays on Charles Williams*. Lewisburg, PA: Bucknell University Press, 1996.

Hyman, Stanley Edgar. "Jessie Weston and the Forest of Broceliande." *Centennial Review* 9 (1965): 509–21.

Inbody, Tyron. "Myth in Contemporary Theology: The Irreconcilable Issue." *Anglican Theological Review* 58, no. 2 (April 1976): 139–58.

Jacobs, Alan. *The Narnian: The Life and Imagination of C.S. Lewis*. New York: HarperCollins, 2005.

Lammers, Ann Conrad. *In God's Shadow: The Collaboration of Victor White and C.G. Jung*. New York: Paulist Press, 1994.

——, and Adrian Cunningham, eds. *The Jung-White Letters*. London: Routledge, 2007.

Kippenberg, Hans G. *Discovering Religious History in the Modern Age*. Trans. Barbara Harshaw. Princeton, NJ: Princeton University Press, 2002.

Knellwolf, Christa, and Christopher Norris, eds. *Twentieth-Century Historical, Philosophical and Psychological Perspectives*. Vol. 9 of *The Cambridge History of Literary Criticism*. Cambridge: Cambridge University Press, 2001.

Knight, Gareth. *The Magical World of the Inklings*. Longmead: Element Books, 1990.

Krissdottir, Morine. *John Cowper Powys and the Magical Quest*. London: Macdonald and Jane's Publishing Group Ltd., 1980.

Kroll, Jennifer. "Mary Butts's 'Unrest Cure' for The Waste Land." *Twentieth Century Literature*, 45, no. 2 (summer 1999): 159–173.

Kuklick, Henrika. *The Savage Within: The Social History of British Anthropology, 1885–1945*. Cambridge: Cambridge University Press, 1991.

Kuper, Adam. *Anthropology and Anthropologists: The Modern British School*. Rev. ed. London: Routledge and Kegan Paul, 1983.

Lentricchia, Frank. *After the New Criticism*. London: Athlone Press, 1980.

Leopold, Joan. *Culture in Comparative and Evolutionary Perspective: E.B. Tylor and the Making of Primitive Culture*. Berlin: Reimer, 1980.

Lincoln, Bruce. *Theorizing Myth: Narrative, Ideology, and Scholarship*. Chicago, IL: University of Chicago Press, 1999.

Lindop, Grevel. "The Third Man; Charles Williams: An Occult Figure of the 1930s." *Times Literary Supplement*, 2 April 2004, 21.

Luckhurst, Roger. "A Writer and His Quirk." *Science Fiction Studies* 26, no. 2 (July 1999): 333.

MacKillop, Ian. *F.R. Leavis: A Life in Criticism*. New York: St. Martin's Press, 1995.

Mali, Joseph. *Mythistory: The Making of a Modern Historiography*. Chicago, IL: The University of Chicago Press, 2003.

Manganaro, Marc, ed. *Modernist Anthropology: From Fieldwork to Text*. Princeton, NJ: Princeton University Press, 1990.

Marcus, Laura. "Mysterious Mary Butts." *Times Literary Supplement*, 24 August 2001, 3–4.

Margolis, John. *T.S. Eliot's Intellectual Development: 1922–1939*. Chicago, IL: The University of Chicago Press, 1972.

Marrett, R.R. *Tylor*. New York: J. Wiley and Sons, Inc., 1936.

McLaren, Scott. "Hermeticism and the Metaphysics of Goodness in the Novels of Charles Williams." *Mythlore* 24, no. 3–4 (winter-spring 2006): 5–33.

McLynn, Frank. *Carl Gustav Jung*. London: Bantam Press, 1996.

Mulhern, Francis. *The Moment of "Scrutiny"*. London: New Left Books, 1979.

Nicholls, Angus. "Anglo-German Mythologics: the Australian Aborigines and Modern Theories of Myth in the Work of Baldwin Spencer and Carl Strehlow." *History of the Human Sciences* 20, no. 1 (2007): 83–114.

Nicholls, Peter. *Modernisms: A Literary Guide*. Basingstoke: Macmillan, 1995.

Nicholson, Ernest, ed. *A Century of Theological and Religious Studies in Britain*. Oxford: Oxford University Press, 2003.

Noll, Richard. *Aryan Christ: The Secret Life of Carl Jung*. New York: Random House, 1997.

———. *The Jung Cult: Origins of a Charismatic Movement*. Princeton, NJ: Princeton University Press, 1994.

Omrod, Sarah J., ed. *Cambridge Contributions*. Cambridge: Cambridge University Press, 1998.

Ortolano, Guy. *The Two Cultures Controversy: Science, Literature and Cultural Politics in Postwar Britain*. Cambridge: Cambridge University Press, 2009.

Owen, Alex. *The Place of Enchantment: British Occultism and the Culture of the Modern*. Chicago, IL: University of Chicago Press, 2004.

Parrinder, Patrick. *Shadows of the Future: H.G. Wells, Science Fiction, and Prophecy*. Liverpool: Liverpool University Press, 1995.

Patton, Laurie L., and Wendy Doniger, eds. *Myth and Method*. Charlottesville, VA: University Press of Virginia, 1996.

Peacock, Sandra J. *Jane Ellen Harrison: The Mask and the Self*. New Haven, CT: Yale University Press, 1988.

Pearce, Joseph. *Tolkien: Man and Myth*. London: HarperCollins, 1998.

Pick, Daniel. *Svengali's Web: The Alien Enchanter in Modern Culture*. New Haven, CT: Yale University Press, 2000.

Radford, Andrew D. "Defending Nature's Holy Shrine: Mary Butts, Englishness, and the Persephone Myth." *Journal of Modern Literature* 29, no. 3 (winter 2006): 126–49.

Robinson, Annabel. *The Life and Work of Jane Ellen Harrison*. Oxford: Oxford University Press, 2002.

Ruddick, Nicholas. "Ballard/Crash/Baudrillard." *Science Fiction Studies* 58, no.19 (November 1992): 354–60.

Saler, Michael. *As If: Modern Enchantment and the Literary Prehistory of Virtual Reality*. Oxford: Oxford University Press, 2012.

——. *The Avant-Garde in Interwar England: "Medieval Modernism" and the London Underground*. New York: Oxford University Press, 1999.

——. "Modernity, Disenchantment, and the Ironic Imagination." *Philosophy and Literature* 28, no. 1 (April 2004): 137–49.

——. "Modernity and Enchantment: A Historiographic Review." *American Historical Review* 111, no. 3 (June 2006): 692–716.

Scarborough, Milton. *Myth and Modernity: Postcritical Reflections*. Albany, NY: State University of New York Press, 1994.

Schakel, Peter J. *Reason and Imagination in C.S. Lewis: A Study of* Till We Have Faces. Grand Rapids: Eerdmans, 1984.

Schleiser, R. "Jane Ellen Harrison." In Ward W. Briggs and William M. Calder III, eds. *Classical Scholarship. A Biographical Encyclopedia*. New York: Taylor & Francis, 1990, 127–41.

Schoenl, William. *C.G. Jung: His Friendships with Mary Mellon and J.B. Priestley*. Wilmette, IL: Chiron Press, 1998.

Schweitzer, Darrell, ed. *Exploring Fantasy Worlds: Essays on Fantastic Literature*. San Bernardino, CA: Borgo Press, 1985.

Segal, Robert A. *Theorizing about Myth*. Amherst, MA: University of Massachusetts Press, 1999.

——, ed. *Psychology and Myth*. Vol. 1 of Robert A. Segal, ed., *Theories of Myth: From Ancient Israel and Greece to Freud, Jung, Campbell and Lévi-Strauss*. New York: Garland Publishing, Inc., 1996.

——, ed. *Literary Criticism and Myth*. Vol. 4 of Robert A. Segal, ed. *Theories of Myth: From Ancient Israel and Greece to Freud, Jung, Campbell and Lévi-Strauss*. New York: Garland Publishing, Inc., 1996.

Selden, Raman, ed. *From Formalism to Poststructuralism*. Vol. 8 of *The Cambridge History of Literary Criticism*. Cambridge: Cambridge University Press, 1995.

Shamdasani, Sonu. *Cult Fictions: C.G. Jung and the Founding of Analytical Psychology*. London: Routledge, 1998.

——. *Jung and the Making of Modern Psychology: The Dream of a Science*. Cambridge: Cambridge University Press, 2003.

——. *Jung Stripped Bare: By His Biographers, Even*. London: Karnac, 2005.

Shippey T.A. *J.R.R. Tolkien: Author of the Century*. London: HarperCollins, 2000.

——. *The Road to Middle Earth*. London: George Allen and Unwin, 1982.

Smith, Jonathan Z. *Map is not Territory: Studies in the History of Religions*. Leiden: E.J. Brill, 1978.

Sterenberg, Matthew. "Tradition and Revolution in the Rhetoric of Analytic Philosophy." *Philosophy and Literature* 34, 1 (April 2010): 161–72.

Stevens, Anthony. *On Jung*. 2nd ed. Princeton, NJ: Princeton University Press, 1999.

Stevenson, Randall. *1960–2000: The Last of England?*. Vol. 12 of *The Oxford English Literary History*. Oxford: Oxford University Press, 2004.

——. *Modernist Fiction: An Introduction*. Lexington, KY: The University Press of Kentucky, 1992.

Stocking, George W. *After Tylor: British Social Anthropology, 1888–1951*. Madison, WI: University of Wisconsin Press, 1995.

——, ed. *Functionalism Historicized*. Madison, WI: University of Wisconsin Press, 1984.

Svarny, Erik. *"The Men of 1914": T.S. Eliot and Early Modernism*. Philadelphia, PA: Open University Press, 1988.

Taylor, Charles. *The Ethics of Authenticity*. Cambridge, MA: Harvard University Press, 1991.

——. *A Secular Age*. Cambridge, MA: Harvard University Press, 2007.

Thisleton, Anthony. "Knowledge, Myth and Corporate Memory." In The Doctrine Commission of the Church of England, *Believing in The Church: The Corporate Nature of Faith*. London: SPCK, 1981: 45–78.

Tickner, Lisa. *The Spectacle of Women: Imagery of the Suffragette Campaign, 1870–1914*. London: Chatto and Windus, 1987.

Turner, Frank M. *The Greek Heritage in Victorian Britain*. New Haven, CT: Yale University Press, 1981.

Veldman, Meredith. *Fantasy, the Bomb, and the Greening of Britain: Romantic Protest, 1945–1980*. Cambridge: Cambridge University Press, 1994.

Vickery, John B. *The Literary Impact of* The Golden Bough. Princeton, NJ: Princeton University Press, 1973.

——, ed. *Myth and Literature: Contemporary Theory and Practice*. Lincoln, NE: University of Nebraska Press, 1966.

——. *Robert Graves and the White Goddess*. Lincoln, NE: University of Nebraska Press, 1972.

Von Hendy, Andrew. *The Modern Construction of Myth*. Bloomington, IN: Indiana University Press, 2002.

Wagstaff, Christopher, ed. *A Sacred Quest: The Life and Writings of Mary Butts*. New York: McPherson & Company, 1995.

Ward, Michael. *Planet Narnia: The Seven Heavens in the Imagination of C.S. Lewis*. Oxford: Oxford University Press, 2007.

Webb, James. *The Occult Establishment*. La Salle, IL: Open Court, 1976.

Weber, Max. *From Max Weber: Essays in Sociology*. Trans. and ed. H.H. Gerth and C. Wright Mills. New York: Oxford University Press, 1958.

Wheeler-Barclay, Majorie. *The Science of Religion in Britain, 1860–1915*. Ph.D. diss.: Northwestern University, 1987.

——. "Victorian Evangelicalism and the Sociology of Religion: The Career of William Robertson Smith." *Journal of the History of Ideas* 54, no. 1 (January 1993): 59–78.

White, Michael. *C.S. Lewis: Creator of Narnia*. New York: Carroll and Graf, 2005.

Winter, Alison. *Mesmerized: Powers of Mind in Victorian Britain*. Chicago, IL: University of Chicago Press, 1998.

Williamson, George S. *The Longing for Myth in Germany: Religion and Aesthetic Culture from Romanticism to Nietzsche*. Chicago, IL: University of Chicago Press, 2004.

Wilson, A.N. *C.S. Lewis: A Biography*. New York: Norton, 1990.

Young, Michael W. *Malinowski: Odyssey of an Anthropologist, 1884–1920*. New Haven, CT: Yale University Press, 2004.

Index

Printed and bound by CPI Group (UK) Ltd, Croydon, CR0 4YY